The Emotionally Intelligent Manager

The Emotionally Intelligent Manager

How to Develop and Use the Four Key Emotional Skills of Leadership

David R. Caruso

Peter Salovey

JOSSEY-BASS
A Wiley Imprint
www.josseybass.com

Published by Jossey-Bass
A Wiley Imprint
989 Market Street, San Francisco, CA 94103-1741   www.josseybass.com

Jossey-Bass books and products are available through most bookstores. To contact Jossey-
Bass directly call our Customer Care Department within the U.S. at 800-956-7739, outside
the U.S. at 317-572-3986, or fax 317-572-4002.

Jossey-Bass also publishes its books in a variety of electronic formats. Some content that
appears in print may not be available in electronic books.

Library of Congress Cataloging-in-Publication Data

Caruso, David.
    The emotionally intelligent manager: how to develop and use the four key emotional
skills of leadership / David R. Caruso, Peter Salovey.
        p. cm.
    Includes bibliographical references and index.
    ISBN 0–7879–7071–9 (alk. paper)
    1. Leadership—Psychological aspects.   2. Management—Psychological aspects.
3. Emotional intelligence.   4. Executive ability.   I. Title: Emotional skills of leadership.
II. Salovey, Peter.   III. Title.
    HD57.7.C369 2004
    658.4'092—dc22

                                                                                2003027933

Printed in the United States of America
FIRST EDITION
HB Printing   10 9 8 7 6 5 4 3 2 1

Contents

Introduction

Have any of these statements been made to you?

Let's not get too excited.
You are being way too emotional about this.
We need to look at this rationally.

We are taught that emotions should be felt and expressed in carefully controlled ways, and then only in certain environments and at certain times. This is especially true when at work. It is considered terribly unprofessional to express emotion while on the job.[1] We all believe that our biggest mistakes and regrets are due to being overly emotional—the times when our emotions get the better of us. After all, emotions are remnants from 300 million years ago, when they were necessary for the survival of our species.[2]

We believe that this view of emotion is incorrect. After 300 million years—give or take a few million—human brains have gotten bigger and more complex but still have the wiring for emotion. The emotion centers of the brain are not relegated to a secondary place in our thinking and reasoning but instead are an integral part of what it means to think, reason, and be intelligent. This is the essence of the work conducted by University of Iowa neuroscientist Antonio Damasio.[3]

The fundamental premise of *The Emotionally Intelligent Manager* is that emotion is not just important but absolutely necessary for us to make good decisions, take optimal action to solve problems, cope with change, and succeed. This does not mean that you jump with joy every time you make a sale or that you sob your heart out when you aren't promoted. Instead, the premise of *The Emotionally Intelligent Manager* replaces the conventional view of emotion with an intelligent view—one that might sound like this:

Let's get excited.

You are not being emotional enough about this.

We need to look at this emotionally—and logically.

The Emotionally Intelligent Manager is organized around an ability-based approach to emotional competencies that was developed in the late 1980s by two psychologists, John (Jack) Mayer and Peter Salovey, and called *emotional intelligence.*[4] This intelligent approach to emotions includes four different skills arranged in a hierarchical fashion. We explain the importance of each of the four emotional skills and provide you with concrete techniques to improve and use these skills in the workplace.

These are the four emotional skills around which we build *The Emotionally Intelligent Manager:*

1. Read People: *Identifying Emotions.* Emotions contain data. They are signals to us about important events going on in our world, whether it's our internal world, social world, or the natural environment. We must accurately identify emotions in others and be able to convey and express emotions accurately to others in order to communicate effectively.
2. Get in the Mood: *Using Emotions.* How we feel influences how we think and what we think about. Emotions direct our attention to important events; they ready us for a certain action, and they help guide our thought processes as we solve problems.
3. Predict the Emotional Future: *Understanding Emotions.* Emotions are not random events. They have underlying causes; they change according to a set of rules, and they can be understood. Knowledge of emotions is reflected by our emotion vocabulary and our ability to conduct emotional what-if analyses.
4. Do It with Feeling: *Managing Emotions.* Because emotions contain information and influence thinking, we need to incorporate emotions intelligently into our reasoning, problem solving, judging, and behaving. This requires us to stay open to emotions, whether they are welcome or not, and to choose strategies that include the wisdom of our feelings.

Each ability can be isolated from the others, but at the same time, each builds on the others. Although we can measure, learn, and develop each skill on its own, the interrelationships among the skills, as depicted in Figure I.1, allow us to employ them in an integrated way to solve important problems.

A Diagnostic Example

Here is a simple example to show how this process model of thinking and feeling works.

You are conducting a product development team meeting with a number of items on the agenda. There is some discussion regarding the items, and once everyone has had a chance to provide input, you ask for consensus agreement before you move on to the next item. Most of the items are discussed efficiently, and you have a good deal of agreement by team members. You find that you are moving quickly through the list.

Figure I.1. Emotional Intelligence.

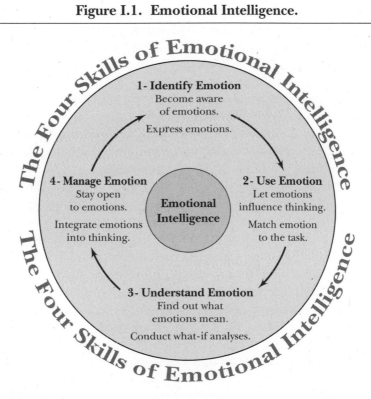

The next item has to do with the latest changes to the product specs requested by your internal customer—the marketing VP. Such changes are not unusual; they have been requested before in this project, and you consider these particular changes to be fairly minor. There is general agreement by the group for the need to alter the plan, and you are about to move to one of the last items on the agenda. But something holds you back, keeps you from moving on, and you pause to reflect briefly before closing down the discussion. It's nothing that anyone has said that gave you pause, but it certainly was *something*. Almost without thinking, you mentally review the requested changes and feel less sure about them. Something does not seem quite right—does not *feel* right to you.

You consider letting this fleeting feeling pass. But even though you have paused for just a few seconds, you see that the pause has had an effect on the group. They seem a bit more attentive and have drawn themselves forward in their chairs. The mood is a bit more serious. One of your senior engineers speaks up and wonders whether the changes, albeit minor, will have an impact on any of the underlying architecture. It's an annoying question, as you have covered this ground a number of times. Again though, you reflect that the vague uneasiness you just felt may have something to do with this very issue. You ask for others' input, and with the now-more-serious focus, a number of team members point out that the product changes are much less trivial than they first appeared to be. You encourage this focused attention and analysis to continue, and in doing so, the team realizes that the system was simply not being designed with such changes in mind. Rather than looking for buy-in, you are now seeking information with which to go back to the marketing VP to demonstrate that the requested changes are not feasible.

What just happened? And why did it happen? Our model of emotional intelligence begins with the awareness, recognition, and identification of emotion. Something held you back from moving on. What was it? First, there was the look on the faces of a few of your more senior developers that indicated some subtle signs of uneasiness and caution. Second, you felt some inner discomfort, recognized it, and did not let it go. Third, you expressed your uneasiness and sense of trouble by looking down at the floor, slightly frowning, and rubbing your hand over your chin.

The second part of our model explains how these feelings influence thinking. The fleeting feelings of worry and concern focused your attention—and the team's attention—on a problem. Your brain, or something inside of you, is saying, "Houston, we have a problem." Your thought processes became more attuned to search for and find errors and inconsistencies. And you did find them.

Our process model then moves to an understanding of emotions, what causes them, and how they change. You determine that the change in the mood of the group is due to some potential issue regarding the requested product specification change. You reason that the growing sense of uneasiness is not due to either the lateness of the hour (the meeting is on time) or to any other external issues. It seems pretty clear to you that everyone is focused—and for good reason.

The fourth and final part of our model indicates that because emotions contain data, we must stay open to them and integrate them. The very last thing you need is another project set-back. And you certainly don't relish having to tell the marketing VP that these latest changes won't fly. Many of us in similar circumstances might try simply to ignore the uncomfortable feelings, discourage them, and direct the team's attention to the next agenda item. But you let the feelings hold sway, allowed them to redirect attention, figured out what was going on, and then stayed open to the wisdom of these feelings to uncover a serious problem.

You have just employed an emotionally intelligent approach to core functions of managing, such as planning, flexible thinking, and adaptability. A focus on emotion does not make you weak or vulnerable; instead, it allows you to be much more able to face up to, and successfully cope with, conflict and change. This approach to managing is not just a reactive, passive analytical tool; it has a strong prescriptive and positive function. It's not enough to uncover problems. The job of the effective manager is to solve problems, and this is where our emotional intelligence approach pays dividends. Let's look at two approaches you, as the team manager, might use to resolve the problem you just discovered: an emotionally *un*intelligent approach and an emotionally intelligent approach.

The Emotionally *Un*intelligent Manager Approach

In most managerial situations, we try to be rational and logical about our management responsibilities. After all, this is what we are being paid to do: to think, to decide, and to act intelligently. We get paid to think, not to worry or to feel. This approach seems sensible, but, as you'll see, is not very effective. Accordingly, you go back to the marketing VP and tell her that the team can't make the launch deadline if these changes are required. She looks surprised and somewhat displeased. That begins a cascade effect. Now in a negative mood, she begins to focus on details, and her search for problems and errors is enhanced. She begins to think about other promises you have made and not kept. You claim that you never actually agreed to the revised specs, and the situation degenerates even further. The result is that she is truly angry with you, as anyone would be in this situation, and you sullenly and reluctantly agree to whatever is asked of you. Not a pretty outcome, is it?

You were completely rational and logical. You were calm and straightforward. And you were also quite ineffective. A truly intelligent approach to managing people must go beyond the search for a holy grail of unsullied rationalism.

A Better Approach

The emotionally intelligent manager prepares and plans for important social interactions. We don't mean that you need to do a month-long strategic planning effort before each meeting you have, but the smart thing to do is to use the skills we've outlined to enhance your interpersonal effectiveness. Let's return to the marketing VP situation.

You know the marketing VP pretty well; you realize that if you just state the problems in a straightforward manner, she will not be very happy. Think about it. After all, you sort of mentioned that the changes didn't seem to be all that major. In fact, you might have even said something like, "I think we can handle that." If anything, she is expecting good news from you. What will happen if you deliver unexpected news? It will be a surprise—an unpleasant surprise at that—and her positive mood will likely turn negative very quickly. If you understand emotions, and if you use your emotional strategic planning ability, you will be able to avoid such an outcome.

In reality, you don't have a rote strategy that you'll employ. You never do, because the exact approach you take must be a function of your emotional situation analysis of how the other person feels at the moment. Is the starting mood positive or negative? Let's say that the VP seems happy and upbeat. That means that your job is to help her to maintain a slightly positive mood, which will enable her to see and to stay open to creative alternative solutions. You understand that you simply cannot announce a major problem and have her maintain her composure, so instead you indicate that you brought the latest changes to your team, and they discovered a number of issues. However, you would like to discuss some ways they came up with to deliver the functionality over a longer period of time while keeping the initial product launch date unchanged.

You'll need to stay attuned to various cues in order to determine how the approach is being received and to modify it accordingly. This won't be easy to do, and it won't necessarily be fun, but this is exactly why they are paying your salary. This is the job of an effective manager. The emotionally intelligent manager leverages the four skills in our model by:

1. *Identifying* how all of the key participants feel, themselves included
2. *Using* these feelings to guide the thinking and reasoning of the people involved
3. *Understanding* how feelings might change and develop as events unfold
4. *Managing* to stay open to the data of feelings and integrating them into decisions and actions

Because *The Emotionally Intelligent Manager* combines passion with logic, emotions with intelligence, readers from opposite sides of the heart-head debate can find value in our approach. Readers who are highly analytical and skeptical about the meaning of emotion or who prefer rationality to emotionality should find *The Emotionally*

Intelligent Manager to be a thinking approach to emotions. Readers who embrace the emotional side of life will find that *The Emotionally Intelligent Manager* provides them with a structured way of viewing their world.

Emotional Intelligence and Effectiveness in Managers

As managers, we have been buffeted by many a management fad and exhortation to develop new skills or risk certain failure. So we've dutifully gone to often terrific and valuable courses on creative thinking, quality circles, and self-directed work teams. We have also been exposed to other training efforts of more dubious quality and utility. Is emotional intelligence just another course, a passing fad? Or is it something new and of lasting value? After all, anyone who has even minimal work experience knows that emotional skills are not a prerequisite for being hired or promoted. The workplace abounds with stories of emotionally unintelligent managers who were considered successful—at least to a certain point.

Have you ever worked for someone who said to you, "As your boss, I can tell you what to do, and you will do it"? Such bosses believe that their autocratic style works well, and they don't have to waste time explaining motives, soliciting cooperation, or engaging in dialogue. We've worked for a person like that. Karen was very "emotional," but she motivated people by playing on their fears. She made promises she never intended to keep, told her boss things he wanted to hear, and acted, in short, like many of the managers we've all seen and worked for. She was a political animal, and that way of operating worked well for her in many ways.

However, Karen did not seem to understand how her actions affected those of us who worked for her. Perhaps Karen would have cared if she had known, but she seemed oblivious to the feelings of her direct reports. Figure I.2 shows that Karen did not have a high level of any of the four emotional skills.

Karen was considered an effective leader by many on the senior management team. She got things done, and her projects were at or under budget. If effective leadership depends on possessing emotional skills, then how come Karen was considered to

Figure I.2. Karen's Emotional Intelligence Skills.

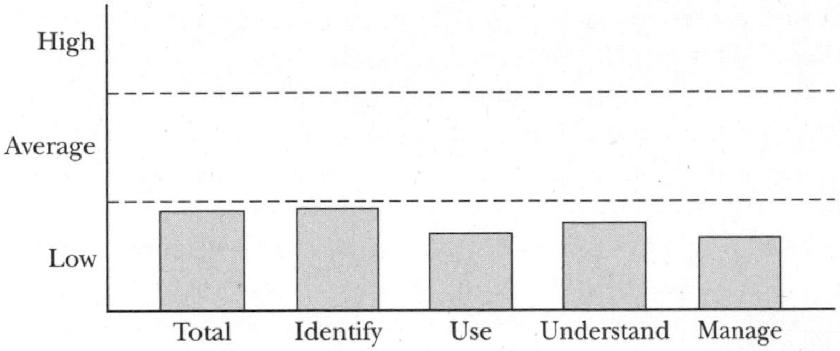

be an effective leader? The moral of this story may be that we are paid to get things done. In a leadership situation, we get things done by directing the work of other people, no matter what it takes.

So are emotions important at work? Do they matter? Does effective leadership truly require strong emotional skills? Karen and many others might well answer a decided *no*.

The Value of the Skills of Emotions

What, if any, advantage does emotional intelligence confer upon managers?

Let's return to Karen for a moment. After a reorganization at her company, Karen's role changed, and she found herself in a matrix management situation in which she had to rely on others to obtain project resources. Telling people what to do no longer was an effective style for Karen. The trouble was that, although she managed-by-fear quite well, the fear tactics didn't work anymore. She had trouble connecting with people in ways that did not involve generating the specter of lay-offs and failure.

A person functioning in amorphous situations marked by rapid change needs to be able to form strong teams quickly and efficiently, interact effectively with people, communicate goals, and obtain buy-in from these self-directed, autonomous groups. In such an environment, the leader must lead by using a set of highly sophisticated skills that involve understanding how people think and feel.

These are the skills of *The Emotionally Intelligent Manager.*

Just to be clear: emotional intelligence does not equal success; emotionally intelligent people are not necessarily great managers, and not all great managers are emotionally intelligent. *Effective management* is our theme here. In this book, we outline a prescription for effective management and leadership that is based on the integral role of the intelligent use of emotion and its impact on thinking, decision making, being motivated, and behaving. An emotionally intelligent manager is not a manager for all seasons, but we strongly believe that such a person will manage, lead, and live in a manner that results in positive outcomes for people. We surmise that truly excellent managers—those who are both effective *and* compassionate—possess a set of abilities that we define and develop in this book.

A New Theory of Leadership

We are not seeking to replace the fine work of theorists and practitioners who have developed sophisticated models of management and leadership. As you'll see, we do not even distinguish between the work of managers and the work of leaders, although we recognize that vast differences exist.

A number of managerial and leadership function taxonomies have been proposed over the years. One way people have differentiated these two roles is to view the role of managers as consisting of planning and implementing activities, whereas the role of leaders is viewed more globally as influencing others in order to accomplish a goal.[5]

These functional analyses offer up an idea of what an effective manager or leader must do, but doing these things right does not necessarily mean you'll succeed. Not only do you need to pull these off but you must also strive to avoid falling into certain traps. Work by the Center for Creative Leadership, for example, indicates that managers face several potential derailers, such as difficulty building a team, difficulty adapting, and problems with interpersonal relationships.[6]

We've distilled the various functions of managers and leaders, along with these potential leadership derailers, into six core areas (also see Exhibit I.1):

Exhibit I.1. What Managers and Leaders Do.

General Function	Examples
Building Effective Teams	Difficulty building and leading a team
	How to lead
	Modeling the way
Planning and Deciding Effectively	Schedule projects
	Plan budgets and resources
	Logistics
	Failure to meet business objectives
Motivating People	Motivate staff
	Generate enthusiasm
	Motivate a team
	Enabling others to act
Communicating a Vision	Create a sense of importance and meaning
	Create an organizational identity
	Develop collective goals
	Inspiring a shared vision
Promoting Change	Promote flexible thinking and decision thinking
	Facilitate creative thinking
	Difficulty changing or adapting
	Too narrow functional orientation
	Challenging the process
Creating Effective Interpersonal Relationships	Conflict resolution among subordinates
	Dealing with firing someone
	Problems with interpersonal relationships
	Encouraging the heart

1. Building Effective Teams
2. Planning and Deciding Effectively
3. Motivating People
4. Communicating a Vision
5. Promoting Change
6. Creating Effective Interpersonal Relationships

Our approach helps inform our understanding of how managers and leaders accomplish these difficult tasks. We'll weave these functions into our discussion of the four emotional intelligence abilities to help you connect those general skills with the specific actions of managers and leaders. You might find, for example, parallels between the four emotional skills and the nature of transformational or charismatic leadership. For instance, we are struck by the critical involvement of the emotions in the practices of exemplary leaders uncovered by the groundbreaking work by Kouzes and Posner.[7]

Nor do we seek to replace the work on managerial competencies, many of which are emotion-focused.[8] Indeed, the competencies of effective managers and leaders described by management professor Richard Boyatzis and expanded on by Daniel Goleman are hypothesized to be based on emotional intelligence.[9]

We have something else—something unique—to offer you: *our focus on emotions per se.* We want you to understand—and to really feel—that thinking and emotions are inextricably linked and that there is little use for such notions as pure logic or cold rationality. We believe that the processes by which managers or leaders create a shared vision, motivate others, and encourage workers are likely based on the intelligent use of emotion and the integration of feelings with thinking.

Our Plan

Emotional intelligence has come to mean many things since the original, scientific work on emotional intelligence was begun by our group in the late 1980s. The overall concept of an emotional intelligence, as well as the general approach to emotional intelligence, was brought to life and to the attention of millions around the world in a 1995 book by science reporter and psychologist, Daniel Goleman.[10] The enthusiastic response to this book resulted in an explosion of interest in the concept, which overnight created a cottage industry of tests, methods, and, unfortunately, many wild claims as to what emotional intelligence is and what it predicts.

We won't be making such wild claims in this book. If you're looking for a miracle cure for leadership woes, then you'll have to look elsewhere. Our approach is based on two principles: (1) to stay true to the original, scientific work on emotional intelligence, which views emotional intelligence as a true intelligence, and (2) to stay true to our philosophy and to the values that have been instilled over decades of scientific training.

We feel that we can stay true to these fundamental principles while offering you valuable ideas and insights. We're very excited about the research that we and others around the world have conducted on emotional intelligence and want to share our insights with you. We hope that you will feel inquisitive enough to be critical about our approach and be excited enough to use it to help you become a more emotionally intelligent manager—of yourself and others.

In this book, we attempt to show you—and to convince you—that emotions do matter—*all the time*. We believe that to ignore their role, to deny the wisdom of your own emotions and those of others, is to invite failure as a person, as a manager, and as a leader.

We'll describe each of the four emotional skills in some detail, providing you with evidence of the importance of the skill in the workplace. Then we'll provide you with a concrete program of development, that is, we'll teach you these emotional skills. Last, we'll show you how you can apply these skills.

If your work is of an individual nature, you can apply these emotional skills to your own work. Developing them might also increase your interest in taking on a leadership role at some future point. If you are currently in a leadership role and experiencing your share of successes, we hope that the approach we lay out in this book can help you acquire another set of skills that will assist you in future situations and roles. If you are already skilled in the domain of emotional intelligence, you might become motivated to use your skills in a leadership role. Whether you are an individual contributor, manager, or leader, you will find ways that our intelligent approach to emotions can be applied to each and every one of your working days.

The Emotionally
Intelligent Manager

PART 1

Learn About the World of Emotional Intelligence

The term *emotional intelligence* seems like an oxymoron to many people. After all, emotions and intelligence are often at odds with one another. The chaotic nature of emotion means that it seems irrelevant, and perhaps even threatening, to the very way in which we think, decide, and work.

In the next two chapters, we appeal to your intellect as we make a case for emotion. Rather than ask you to throw away reason and logic, we tap into your analytical powers to help you make sense of emotion. We first outline a set of fundamental principles behind the concept of an emotional intelligence. Then we present you with an analytical tool—a process model we call an Emotional Blueprint—to help you view emotion as an organized and adaptive system.

CHAPTER 1

Emotions and Reasoning at Work

Rule of Reason or Rule of Emotion?

Throughout *The Emotionally Intelligent Manager,* we argue that the integration of rational and emotional styles is the key to successful leadership. It is clear that good decisions require emotional and logical skills. But too much of one or the other, or the incorrect application of either, can present problems. (Determine your approach with the help of Exhibit 1.1.)

We all know that emotions can derail us. We have seen this time and time again, both in the business world and, even more so, in the world of sports. Consider two cases, one from professional tennis and the other from professional golf.

Tennis player Althea Gibson was neither physically nor financially healthy during the last years of her life. She had fallen from the peak of her career to become a worker in the local recreation department in one of the less wealthy cities in the area. Perhaps this should not be much of a surprise, as she had lived, early on, a self-described "wild" life. She dropped out of school and, after failing to win one of her first tournaments, almost decided to leave the sport.[1] There is more to her story, as we shall see.

During the British Open in July, 2001, golfer Ian Woosnam's caddie, Miles, made a fatal error: he had placed an extra driver in the bag, costing Woosnam a two-stroke penalty. Woosnam threw the extra club on the ground in anger, and his frustration led him to bogey the next two holes.

Exhibit 1.1. Assessment of Your Workplace Decision-Making Style.

Indicate whether you agree or disagree with each of the statements below:

It is important to control emotions at work.
Decisions need to be made on logical and rational grounds.
People should try put their personal feelings aside.
Overly emotional people don't fit in well in the workplace.
Expressing feelings should be limited.
Emotional awareness is less important than logical thinking.
At work, people should emphasize logic over feeling.

If you *agree* with these statements, then you are endorsing the rule of reason in the workplace. You probably value rational, logical thinking, and although you can be emotional, you are able to control your emotions so that they don't control you.

If you *disagree* with these statements, then you are endorsing the rule of emotion in the workplace. Perhaps you find emotions to be an integral part of your work-life and are not able to separate thinking and feeling.

Does it matter? Endorsing the rule of reason or the rule of emotion suggests something important about your management style.

One might think that it was Gibson's lack of emotional control and Woosnam's frustration that hurt their games. But there is quite a bit more to these stories.

Althea Gibson won fifty-six international tournaments and five Grand Slams. These achievements would be enough to label Gibson as a real talent, but what makes her so remarkable are the obstacles she faced and overcame in order to be allowed even to set foot on the courts. She was born in South Carolina into a sharecropper's family but soon moved with her family to the Harlem section of New York City. Having been discovered and mentored for her tennis abilities, Gibson became a highly motivated and very disciplined tennis player. But Gibson wanted more. She wanted to compete on a larger playing field, namely, on the grass courts of the all-white country clubs and associations that were closed to African Americans. After years of struggle, Gibson became (in 1950) the first African American ever to play in the U.S. national tournament. Some years later, she would also become the first African American woman to hold a membership card in the women's professional golf group, the Ladies Professional Golf Association.

Retiring at the peak of her career in order to make ends meet, she never made it big financially. Gibson later became a coach and mentor to hundreds of kids over the course of many years, working in the East Orange New Jersey Recreation Department. She never sought the limelight, nor did she attempt to become a spokesperson for a cause. Instead, she faced each struggle with determination and provided young kids, who might have reminded her of herself as a child, with a hope and a dream and a belief in self. Gibson's emotions did *not* sideline her, they helped her.

There is also more to the story of the forgetful caddie. The expectation was that the caddie would be fired on the spot. Asked about the caddie's error after the game, Woosnam said, "It is the biggest mistake he will make in his life. He won't do it again. He's a good caddie. I am not going to sack him. He's a good lad. He should have spotted it. Maybe he was a little bit nervous. It is the ultimate sin for a caddie."[2]

Woosnam seems to have been able to take the feelings of frustration and use them in a constructive manner. He did not forget them nor did he try to deny them; instead, he integrated them into his play and into his thinking. His decision not to fire Miles also shows sophisticated thinking and reasoning that included emotion.

So what if Woosnam was a decent guy on the links? What counts is performance, and in golf it's quite easy to measure performance. For this reason, it's interesting to note that Woosnam recovered his game that day and finished an even par, narrowly missing a chance to win the Open. Woosnam might not be one of golf's all-time greatest, but he won the Masters at Augusta in 1991 and was the oldest player to win the Wentworth Cup in 2001.

Would Woosnam have been better off if he had immediately fired the errant caddie? The final postscript to this story is that the caddie was indeed fired a few weeks after this incident when he slept late and missed a tee-time!

Can You Be Too Emotional?

We still hear of many situations in which people's emotions get the better of them. Surely, there are times when we can be too emotional. Perhaps tennis star Andre Agassi's story meets this definition.

It seems that Agassi had experienced quite a bad day on the court when he was heard to mutter an obscenity. The referee warned him, but "the incident threw Agassi into a funk. A moment later, he was slapping easy ground strokes into the net." He lost the match.[3]

Agassi's *moods* seemed to get the best of him. This would seem to be a clear-cut case for the need to have balanced and reasonable emotions and to control one's emotions. There is such a case for tight emotional control, but it's not a case we're going to make. Nor is the notion of being "too emotional" one that is recognized by the emotionally intelligent manager.

Agassi's temper tantrum and resulting performance meltdown is not an argument for less emotion but for *appropriate* emotion. Anger is a powerful emotion, and it rises from a sense of injustice or unfairness, or being blocked from achieving an important goal. In Agassi's case, his temperament—the way he is wired—and not the external situation created his frustration and his anger. And his inability to allow anger to motivate him to achieve his objective—winning the match—resulted in the negative outcome.

What Role Should Emotions Play at Work?

The sports world may have room for emotion, but is there any room for emotion in the boardroom? Many leaders would say there is not and, furthermore, there should not be. Business decisions need to be carefully considered, and many would probably agree that the more reasoning and rationality involved the better.

Others feel that emotions play a role, sometimes an integral or equal role, in business. Which type of manager, as shown in Exhibit 1.2, are you most like, Manager A or Manager B?

Many managers we have worked with have the characteristics of Manager A. Indeed, our Manager A clients often tell us that their job is to make optimal decisions by considering all the critical data in an orderly and logical fashion. After all, managers (and leaders) are charged with making good decisions. However, making good decisions and being an effective manager of self and others cannot—and does not—happen in the absence of emotion. Emotions are at work, and they work with and for us, as we'll see in the next section.

Exhibit 1.2. Comparison of Managing Styles.

Manager A	Manager B
I try to keep emotions at arm's length.	I try to be aware of my emotions.
Emotions are not important at work.	Emotions are important.
Emotions should not influence me.	My emotions influence me.
Emotions need to be isolated at work.	Emotions should be part of work.

Do Emotions in the Workplace Matter?

Scientists have learned a lot about the role of emotions in the workplace by conducting thousands of research studies. Some of the results of these studies may surprise you. For instance, how managers *feel* is a useful indicator and predictor of organizational performance.[4] In fact, research by Sigal Barsade, a professor at the Wharton School of the University of Pennsylvania, demonstrates that how a management team feels has a direct impact on a company's earnings. She discovered that a top management team that shares a common, emotional outlook that is positive will have 4 to 6 percent higher market-adjusted earnings per share than companies whose management team consists of members with diverse emotional outlooks.[5]

In a nine-week-long research study by University of Queensland's Peter Jordan and Neil Ashkanasy, teams consisting of members low in emotional intelligence ended up at the same level as did teams of people with high EI.[6] At first blush, these results are not something that the high-EI manager might expect. What is striking is the difference in performance during the *first* weeks of the study. The high-EI teams were able to get their act in gear a whole lot faster than the low-EI teams. Eventually, the low-EI teams did catch up to their more emotionally intelligent peers. The lesson learned from this study is that team emotional intelligence doesn't much matter—as long as you don't mind weeks of lost team productivity and hundreds of worker hours wasted.

Emotions at a team level have a powerful impact in other ways as well. You might call it team spirit or morale, but all of us have experienced how the mood of a group can change. And how we feel does seem to influence our performance.[7] Sometimes it happens slowly and subtly, but sometimes you can almost feel a chill come over the group; at other times, a sense of excitement permeates the air. The spread of emotions from person to person is a phenomenon known as *emotional contagion*.

Emotional contagion has powerful effects on a group. Consider the experiment in which several groups of people were asked to simulate an end-of-the-year bonus pool discussion.[8] Their role was to get as large a bonus for their employees as possible, while still attempting to make the best decisions for the organization as a whole. One of the people in the group, unbeknownst to the discussants, was a trained actor who behaved in a negative manner with some of the groups and in a positive manner with the other groups. Videos of the groups made it clear that the actor had an impact on the groups' mood, depressing it in the negative condition and enhancing it in the positive condition. The research participants also reported changes in their mood, but they did not seem to realize why their mood had changed. Even more important, the positive groups showed a lot less conflict and much more cooperation than did their negative-mood counterparts.

But emotional contagion, on its own, is neither intelligent nor unintelligent. The strategic application of emotional contagion is what makes it part of the repertoire of the emotionally intelligent manager.

How leaders feel also affects how, and how well, they influence people, which, after all, is the core of leadership. A leader who is feeling sad is more likely to generate arguments that are persuasive and well thought out. Sad moods, in general, help people think in a more bottom-up, systematic manner than do happy moods. The same leader, feeling somewhat happy, will probably generate creative and original arguments in a bid to influence others. This leader will also come up with a whole lot more arguments when feeling happy than when feeling sad. And in general, emotions at work influence judgment, job satisfaction, helping behavior, creative problem solving, and decision making.[9]

What makes all of this either smart or dumb is whether you realize the role that emotions play and what you do with that knowledge. Do you try to get your team to generate creative messages when they are down in the dumps? Or do you use this time instead to critically evaluate and edit a prospectus? The emotionally intelligent manager matches the mood to the moment.

We don't expect most managers to know how to do this. You might have taken courses in accounting and marketing, but we'll bet that you never took a course on emotion management strategies, emotional identification skills, or emotion generation. So consider this book your course on emotions at work—why they matter, how they operate, and how to leverage the power of your emotions to be a better manager and leader.

Your emotional education starts with the six basic principles of emotional intelligence, which we discuss next.

Six Principles of Emotional Intelligence

Our approach to emotional intelligence begins with these six principles:

1. Emotion is information.
2. We can try to ignore emotion, but it doesn't work.
3. We can try to hide emotions, but we are not as good at it as we think.
4. Decisions must incorporate emotion to be effective.
5. Emotions follow logical patterns.
6. Emotional universals exist, but so do specifics.

PRINCIPLE 1: EMOTION IS INFORMATION

Emotions Are Data

Emotions contain data about you and your world. Emotions are not random, chaotic events that interfere with thinking. An emotion occurs due to some factor that is important to you, and it helps motivate you and guide you to success. At the most basic level, emotions can be viewed as:

- Occurring due to some sort of change in the world around you
- Starting automatically
- Quickly generating physiological changes
- Changing what you were paying attention to and how you were thinking
- Preparing you for action
- Creating personal feelings
- Quickly dissipating
- Helping you cope, survive, and thrive in your world

Figure 1.1 shows graphically the function of an emotion. Emotions are a signal, and if you pay attention to what an emotion is signaling, chances are the emotion is going to help you out of a tough situation, prevent something bad from happening, or help bring about a positive outcome.[10]

Emotions Are Mainly Data About People

Principle 1 has an important subprinciple: emotions are primarily signals about people, social situations, and interactions. Emotions tell you a lot about you—how you feel, what's happening to you, what's going on around you. But emotions likely evolved in order to ensure our survival by helping us work together. Psychologist Paul

Figure 1.1. Function of an Emotion.

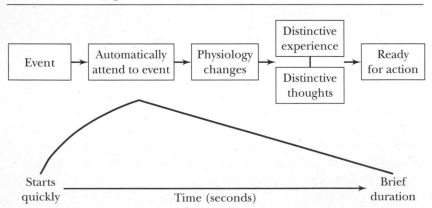

Ekman believes that this is the key function of our feelings: "Typically, the events that call forth emotion are interpersonal actions."[11]

When we are angry, we send a signal to other people to leave us alone or to give back what they took from us—"or else." Our smile of happiness shows that we are open and accepting and, most important, approachable. The interpersonal, or social, nature of emotion is what makes these data sources of such vital importance in the lives of all managers and leaders.

Emotions Are Not Always Data-Driven

If emotions are this wonderful source of data that we need to embrace, then what about those stories you have heard about how emotions derail people, how destructive they can be, and about the need to rein in our emotions? It's a great question. As Figure 1.1 illustrates, emotions are real-time feedback signals that come on quickly and dissipate just as rapidly. But what gives emotions a bad name and gets us into trouble, is something related to emotions: *moods*. Scientists often distinguish between emotions and moods. Emotions have a definable cause. Moods are feelings that last a long time, often occur for unknown reasons, and can be part of our body chemistry. Sometimes the "aftershocks" of emotions are felt as lingering moods. It's likely that calls to carefully regulate and control emotions, as well as the view that emotions are often irrelevant and give rise to undue stress, are really calls to examine our moods.[12]

The emotionally intelligent manager must be able to differentiate between the experience of an emotion and the influence of being in a certain mood. This requires great skill, knowledge, and practice, and it's something that we will help you develop.

Emotions Help Us Survive

Emotions are critical to our survival as individuals and as a species. In fact, emotions are not unique to humans. The survival and development of a species depends on a number of behaviors, including attending to emergencies, exploring the environment, avoiding danger, maintaining bonds with other members of the group, protecting oneself, reproducing, fighting against attack, and giving and receiving care.[13] Emotions were hard-wired millions of years ago through evolution to protect us from threats to survival, as suggested by Exhibit 1.3.

Yet is it possible that, after millions of years of evolution and change, emotions have indeed become useless vestiges of an earlier and more dangerous existence? In current times, with the advances in technology and a general growth of civilization, do these "primitive" emotions interfere with survival and success in the modern world? This is a very logical and sensible argument. But it is very wrong. The world that we live in is exceedingly complex, and accessing our emotions is still important to behaving adaptively and surviving.

Let's take fear, for example. Fear is a powerful emotion that certainly has an important role to play in the lives of even the most "civilized" of nations and peoples. When we worry about something, we are potentially motivated to act in order to alleviate the fear.

Of course, fear can also paralyze us and prevent us from achieving important goals: fear of rejection leads us to avoid relationships with people; fear of failure causes us to delay our plans. But emotionally intelligent managers integrate their emotions and their thinking in ways that are adaptive and productive. The intelligent use of fear involves using it to energize us to address things that are important: feeling nervous about a major presentation can motivate us to work harder; worry about an upcoming business meet-

Exhibit 1.3. The Survival Value of Emotion.

This emotion:	Motivates this behavior:
Fear	Run, there's danger!
Anger	Fight!
Sadness	Help me, I'm hurt.
Disgust	Don't eat that, it's poison.
Interest	Let's look around and explore.
Surprise	Watch out! Pay attention!
Acceptance	Stay with the group for safety.
Joy	Let's cooperate; let's reproduce.

ing can provide the energy we need to go back and review our notes, catch some glaring inconsistencies and problems, and achieve a more successful outcome; anxiety can facilitate performance just as easily as it can debilitate it.[14]

Emotions motivate our behavior in ways that are adaptive and helpful to us. Emotions are not extraneous. They don't just add interest to our lives; they are critical to our very survival. Almost every theory of emotions suggests that emotions convey important information about the environment that helps us thrive and survive. Different emotions have evolved to help us meet these and other needs.

Emotions are also linked to action. Consider a situation in which you're angry with certain team members for failing to show up at the meeting you called. That's only natural. These no-shows are an obstacle in your path. Rather than physically attacking them, however, you can contact them, express your displeasure constructively, and gain their assistance.

Positive emotions like happiness and joy are also a part of our work life—alas, a small part for many people. For example, when you make that huge sale, and there are high-fives all around the trading floor, the team experiences a feeling of *joy*, motivating them to repeat that experience all over again. Quite simply, emotions convey information and meaning and motivate action.

In Exhibit 1.4, we have revised Exhibit 1.3 to suggest ways in which emotions motivate behaviors that, although they may not have survival value, can be relevant in everyday workplace situations.

PRINCIPLE 2: WE CAN TRY TO IGNORE EMOTION, BUT IT DOESN'T WORK

Most of us would admit that emotions influence performance in some areas of our life and that this is normal and even desirable. We see the impact of emotion in sports, as we attempt to psych out our opponent or energize our team. "Attitude"—mood and emotion—is critical in all sports.

But what about a job in which logic is essential? Surely, emotions cannot, and should not, play any sort of role in highly rational and analytical decisions. In a classic study, psychologist Alice Isen discovered that even presumed bastions of rationality—physicians—

Exhibit 1.4. The Way Emotions Motivate Us Now.

This emotion:	Motivates this behavior:
Fear	Act now to avoid negative consequences.
Anger	Fight against wrong and injustice.
Sadness	Ask others for their help and support.
Disgust	Show that you cannot accept something.
Interest	Excite others to explore and learn.
Surprise	Turn people's attention to something unexpected and important.
Acceptance	I like you; you're one of us.
Joy	Let's reproduce (that event).

alter their thinking and decision making, depending on their mood. In an experiment with radiologists, she found that their diagnoses were both faster and more accurate after they were given a small gift (presumably mildly elevating their moods).[15]

We told you earlier how emotional contagion influences the effectiveness of groups. It is remarkable that although emotions have a major impact on judgment, we are almost completely unaware of their effects. It doesn't matter whether you believe it or not, or whether you are aware of it or not, emotions and thinking are intertwined.

You can try to fight against Principle 2, but it won't work. Social psychologist Roy Baumeister found that when people try to suppress the expression of emotions, they end up *remembering* less information.[16] It seems that emotional suppression takes energy and attention that otherwise could be expended in listening to and processing information.

This is not to suggest that we must continuously be awash in emotion. Instead, we can process the underlying information, as well as the emotional component, of the situation, through strategies that do not involve suppressing the expression of our feelings. One such strategy is emotional reappraisal, wherein we look at the issues but attempt to reframe them in a more constructive and adaptive way. We view the situation as a challenge to be addressed, or we try to gain some sort of lesson from the situation.

Don't get us wrong. Emotionally intelligent managers don't merely fix a smile on their face every morning and try to put a positive spin on everything the rest of the day. In fact, emotionally intelligent individuals try to *avoid* Pollyanna-like positive reactions to all things all the time. That is not an effective way to deal with problems—or to avoid dealing with them. An emotionally intelligent manager experiences the emotions and *then uses* the power of emotion as a springboard to a successful, productive outcome.

PRINCIPLE 3: WE CAN TRY TO HIDE EMOTIONS, BUT WE ARE NOT AS GOOD AT IT AS WE THINK

Managers and leaders often don't share certain types of information with their people, or they try to cover up how they feel in order to protect themselves or others. We say that everything is fine when it is not; we claim that we're not worried when we are.

Organizations are notorious for their attempts at controlling emotions, especially the display and the expression of emotion. In many service-oriented jobs, employees are explicitly taught to suppress their feelings and to put on a happy face. This is the concept of "emotional labor," an idea that sociologist Arlie Hochschild first brought to wide attention.[17] There are a few ways that people try to display the emotions that their employer demands. One is through surface acting, when you feel one way but don't show the true, underlying feeling. In deep acting, you actually try to change your current feeling to match the desired feeling. As you might expect, surface acting, as well as emotional labor, have been linked to performance burnout and job turnover, among other issues.[18]

Emotional suppression in organizations takes many other forms. In a process known as *normalizing* emotion,[19] we do not show strong emotions or emotions that the organization or group deems inappropriate. What may surprise you are the sorts of emotions that people are taught not to show at work. Think about your own observations of organizational life. What emotions do you see people show, and what emotions are rarely displayed?

If you said that anger is an emotion that gets covered up and suppressed at work, that may be true for your workplace, but it certainly is not the case in general. In one workplace study, anger was the most likely emotion to be expressed to the person who provoked it.[20] In fact, this study found that 53 percent of people expressed their feelings of anger. The emotion that was least frequently expressed at work was the feeling of *joy;* only 19 percent of people said they expressed this emotion while at work.

At first blush, these results seem counterintuitive. Anger is a powerful, negative emotion that people cover up and try to suppress, whereas joy is a positive emotion that seems more appropriate to display. But the emotional norms of organizations dictate that the expression of joy is not professional. After all, this is work, and we're not supposed to be having that much fun at work. Anger, on the other hand, is the expression of power and authority, of showing others who's the boss. We're not saying that this is the way we should live our work-lives. We believe that the expression of joy is an important part of the emotionally intelligent manager's tool kit, and we need to celebrate our successes more often and encourage each other to reproduce that success.

These attempts at disguising our emotions, although they are consciously made, may not work terribly well. Ekman's research on facial expressions and lying indicates that it is possible to spot a liar by observing pauses in a person's speech, speech errors, and fleeting emotional displays. Our desire to protect emotions or to engage in purely rational pursuits in the workplace can end up in decision-making failures and create an atmosphere of mistrust.[21]

You can try to be the management tough-guy loner type—a John Wayne of organizational effectiveness—and it will work some of the time. But not all of the time. Your feelings and emotions will be read by some of the people most of the time and all of the people some of the time.

PRINCIPLE 4: DECISIONS MUST INCORPORATE EMOTION TO BE EFFECTIVE

Our feelings have an impact on us and on others, whether we want them to or not. Quite simply, no decisions are made without emotion. As we noted earlier, according to neuroscientist Damasio, rational thinking cannot occur in the absence of emotion.[22]

The fundamental error often made by Western philosophers and researchers is to separate mind from body. In doing so, we have created a split-personality view of ourselves as rational creatures (with minds, or thoughts) who must fend off irrational impulses (originating in our bodies, or emotions). Such a view seems to be shared by many people, even today. We distrust emotion as unreliable, irrational, and unwanted impulses that bring us back down to a lower evolutionary level. Such a view is embedded in a "pop" psychology approach to emotional intelligence; consider this quote from a magazine article trumpeting, "What's Your EQ?":

> Primitive emotional responses held the keys to survival: fear drives blood to the large muscles, making it easier to run; surprise triggers the eyebrows to rise, allowing the eyes to widen their view and gather more information about an unexpected event. Disgust wrinkles up the face and closes the nostrils to keep out foul smells.
>
> Emotional life grows out of an area of the brain called the limbic system, specifically the amygdala, whence come delight and disgust and fear and anger. Millions of years ago, the neocortex was added on, enabling humans to plan, learn and remember.[23]

Perhaps this passage illustrates the most critical point of divergence between many approaches to the topic of emotional intelligence and ours. In our approach, we recognize that emotions make us truly human and undergird rationality, and, as such, emotions must be welcomed, embraced, understood, and put to good use.

Although we'll teach you the importance of strategies such as regulating and managing moods and emotions, we emphasize the fuller experience of emotion, not blocking it out or rationalizing your experience. It means that there are times as a manager, a team member, an individual contributor, when one might feel hurt, badly hurt. But if it doesn't hurt badly at times, you're probably not making emotionally intelligent—and effective—decisions.

Different Moods Influence Our Thinking in Different Ways

Psychologists Gordon Bower and Alice Isen, among others, have studied the interaction of mood and thinking for many years.[24] They have found that emotions influence our thinking in different ways.

Positive emotions tend to open us up to our environment for exploration and discovery. The *broaden and build* theory of Barbara Frederickson suggests that positive emotions do more than make us feel good.[25] Positive emotions:

- Expand our thinking
- Help generate new ideas
- Encourage us to consider possibilities

Generally, pleasant or positive emotions motivate us to explore the environment, broaden our thinking, and enlarge our repertoire of behaviors. Positive emotion dares us to be different. It helps us see new connections and generate new and novel solutions to problems.

Positive emotions have other effects on us. For example, happiness motivates us to play or to interact with others; smiling and laughing signal others that we are friendly and approachable. In this way, positive emotions promote social bonds and stronger social networks.

Positive emotions also inoculate us against negative events and emotions. If people are asked to watch a film that induces strong negative emotions and are simply asked to smile after watching the movie, they tend to recover more quickly from the physiological impact of the stressful event.

In one study, Lee Anne Harker and Dacher Keltner studied the yearbook photos of more than one hundred women college graduates. They rated the faces on how happy they were and then tracked these individuals over thirty years. The women who expressed positive emotion in their photos were more likely to have stronger social bonds and more positive social relationships than the women who were not smiling.[26]

Negative thinking has received bad press of late. Yet negative emotions are also important, as they can enhance thinking in very useful and practical ways. Some of the effects of negative mood or emotion on thinking include:[27]

- Providing a clearer focus
- Allowing details to be examined more efficiently
- Motivating a more efficient search for errors

Negative emotions call for us to change what we are doing or thinking. They narrow our field of attention and perception, and they motivate us to act in very specific ways.

Compared to positive emotions, negative emotions tend to be experienced more strongly, and there may be an evolutionary explanation for this phenomenon. There are greater survival costs for an injury or an attack than there are potential rewards for finding something interesting out in the wild. Therefore, negative emotions that signal the chance of danger must be more carefully attended to, and if they are experienced more strongly than positive emotions, then we are less likely to end up on some predator's dinner table.

We all love positive emotions and recognize their positive effects on health and well-being, but there should be a fond place in our hearts for the so-called negative emotions such as fear, anger, and disgust. There's a time for peace—happy emotions—and there's a time to fight—to feel negative emotions. Management is not about avoiding conflict and making everyone happy all the time. Management is more about effectiveness, and effectiveness requires a range of emotions.

PRINCIPLE 5: EMOTIONS FOLLOW LOGICAL PATTERNS

Emotions come about for many reasons, but each emotion is part of a sequence from low to high intensity. If the event or thought that initiated a feeling continues or intensifies, then it is likely that the feeling also gets stronger. Emotions are not randomly occurring events. Each emotion has its own moves, sort of like in a game of chess. You just have to know which piece you have and the rules that govern that piece.

Robert Plutchik, a well-known emotions researcher, proposed a model of emotions that explicitly presents them along an intensity continuum, so that emotions intensify as they go from lower to higher on the diagram.[28] The eight primary emotions are arranged in a circle, with opposite emotions on opposite sides of the circle. His model also indicates how emotions can combine with one another to form more complex emotions. The terms in the open spaces are called primary dyads or a mix of two of the primary emotions. A graphic model of Plutchik's work is shown in Figure 1.2.

This map of emotions provides us with just one of many pieces that we need to understand and manage our emotions better.

Figure 1.2. An Emotional Map.

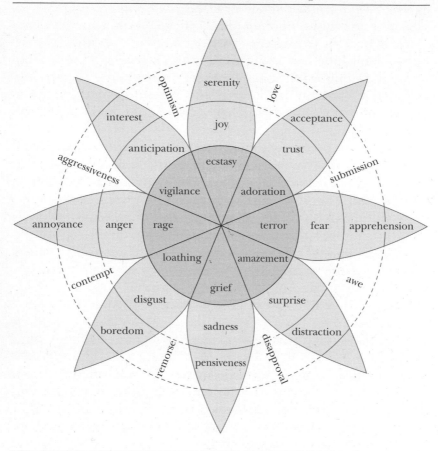

Note: The figure is reprinted by permission of *American Scientist,* magazine of Sigma Xi, The Scientific Research Society.

Consider this example of the importance of understanding the rules of the emotion game.

Jenna is in sales, and Joe is a customer. It came as a real surprise to Jenna that Joe was angry. His anger seemed to come out of nowhere. In reality, there were many warning signs of Joe's impending anger. It didn't just materialize; it was the next logical step in the progression of Joe's emotions.

Here's what happened. Joe started with a mild feeling of annoyance when Jenna told him that the new system would be delayed a week or so. But Joe was not angry. "These things happen," he reasoned at the time. When a week went by and there was no word from Jenna, Joe called her. She casually mentioned that they couldn't do the install for another week because they were so busy. Now Joe's minor annoyance transitioned into a feeling of frustration. But when still another week went by and Joe called Jenna's office, only to find out she was on vacation, then Joe was pretty mad.

Your emotional knowledge can serve as a crystal ball of sorts. When applied with care, it can reduce surprises and predict the future.

PRINCIPLE 6: EMOTIONAL UNIVERSALS EXIST, BUT SO DO SPECIFICS

Emotional intelligence "works," in part, because there are universal rules of emotions and their expression. Much is made of cultural differences in social behavior, and with good reason. Customs and manners do vary markedly from country to country, as well as within regions of larger or diverse nations. But the case of emotions is a special one. We know that cultural universals exist in emotions. A happy face is seen as a happy face by people all over the globe. A face of surprise is interpreted the same way by a Wall Street investment banker and a New Guinea tribesman. Even non-humans display and recognize emotional expressions in fellow creatures. Those of you with dogs know this. Can't you tell when your dog is happy or sad or angry?

Perhaps we all recognize a smiling face for what it is because there are universals in the underlying causes of different emotions. Thus we are happy when we achieve or gain something, and we are sad when we lose something. At its core, an emotion signals something important and therefore communicates a universal signal to all peoples.

But life is more complex than the universal picture we are painting, and there are, indeed, emotional specifics. Some of these specifics have to do with display rules, secondary emotions, and gender.

Emotional Display Rules

Even though all of us may be able to identify happiness in people's expressions clearly, and even though we may all experience happiness for similar, underlying reasons, it doesn't mean that we all *show* our happiness the same way. This brings up the concept of *emotional display rules*. Our society and culture teach us when it's okay to show how we feel and when it's not. We learn these rules early in life, such as when little boys are told that "big boys don't cry," or when, feeling absolutely miserable, we tell our officemate that we're doing "fine" in response to his daily greeting, "Hey, how 'ya doing?"

Emotional display rules are a form of hidden knowledge. This is knowledge that we are aware of, but we're not quite sure where we acquired it. Display rules vary from organization to organization. The creative culture of a New York advertising agency may encourage the display of joy, surprise, and interest, whereas a buttoned-down, Park Avenue law firm prides itself on its quiet restraint.

Cultures also have their own sets of emotional display rules.[29] When in France, we were initially surprised when our hosts kissed us goodbye—on both cheeks! That would not have gone over very well in the United States, but in France, it's perfectly acceptable to express your feelings of happiness in this way. In the United States, we might simply smile and say a word of thanks. In Japan, a colleague may *feel* angry with you, but all you see on his face is a smile.

Secondary Emotions

Closely linked to the notion of emotional display rules is the concept known as *secondary emotions,* or as they are called in some cases, *self-conscious emotions.* Unlike the basic emotions of anger, fear, and joy, these secondary emotions have a strong social or cultural component to them. Consider the feeling of embarrassment. We feel embarrassed when we commit some sort of faux pas, and we are "caught" by someone else. This general rule of embarrassment probably applies to all people and cultures, but what sets the emotion called embarrassment apart from its more basic colleagues is that the actions that bring on the feeling are tied to culture.

If you walk into a meeting of the board in mud-stained clothes, you might feel a bit embarrassed. But walk into your local garden center dressed that way to pick up a bundle of fertilizer, soil, and annuals, and you might not feel embarrassed at all. The context is the key. Different cultures have different social norms for behavior, and what is accepted in one environment may give rise to embarrassment in another. During our first stays in Japan, visiting our colleagues at EQ-Japan in Tokyo, for instance, both of us were at first a bit surprised when our genteel and polite hosts started loudly slurping their noodles at lunch. If one of us did that in a midtown Manhattan restaurant in front of a client, we'd be plenty embarrassed. In Tokyo, the norms are different, and so noodle slurping is not embarrassing to our Japanese colleagues. In contrast, we unknowingly embarrassed our Japanese hosts when we hugged them good-bye. And when we realized later what we had done, we too felt ashamed and embarrassed.

Gender and Emotions

Gender has important effects on emotions and emotional intelligence. Our own work, for example, suggests that women may have a slight advantage in the hard skills of emotional intelligence.[30]

Even though women, as a group, may be more emotionally intelligent than men, women are devalued relative to men when they engage in certain leadership behaviors, even though they might be effective. For instance, it's acceptable for us, as males, to be assertive and in-your-face at work. Our female counterparts, however, are perceived a lot differently when they act in an assertive manner. A female executive expressing happiness may be seen as being "typically female" and soft, whereas a guy can get away with his high-five in the hallway. Gender role norms in the workplace mean that what is acceptable for a male executive is not always acceptable for a female executive.[31]

◆ ◆ ◆

In the remainder of this book, we explore emotional intelligence in depth and provide both an explanation of its importance and techniques for acquiring or improving one's work and management style.

CHAPTER 2

An Emotional Blueprint

If there is one theme that captures the primary message of this book, it's this: *emotions are important*. They are relevant to our everyday lives. They are not merely vestiges of our evolutionary past, like our wisdom teeth or appendix. Nonetheless, for all the importance of emotions, they receive so little attention in our formal education that we are woefully inadequate when it comes to understanding and dealing with them.

A Blueprint for Thinking and Feeling

We believe that it is difficult, yet possible, to become an emotionally intelligent manager. At first, learning to identify and use the data in feelings might be somewhat awkward and mechanical. It might seem like following a difficult schematic diagram or a set of instructions for assembling a complex machine. Whereas some of us learn the underlying principles over time and can dispense with detailed assembly instructions, others of us will always need the schematic or explicit steps. The good news we offer all managers is that we have developed a schematic diagram for emotions—a set of detailed, how-to instructions. We call this an Emotional Blueprint (see Figure 2.1).

The Emotional Blueprint is based on a chapter by John D. Mayer and Peter Salovey in a 1997 book called *Emotional Development and Emotional Intelligence*. The original work on emotional intelligence in the scientific literature was published in 1990 by Salovey and Mayer as a journal article in *Imagination, Cognition, and Personality*. Their research was motivated by the gap between the

Figure 2.1. Emotional Blueprint.

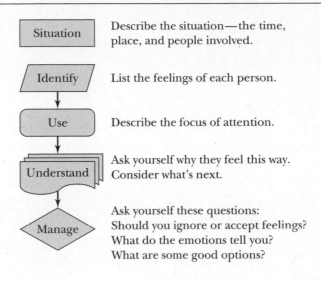

Situation	Describe the situation—the time, place, and people involved.
Identify	List the feelings of each person.
Use	Describe the focus of attention.
Understand	Ask yourself why they feel this way. Consider what's next.
Manage	Ask yourself these questions: Should you ignore or accept feelings? What do the emotions tell you? What are some good options?

importance of emotions and the level at which the average person understands them.[1] It was also influenced by the work of people such as Howard Gardner, with his theory of multiple intelligences, as well as by Robert Sternberg's discussions of practical and successful intelligences.[2] More to the point, the key idea behind emotional intelligence is that our emotions, in effect, make us smarter. Rather than get in the way of rational thought, they help to shape it. Since that time, these ideas have been further explored and developed into a sophisticated, yet beguilingly simple, set of skills that we term the *ability model of emotional intelligence*. This model provides a framework to help us learn about emotions and manage them effectively.

In this model, emotional intelligence is viewed as an actual intelligence consisting of four related abilities, which you'll recognize as the abilities we described in the Introduction (see Figure I.1):

1. Read People—Identify Emotions: This refers to the ability to identify accurately how you, and those around you, are feeling and your ability to *express* these feelings. More than awareness, this ability stresses *accuracy* of awareness.

2. Get in the Mood—Use Emotion: This special ability helps you determine how emotions help you and how they work in harmony with thinking. Your ability to use emotions changes your perspective, allowing you to see the world in different ways and to feel what others feel.
3. Predict the Emotional Future—Understand Emotions: Emotions have their own language, and they have their own logical moves. The ability to understand emotion means that you can determine why you feel the way you do and what will happen next.
4. Do It with Feeling—Manage Emotions: Emotions convey important information, so it is valuable to be open to our emotions and to use this information to make informed decisions.

Emotional intelligence, then, consists of these four abilities: to *identify* how people feel, to *use* emotions to help you think, to *understand* the causes of emotions, and to include and *manage* emotions in your decision making to make optimal choices in life.

Each of these four abilities is separate from the other abilities and can be defined, studied, measured, developed, and used independently. But the four abilities also work together. The four-part model provides a blueprint for leading more effective lives. The model applies to almost any realm of our life, as we tap into these emotional skills to understand ourselves and other people better.[3]

Emotional Blueprint in Action

Keeping a team together and motivated is one of the most difficult tasks for managers. This task is made even more complex and challenging when the team experiences change. The Emotional Blueprint can help us understand better how to effectively manage a team through such turbulent times. Consider, for example, the situation that one of our managerial clients, Don, experienced when his team went through a significant change.

The Manager Who Did Not Manage Emotions

Don was a great manager. He was extremely effective in many ways, as reflected by his own job satisfaction, the satisfaction of the people reporting to him, and his ability to complete projects on a schedule that met his clients' needs. That is why Don was initially quite surprised when his operations group at a high-powered Wall Street firm suddenly experienced an unanticipated change: a noticeable drop in morale and productivity.

Recounting the history of his group, Don related that some problems had arisen during and after a partial staff relocation eight months earlier. In his inimitable, hands-on manner, Don had addressed each of these problems, resolved the issue, and moved on. He continued his detailed analysis of the group, discussing other problems they had experienced, the nature of their projects, and a host of other, possible causes for the precipitous productivity drop.

The list of potential causes was long, but Don dismissed each one, and it did seem that none of these could have had such a major negative impact on this previously high-functioning team. Don's analytical skills were as strong as his managerial and technical skills, and he was quite open to possible personal failings. His systematic analysis was detailed, rational, and logical—and wrong.

While readily addressing the concrete concerns, Don failed to conduct an emotional analysis of the situation. The problems that arose after the move—problems with new parking spaces, different tax forms, faulty air conditioning—were actually symptoms of something else. The "something else" in this case turned out to be the feelings of the department members who now had a shorter commute but no longer felt part of the community. The something else was also the feeling of loss experienced by the people who stayed behind in the original Wall Street offices.

It was only with the accurate identification of the root cause of the morale and productivity problem that corrective action could be taken and a positive result achieved. It was only when Don addressed the real issues that he was able to turn the situation around by meeting the deeper, unspoken needs of his staff. Some people believe that it's not in a manager's job description to have to deal with people's feelings (unless, of course, you're a psychologist!). We argue that this is exactly what a manager's job description should include: identifying how people feel, using their feelings to direct their thinking, understanding the reasons for these feelings, and managing to stay open to the data in feelings and use the information to make optimal decisions.

Don's Emotional Blueprint

Don was a smart guy. Because our intelligent approach to emotions does not place analytical abilities, or IQ, in opposition to emotional intelligence, we see Don's "smarts" as a benefit, not as a handicap in his acquisition and use of the skills of emotional intelligence.

In fact, Don turned out to be a quick study in the realm of emotions. With a bit of guidance and information, he was readily able to use our Emotional Blueprint. This is what the Blueprint consists of (see Exhibit 2.1).

If you were in Don's shoes, you might first tune in to the feelings of the group as well as your own. Tuning in is only part of this step, because even though you're tuned in, you may be tuned to the wrong channel! In other words, it takes more than paying attention. You have to pay attention to the right things and draw the correct conclusions. What would you learn? You might be able to tell from gestures, tone of voice, forced smiles, and the like that people are feeling down. Morale seems to be sinking like a stone.

Your next step is to use these feelings to help guide your thinking. For Don, it means that he feels what his team feels and so sees

Exhibit 2.1. An Emotional Blueprint.

Step	Goal	Action
Identify Emotions	Get complete and accurate data.	Listen, ask questions, and paraphrase to ensure you understand how your team feels.
Use Emotions	Have feelings help guide your thinking.	Determine how these feelings influence your thinking and that of the team.
Understand Emotions	Evaluate possible emotional scenarios.	Examine the causes of these feelings and what may happen next.
Manage Emotions	Determine underlying, root cause and take action to solve the problem.	Include the rational, logical information available with the emotional data you just gathered to make an optimal decision.

the world and feels the world through their eyes. He senses that his people are giving up and perhaps losing hope. They are focused on problems, on what is wrong with the organization. It's not a pleasant feeling, nor is it encouraging, but it is what it is: an accurate appraisal of a worsening situation.

Don has to engage in some heavy analytical lifting now. He must analyze why his group is losing all hope. What is the source of their feelings? What happened? Perhaps even more important, Don has to predict the future and figure out how people *will* feel in the future. Because he is analytical by nature, Don can apply his sophisticated what-if reasoning skills (we talk more about "what-ifs" in Chapter Five) to the situation and determine that *if* the situation continues, people may give up, be motivated to leave the organization, or fall prey to despair or anger.

The situation isn't going to get better if Don continues his present course. That seems clear. The fourth emotionally intelligent step Don takes may be the most difficult one of all. When we are feeling lousy, we try to push those feelings and the accompanying thoughts away. We don't like feeling bad, so we do almost anything not to feel bad. Unfortunately for Don, he must stay open to these negative, difficult feelings. To do otherwise means he is not doing his job, or not doing his job well, in any case.

These feelings are the crux of the matter; they hold the key to the team problem that Don is facing. He guards against suppressing his and his group's frustration and sadness, and he integrates this information into his decision making and behavior. This is where Don has a moment of insight and realizes that he must directly address how his people feel about the move, not just the concrete issues that are disguising the real problem of loss. Being an emotionally intelligent manager means that there will be times, perhaps plenty of times, when you must open yourself up to strong feelings, both positive and negative. Before allowing this to happen though, it is essential that you develop the skills that allow you to fully engage these strong feelings and not to get overwhelmed by them. This book can help you develop this skill.

Don's action plan, based on his Emotional Blueprint, is shown in Exhibit 2.2. As you can see, Don has to alter his strategy and behavior, using his reanalysis of the situation and his correct identification of the root cause of the team's performance problems.

Exhibit 2.2. Don's Emotional Blueprint Action Plan.

Step	What Don Discovers
Identify Emotions	The team feels isolated, alone, and sad.
Use Emotions	They are focused on negatives and fault-finding.
Understand Emotions	They feel abandoned. As the situation continues, they may feel upset and angry.
Manage Emotions	It may have been a mistake not to move with the group, but I need to stay open and try to solve the real issue.

This is what emotionally intelligent managers do. Do they walk through every decision step-by-step in this fashion? Probably not. But it is the way they think and feel and act.

The exciting thing about this Emotional Blueprint is that we can provide *you* with the drafting tools you need to create your own blueprint for each important situation you face. We can teach you to see and feel the world in a different manner. It is not easy to do, but even if you simply start by asking these questions, you'll come out ahead. (When you are ready, Appendix 2 provides detailed Emotional Blueprint questions.)

◆ ◆ ◆

The world of emotion is complex and confusing, but the Emotional Blueprint can help you navigate your way through the turbulence. To get the most out of our intelligent approach to emotions, and the Emotional Blueprint, we'll share critical information about each of the four emotional skills, show you how to develop each of the skills, and then show you how to apply the skills to your daily work-life. In the next several chapters, we take a look at each of the four abilities in greater detail.

PART 2

Understand Your Emotional Skills

The Emotional Blueprint offers an approach to emotion that is intelligent. It does not threaten the importance of logic or reason. This blueprint describes four different, but related, emotional abilities. The best way to help you really understand the blueprint is to take it apart and figure out how it works.

That's what we do in Part Two. We describe each of the four emotional abilities in greater detail, give you examples of people high and low in each ability, and demonstrate to you why the ability is important. To show you that we are in earnest about emotional intelligence being similar to the traditional notion of intelligence, we close this section by sharing with you how we can objectively measure a person's four emotional skills.

CHAPTER 3

Read People
Identifying Emotions

What does it mean to be able to identify emotions accurately—to take the first step described in our model? Managers with these skills are described by the statements in Column A in Exhibit 3.1. Managers who struggle with this skill are often described by statements such as those listed in Column B.

Let's take a look at two people, each of whom is better described by one of these lists of attributes than the other.

What Does It Mean to Identify Emotions?

Managers have to work with people. As simple and obvious as this sounds, it is not always easy to do well. Failures of interpersonal

Exhibit 3.1. Identifying Emotions.

Column A: Skillful	Column B: Not Skillful
Knows what people feel	Misreads people's emotions
Will talk about feelings	Doesn't talk about feelings
Can show how they feel	Never shows feelings
Expresses feelings when upset	Does not know how to express feelings
Smiles when happy or pleased	Maintains neutral expression
Reads people accurately	Fails to identify how others feel
Good at recognizing own feelings	Misunderstands own feelings

relationships at work can occur for many different reasons. In Bill's case, the reason seems to be his struggle in figuring out how people feel.

Bill Just Doesn't Seem to Get It

Bill, age forty-five, was an outgoing and energetic person. He was considering a career change to consulting, as he had extensive experience in his industry and was well educated. However, Bill's colleagues reported that Bill wasn't always effective with them or with clients in general. In the words of one colleague, "Bill isn't always there. He seems a bit 'off' at times. He just doesn't seem to get it."

Bill didn't pick up on others' nonverbal signals. During a conversation, when it was clear to most people that the discussion wasn't going anywhere, Bill would obliviously continue to expound on his points and end up completely losing the audience.

He also didn't seem able to appreciate his own emotional state of mind. For instance, Bill had a mild temper problem. After an especially difficult week in the office, it appeared that Bill was quite angry. He would fling his briefcase around, speak gruffly to his secretary, and generally stomp around the office. Asked how he was feeling, he replied, "Fine, I'm fine." One colleague ventured to say to Bill, "It seems like you're really angry with the way that deal is going," only to have Bill almost yell at him, "I am not angry! Understand? I am not angry!" And he really meant it! He was oblivious to his own emotions and to those of others.

Bill's ability to identify emotions was modest, at best.

Bob Gets It

Bill lacked basic emotional awareness, but many managers who are aware of emotions can't accurately identify them. Having emotional awareness and accurate emotional data is the basis for most effective relationships, as the case of Bob illustrates.

Bob was a hail-fellow-well-met sort of guy. A second-generation Italian American, Bob had risen from junior bookkeeper to managing partner at one of the biggest public accounting firms in the world. The first impression Bob usually gave people was that he was unsuited for a role as a managing partner. He was big and brash and loud. His speech and mannerisms reflected his blue-collar background rather than the upper-crust polish evident in his fellow partners.

It was surprising that not only had he survived but he had thrived in this staid, conservative environment. However, that surprise was based on externals. As we worked with Bob, we came to discover many qualities that were hidden below the surface—qualities that his colleagues knew about and had appreciated for more than two decades.

Bob had a great sense about people, and he could zero in on the mood of the room or, as he said it, "I feel the vibes in the organization." He was an astute observer of people and, even as he talked to you, you could feel that there was continuous thinking and processing going on in Bob's head.

At times, he surprised people with his insights on how a client felt about a proposal or how a meeting went. On one occasion, when everyone else agreed that the meeting had gone well and the client seemed pleased, Bob differed. He insisted that there was more to it than that and that there were still unresolved issues in the client's mind. It turned out that Bob was correct. Bob's ability to identify emotions accurately was strong.

How Do We Identify Emotions?

As we noted in Chapter One, the ability to identify accurately how other people feel is critical, not just to success and happiness but perhaps to our very survival. This point was dramatically illustrated (with examples from many different species) by Charles Darwin in his wonderful book *The Expression of the Emotions in Man and Animals*.[1] Recognizing the difference between a stranger who is friendly and ready to help you and a stranger who is unfriendly and ready to attack you can spell the difference between living another day and ending up dead.

In our Emotional Blueprint, identifying emotions is ability number one. This ability consists of a number of different skills, such as accurately identifying how you feel and how others feel, sensing emotion in art and music, expressing emotions, and reading between the lines. Perhaps most critical is the ability to detect real versus fake emotions.[2]

Accurate Awareness

Without emotional awareness, how can we distinguish whether we are feeling tired or sad, happy or nervous? Awareness is the essential building block for emotional intelligence.

The ability to introspect has been highly touted among self-help advocates as a critical component of personal growth and development. What most self-help gurus fail to understand is that introspection and reflection can lead to worsening mood and can result not in insight but in feelings of depression and shame.[3] Awareness is certainly an important component of emotional intelligence, but it must be accurate and not obsessive. We must know how we feel and be able to label our feelings appropriately if we wish to better understand ourselves and others. When we attempt to determine how we feel, we have to be fully aware of gradations and shifts of feeling. It's important to know whether we're frustrated during a sales presentation, or bored, or just tired. This information provides insights about the sales message itself.

Expression of Emotion

If emotions serve as a sophisticated but efficient signaling system, then we not only need to be able to decipher signals but send them as well. Expressing emotion is relatively easy, but doing so accurately is somewhat more difficult. Some people are "hard to read," and the signals they send are either not clear or too subtle to be detected. Others are *purposefully* unexpressive. They may feel that it is inappropriate to express themselves, or they may be afraid of emotional expression for more personal reasons. In this case, they have the ability to express emotion, but they choose not to do so. Cultural and organizational display rules, which we discussed earlier, also come into play.

The *inability* to accurately express emotion means that we do not send signals about ourselves and, as a result, our needs may not be met. If I am sad regarding a lost computer document that I required for a major meeting later that day, I need support at that time. My expression of sadness is likely to increase the chances of being supported, which, in this case, means someone taking time to help me recover the lost file. In another situation, if I am calm and at ease but communicate a message that says something different about my emotional state, another person may incorrectly perceive me as a threat and take action against that perceived threat. "I didn't think he really cared" is something that many managers will say about an employee who masks his passion for the job.

The ability to communicate has survival value in other ways. Our interpersonal communications consist of both verbal and non-verbal cues. Our tone of voice, gestures, posture, and facial expressions are conduits for information. If the information enhances the verbal message, it is likely that the message will be communicated in a more accurate and meaningful way.

Paul Ekman, a psychologist in the field of emotional expression, has studied people's ability to express emotions. Even though emotional expression begins to develop in infancy,[4] Ekman finds that people differ greatly in their ability to express various emotions.[5]

Ability to Read People

Right now, you are feeling a certain way—perhaps content and satisfied. Then a colleague approaches you and asks why you look so unhappy; he asks what the problem is. In this case, your colleague's perceptions are not accurate. He may definitely feel that you are unhappy, but if you are not, then his perceptions are off-base.

The ability to read facial expressions and identify the emotion expressed in that face accurately is a core skill. This ability is essential to our interpersonal survival and, perhaps, to our physical survival as well. Emotions are a signaling system, and emotions contain important data, as we mentioned earlier. If we are unable to read these signals, then our data and information about a situation is either incorrect or flawed.

Distinguishing between a person who is enraged and a person who is calm can make a critical difference in our own well-being. Determining friend from foe is only part of the importance of this ability. Perceiving emotion accurately allows us to approach a situation with some finesse.

By the way, it's not just people who display emotion. Our four-skill model of emotional intelligence also posits that this ability extends beyond emotional displays to the perception of emotion in art forms such as music and sculpture and paintings. Art makes us think and feel. Art moves us, not just intellectually but emotionally as well. The power of music to convey emotion is well understood, or rather, well "felt" by most of us. Think of the chill of suspense that certain musical scores provide or the happiness you feel listening to certain tunes. Also consider the billions of dollars that are spent on advertising, trade shows, logo design, and branding. These seek to influence how people feel about a product, as well as how they think about it.[6]

Ability to Read Between the Lines

Accurate emotional identification also means that you can't be easily fooled by people who are expressing an emotion they don't actually feel.[7] Although it is very easy to be able to smile on demand—witness many photographs with everyone smiling—it is harder to create a true smile if you are not feeling happy.

Sometimes, people who are not emotionally aware pay a little bit of attention to facial and emotional expressions—just enough to see that there is an emotional display. What they miss, however, are the subtle cues that help to distinguish genuine from manipulated expressions of emotion. And sometimes you may be paying a great deal of attention to emotional displays but still misread the emotion.

Some managers who don't pick up on emotional cues at all, especially false cues, accept others at face value. They don't go beyond the surface expression of emotion because they don't see any need to do so. The result is that they see a smile, but it doesn't occur to them that it might be a forced smile—one in which the mouth is smiling but the eyes are not crinkling as they should. This leads them to an incorrect conclusion, wrong basic assumptions, and faulty emotional information.

Why Is Identifying Emotions Important?

The advice offered to Professor Harold Hill in *The Music Man*[8] ("but you gotta know the territory") applies not just to sales but to all our interactions. That is, you need to have a basic understanding of a person or a sales territory in order to be effective.

Data for Decisions

Accurate emotional identification results in core emotional data that are required for decisions and actions. Without this base of data, how can we hope to make good decisions and take appropriate action?

Even slight inaccuracies can have a major downstream impact on our lives. It's like what happens when we take a compass bearing and follow it to some distant point. If that point is not far away, a slightly inaccurate reading has little impact on us. But a compass reading that is off by just one or two degrees, over a journey of hundreds of miles, can lead us to a point very far distant from our intended destination.

Accurate emotional identification is important, even in seemingly routine managerial tasks such as budget planning. Consider a meeting in which you present your annual budget to your direct reports and seek their buy-in and agreement. Lots of things need to happen correctly for you to get the data you need. First, your direct reports have to feel that you want feedback. Whether that message gets communicated or not will depend on the way you express emotion. You may subtly invite comment, or you may send signals indicating that you really don't want any feedback. Second, your ability to read between the lines and pick out the accurate emotional signal in all of the noise of the team's moods requires a fair amount of skill. One of your managers says that the plan looks fine to him, but he sure does not seem fine to you, as he shifts nervously in his chair. Another direct report complains that not enough money was allocated for his people, but there doesn't seem to be much passion behind the complaint. Likely enough, he's just trying to pad his budget against possible cutbacks later in the fiscal year.

Opportunities to Explore

Recognizing negative emotions accurately is a key to our well-being and, in some cases, to our physical survival. Accurately reading positive emotions may not have immediate survival value (at least for humans; in animals it may be an important cue for a mating opportunity), but it does help us develop and grow. Opportunities to explore our environment, to experiment, and to invent arise from positive emotions. We approach situations and other people when we perceive positive emotions. Wouldn't it be useful if we could detect the subtle signs of interest during a sales presentation or when we are interviewing for a job? Would that be a hint that you could use? Perhaps the encouragement you also seek?

Your ability to be aware of positive emotions and to recognize them accurately can provide you with extremely important information about your world. It's easy to dismiss the hunches or the gut feelings we have, and perhaps some of us should if our emotional read is inaccurate. But if we are accurate, then attending to positive feelings means we are onto something good. It's like the game kids play when they search for a hidden object, and the person who hid the object tells them whether they are getting colder (further away) or warmer (closer). Positive—warm—feelings can signal that we are on the right track.

Social Interaction and Communication

Nonverbal information is often the basis for successful social interaction. This information consists of gestures, voice tone, and facial expressions. If we focus on a person's words alone, we are at serious risk of misunderstanding the underlying message.

Although the concept of body language received bad press some years ago, when it was exploited as a tool to pick up potential romantic partners, a great deal of research has been conducted in the area of nonverbal communication.[9] Estimates vary, but as little as 10 percent of the information in an interchange between two people comes from their actual words, and the rest from tone of voice, gestures, and facial expression.[10]

Accurately identifying facial expressions and accurately expressing emotions is therefore a key to appropriate and successful interpersonal interactions. The person who is not skilled in identifying their own or another person's emotions through subtle cues is likely to behave quite boorishly, whether intending to or not.

◆ ◆ ◆

Once you've identified the emotions, it's time to examine how these emotions influence thinking.

CHAPTER 4

Get in the Mood
Using Emotions

What does it mean to use emotions to help thinking? Those with that ability may be better described by the statements in Column A of Exhibit 4.1. People who struggle with this skill are often described by statements such as those listed in Column B.

Let's take a look at two people, each of whom is better described by one column than the other.

When the Lack of Emotion Limits Your Thinking

If ever there was a case from our practice that argues against the need for pure, rational thinking, it's this one. Perhaps not every

Exhibit 4.1. Using Emotions.

Column A: Skillful	Column B: Not Skillful
Creative thinker	Practical and concrete
Inspires people	Doesn't motivate others
Focuses on what's important when emotions are strong	Forgets what's important when upset
Emotions *improve* thinking	Feelings are flat or distracting
Can feel what others are feeling	Emotions are self-absorbed and not influenced by others' feelings
Feelings help to inform and change beliefs and opinions	Beliefs and opinions are unchanged by emotions

manager needs to be a creative genius, but most managers, at some point, have to think differently. This is where your ability to use emotions to facilitate the right kind of thinking fits in. And this is the ability that Alison, a marketing manager, didn't have. Although Alison was in marketing, her focus was more on sales than on marketing, per se. She was an upbeat person with strong social skills; she was intelligent and possessed good analytical skills.

Alison spoke eloquently about her feelings. She evidenced a lot of insight as well, except when it came to certain negative feelings. When the conversation turned to these feelings, she would become uncomfortable and change the subject. Alison tried really hard to seem cheerful and pleasant.

Although Alison was comfortable feeling and expressing positive emotions and optimistic thoughts, she could not allow herself to access negative emotions, especially embarrassment, guilt, and shame. She actively fought against those feelings.

There was another surprising side to Alison: she had trouble generating creative, new ideas. She was very grounded, practical, and concrete and did not value imagination. For a compassionate and insightful person, Alison did not have a lot of empathy for people she called "complainers" and "whiners." She said that they had no excuse for focusing on the negative aspects of their lives.

Alison's ability to facilitate thinking by using emotions was weak. She did not want to, and perhaps was unable to, generate emotions, experience them, and use them to help her think, process information, make decisions, and feel empathy for people. That may be fine with Alison and perhaps with some managers, but being closed off to emotion is often reflected by a rigid thinking style.

Where Breakthrough Ideas Come From

Julia was a research analyst for a major Wall Street firm. It turns out that her career was not so much a choice she made but more of a tradition she followed. Her father had founded an investment firm and groomed and trained his daughter, his only child, to take her place as the heir to his throne. The analyst position was her first step toward obtaining the real-world experience and training required before moving to dad's firm.

Because one of her most important career values was monetary compensation, it seemed that Julia had it made. Yet her career was not a satisfying one. There was something missing, and Julia was determined to figure out what it was. She had a number of interests and passions, and it appeared that her current job, while meeting one need, was much too narrow in scope. She needed a much larger canvas on which to paint her life's work.

It was fascinating to hear Julia talk about her career, her colleagues, and her ideas. She had a great imagination and a good deal of empathy for people. Julia was truly able to feel what others felt, and she related well to others' emotional experiences. She took these experiences and blended them with her thoughts, resulting in extremely insightful and creative ideas. In a word, Julia had tremendous ability to use emotions to facilitate thinking.

Although she worked diligently on examining career alternatives, she resisted suggestions about a major career change that would allow her to pursue her interests and a career that rewarded her empathic and creative skills. It took some months, but after strongly rejecting the ideas, she came to realize that the financial services world was not for her. She was recruited by a start-up firm that was in the industry she had tracked as an analyst. Rather than becoming their financial analyst, though, Julia was brought on board as their vice president of marketing and new-product development. Here was a career that allowed her to leverage her strong creative abilities.

What It Means to Use Emotion to Facilitate Thought

Rather than view emotions as unwelcome visitors, we need to embrace them as a key component of thinking and cognition. One of the most important messages that we want to communicate is that emotions can *enhance* our thinking.

This was not always the case in the enlightened science we call psychology. Where the role of emotion in thinking is concerned, it can be a bit embarrassing to quote from the early history of psychology. Take, for instance, what a psychologist had to say about the role emotions play in our lives: "[Emotions cause] a complete loss of control . . . [and there is] no trace of conscious purpose."[1]

During the heyday of behaviorism during the last century, many psychologists thought that emotions were not important aspects of conscious experience.

Much has changed since this claim was made. Investigators now agree that emotions can work together with thought in interesting and unusual ways. Those who study the role of emotion in cognitive processes provide us with a firm understanding of ways in which our emotions influence our thinking—for better and for worse.

Emotions can assist our thinking, enhance our problem solving, and aid reasoning.[2] For example, if we are in a positive mood, we can generate new and interesting ideas, and we tend to be better at inductive problem solving, such as generating a new marketing plan. If we are in a more negative mood, we focus on details and are better at solving deductive reasoning problems, such as checking a financial statement for errors.[3]

It is important to stress that not everything that links emotion and thought is emotional intelligence. To be emotionally intelligent, emotions must enhance and assist our thought processes in some meaningful manner, not just influence them. For instance, the powerful memories conjured up by Proust's madeleines is not emotional intelligence, unless the author were to generate such an emotion in order to purposefully engage in creative thinking.[4]

Paying Attention

Emotions contain important data and information, but they also serve to bring our attention to bear on significant events in our environment. Thus when we are afraid, we pay more attention to the environment around us; we scan for a possible threat. When we are happy, our energy and attention are freed up, allowing us to explore the environment and to make new discoveries. Consider this example of how emotions assist thinking.

You're sitting in the train on your way to work. You are not sure why you feel uneasy, but you do. You're feeling worried and somewhat tense. You start to think about the budget spreadsheet in your briefcase that you will hand to internal audit when you arrive at the office later that morning. You absent-mindedly remove your laptop from your briefcase and begin to review the spreadsheet. You are startled to see a really egregious error on the second page. Feeling nervous but energized, you focus all your mental resources on the task, scanning every number on every line. You re-enter all the formulas and recompute all the numbers. You catch one more error, a fairly minor one. All of a sudden, you realize that the train has stopped; it has arrived at your station. You grab your bag in one hand, your coat in the other, and make a mad dash for the exit door, hurling yourself out the door just in time.

Nervousness and worry are often unwelcome, especially late at night when you are trying to get some sleep. But these emotions were used in an intelligent way in the spreadsheet situation. The feelings focused your thinking on a critically important task, helped you to concentrate on the details, and assisted you in error detection.

Taking Another's Perspective

To understand another person's point of view may be relatively easy. To truly see the world and experience it from a different perspective is much harder. This ability to experience what another person experiences or to feel what a certain course of action would be like requires us to generate an emotion or a set of emotions. Once we are in that mind-set, or feelings-set, we are better able to understand, from a thinking and emotional level, what it is like to be that person or to be in that situation.

Consider this scenario. You are a regional sales manager, and your team has not met its current quarterly sales goal. Not pleased with yet another problem quarter, you call a sales meeting, making it clear that everyone must attend. As the fifteen sales people enter the conference room, one seems more glum and despondent than the others. You start to feel a bit down yourself, and in doing so, you realize that they certainly don't need to be yelled at or made to feel even more pessimistic about the future. You feel what they are feeling, and this allows you to have more empathy for your staff. The sales problem is still real, but rather than demand that the sales staff turn things around, you open the meeting with, "I think I know how everyone here today feels. I'm feeling the same way." Surprised looks greet you, and as you continue, these looks turn to hopeful ones. "He's not going to fire us!" runs through everyone's mind, "He's on our side!" With this feeling of empathy and camaraderie, you can now turn your team to achieving a common goal: a successful next quarter.

Thinking Differently

Moods have a direct impact on thinking. As our mood shifts, so does our thinking. Those who are able to harness moods and alter them are more likely to engage in creative thinking, seeing the world in one way and a different way soon after that.[5]

When we say we are in a rut, we usually mean that everything around us is familiar, and we lose our sharpness of seeing and thinking.[6] Our senses are dulled, as are our minds. Thus when we travel to a faraway place, our attention is heightened and we see new things. Those who can shift their moods can take a "virtual vacation," anytime and anyplace. Their thinking and perspective shifts at will, thus enabling them to generate new ways of viewing the world.

A decision consists of logic as well as emotion, and if we can generate an emotion or a set of emotions that mimic some future or possible event, we can transport ourselves and walk around in this future world. How many times have you heard a story of a person who takes a new job, full of excitement, only to discover within weeks that the job isn't the right job, or what they expected? They did all of their due diligence during the job search, negotiated a great offer, met with all of the key players, and yet it still didn't work out. The one thing the job-seeker failed to do was to figure out how he would feel working at this new job. He didn't, or couldn't, create a sort of emotional fantasy world in which to spend a virtual day feeling what it would be like in that stifling environment.

Using Emotions to Problem Solve

John came into work with a smile on his face and in a very happy and upbeat mood. He sat down at his desk, and his boss came over to ask John to have a look at the marketing plan for the following year. John gladly agreed to do it and said he'd get it done right away. He worked quickly and sped through page after page of detailed charts and figures. There were still a few errors in the plan, and he circled them, noting what the corrections were in the margins.

The revisions were made the next day, and another version of the plan was prepared for presentation to the corporate office. Given the importance of the document, the manager wanted John to have a final, last look to make sure that all the changes were made. John walked into the office slowly, a bit downcast. "Everything okay?" his boss asked. "Oh, yeah, I'm fine," John replied with a slight smile. He wasn't depressed, but he was in a slightly negative mood. In this calm state of mind, John went immediately to work on the final edit. After checking that the first revision had been made, he continued to scan the document and was surprised to find another error—one that he had failed to catch the day before. Concerned, he flipped to the front of the document and did a painstaking analysis of every line. By the end of his review, he had found five new errors, two of which were fairly important.

Why did John do a better job analyzing the plan the second time? Was it because he was more familiar with it? Not likely, as such familiarity can actually decrease attention to detail. The only discernable difference was that the first day John was feeling upbeat, and on the second day his mood was slightly negative. Does it really matter if you are in a positive and happy mood when you are asked to proofread and review a marketing plan? It certainly does, and the ability to use emotions to facilitate thinking recognizes that thinking is assisted differently by different moods.

Why You Need to Use Emotions

The ability to use our emotions intelligently may underlie creative thinking. When people are able to get into and out of moods, they see things from different perspectives, and this perspective shift can often result in new ways of viewing the world.

This mood-generating ability may also play a role in *empathy*—feeling what other people feel. In order to relate genuinely to others, whether they are employees, bosses, or customers, we need to be able to understand them and their feelings. If a team member is feeling anxious, and we are able to generate a feeling of anxiety, we can have empathy for the person. In turn, our sense of empathy allows us to form strong bonds with the individual.

As certain moods facilitate certain types of thinking, we can be more efficient, generating, for example, a neutral mood before we proofread an article and a positive mood just before we go to a sales award ceremony.

Because thinking and feeling are vitally linked, people who are good at using emotions to facilitate thinking can be better at motivating others. They may have an intuitive sense of what inspires people, motivates them, and excites them. This is the essence of management and leadership, and these skills have a strong emotional component to them, as recognized by this definition of leadership: "Leadership, which embraces the emotional side of directing organizations, pumps life and meaning into management structures, bringing them to full life."[7]

In addition, leaders lead through words as well as through powerful icons of meaning, or symbols. Symbolic management relies on the use of these powerful ideas to focus and direct organization and "symbolic management is effective because it draws on the qualities of the heart and of the head—and, at times, it entirely bypasses the latter for the former."[8]

Certainly, symbolic management and leaders' facility in creating meaning tap into their ability to express emotions. But that ability also has to do with the interwoven nature of feeling and thinking—the ability to match the emotion to the message in order to communicate on a deep and meaningful level. Consider some of the memories you may have of certain leadership moments. People from the United States can often recall not only the words but the stirring tone of civil rights leader Martin Luther King Jr.'s "I have a dream" speech. Tragically, many vividly recall exactly where they were when they heard that Reverend King had been shot.

As England was plunged into one of its darkest moments, Prime Minister Winston Churchill roused not only the island nation but the world, when he spoke these words before the House of Commons:

> We shall not flag nor fail. We shall go on to the end. We shall fight in France and on the seas and oceans; we shall fight with growing confidence and growing strength in the air. We shall defend our island whatever the cost may be; we shall fight on beaches, landing grounds, in fields, in streets and on the hills. We shall never surrender.[9]

Let's take a look at some ways in which feelings and thinking interact.

Thinking Does Not Happen Without Emotion

Although we may take pride in ourselves as rational beings, decisions are not made with rationality alone; they depend on the interplay of emotions and thinking. In fact, as neuroscientist Damasio notes, "Appropriate emotions speed up decision-making enormously."[10]

How Moods Influence Thinking

Would you ask your boss for a raise when she was in a grouchy and grumpy mood? Most people would not, reasoning that she would be less likely to offer a reasonable raise when in a bad mood.

People do seem to know which moods are helpful and which moods are not in a particular situation. It's just that they don't always *know* that they know it. Even people stereotyped as anti-feeling depend heavily on emotionality. Take the case of the local high school football team. The coach knows when it is important to psych the team up and to get them thinking that they can win just this one game. Likewise, the coach knows that there are times when he needs to bring the pregame jubilation down a notch or two so his team will be able to better focus on executing the game plan.

How Emotions Influence Decision Making

Physicians are often viewed as pillars of rationality. Their years of medical training are scientifically and intellectually rigorous—so, of course, they would seem to be the last group to be influenced by fleeting moods. But that is not quite the case, as Alice Isen, a psychologist at Cornell University, discovered. In her experiments, already mentioned in Chapter One, she gave a small gift to medical students and doctors, with the result that their diagnoses were often more accurate and made more quickly. The finding that is most intriguing to us is that the "happy" doctors provided diagnostic notes that made helpful suggestions for treatment and included offers for further consultation.[11]

How can a cognitive decision-making process be influenced for such a seemingly inconsequential reason? Isen reasons that a gift, even a small one, induces a happy and positive mood. In a positive mood, people are then more likely to feel generous and helpful. But positive moods can also enhance creative problem solving, which may be the reason for the more accurate medical diagnoses.

How Emotion Controls Attention

Research by psychologists such as Gerald Clore (among others, such as our collaborator John D. Mayer) demonstrates that how we feel influences what we pay attention to and how we think, remember, and make decisions.[12]

Clore, for example, induced a happy or a sad mood in research subjects. He then asked them to perform a cognitive, or thinking, task such as judging what they thought of a political candidate or describing their attitudes toward a consumer product. Clore found that changes in mood had a direct impact on people's judgments.[13]

Mood and Memory Are Linked

Even our memories are linked to our emotions. The closer the match between the mood we experienced during learning and the mood we're in when we try to remember what we learned the more we remember. This phenomenon—remembering information better when in the same mood as when the information was acquired— is known as mood-congruent memory, or affect-dependent recall.

It's a straightforward relationship: if you are in a positive mood when you learn new information, it will help to be in a positive mood when you need to recall that information. Likewise, if you were a bit down when you had a conversation with a client and later need to remember what the client said, you might remember more information when you are in the same sort of mood.

That's an important lesson for the emotionally intelligent manager. For example, have you ever given a problem employee negative feedback, only to find that the person remembered only the positive things you said? If so, you are not alone. This happens for many reasons, but consider for now the mood and memory link. You gave your problem employee (let's call him Henry) the feedback in a very somber, serious, and grave manner. Later that week, it's reported to you that Henry felt that the meeting "went fairly well." In fact, Henry told a colleague of yours that "there are one or two things I need to work on, but the boss thought that I was doing a good job overall."

Contrary to what you may think, Henry has not lost touch with reality; neither have you. The negative feedback was given under a negative mood condition. The positive feedback, which does have some basis in reality, is recalled when Henry is feeling his usual happy self. He's primed his memory pump to recall only the positive feedback, as scanty as it was during your conversation with him.

This effect is heightened for memories with a great deal of emotionality. In general, such emotion-laden memories are recalled better, and over longer periods of time, than are memories that are less intense. Perhaps that's why it is worth spending more time on your presentation to the board so that the message appeals to head *and* heart.[14] The examples, illustrations, and stories that you tell in a meeting or a formal presentation create an emotional tone whether you realize it or not. It is up to the emotionally intelligent manager to match the mood with the message for maximum impact.

The emotionally intelligent manager is aware of the various connections between emotions and cognitive processes—attention, memory, thinking, reasoning, problem solving—and then attempts to match emotions, whenever possible, to the task at hand or to select tasks based on how a person is feeling.

◆ ◆ ◆

Feeling for others, establishing rapport, building trust—these are the tasks with which every team leader is confronted. These are also tasks that call for an intelligent integration of emotions with thinking. Generating a vision and communicating it to others so that they remember it, believe it, and buy in to it will likely have a lot to do with more than just the words. It's the feeling behind the words that will have the biggest impact on your message.

Emotions are not as chaotic as some people may believe. The next chapter examines rules of emotions.

CHAPTER 5

Predict the Emotional Future
Understanding Emotions

What does it mean to be able to understand emotions—step three of our model? Managers with this ability may be better described by the statements in Column A in Exhibit 5.1. People who struggle with this skill are often described by statements such as those listed in Column B.

Let's take a look at two people, each of whom is better described by one column than the other.

Exhibit 5.1. Understanding Emotions.

Column A: Skillful	Column B: Not Skillful
Makes correct assumptions about people	Misunderstands people
Knows the right thing to say	Gets on people's nerves
Makes good predictions about what people may feel	Is surprised by how people feel
Has rich emotional vocabulary	Finds it hard to explain feelings
Understands that one can feel conflicting emotions	Experiences on-or-off emotions, with few shades of gray
Has sophisticated emotional knowledge	Has only a basic understanding of emotions

Suzanne: Poor Manager of Conflict

Suzanne managed a twelve-person computer help-desk for a large retail organization. Her department experienced a series of problems, small ones at first, but problems that were cascading into a major headache for Suzanne and for the company. One employee, Mary, was threatening legal action for discrimination, and another, George, had already filed for a work-related stress disability claim.

These problems did not come as a surprise to Suzanne, because she was aware of how Mary and George were acting. But she was very upset when human resources called her about Mary's discrimination complaint, and she was shocked to hear that George was going out on disability. When quizzed about the discrimination complaint, Mary indicated that she did not feel "respected" by Suzanne or her departmental peers. In a conversation with George as he packed his briefcase to leave the office, he complained over and over again about how unfairly he was being treated and how his efforts were never recognized. Suzanne had no idea where these problems originated. In fact, these two events, though unrelated in Suzanne's worldview, were based on the same underlying cause.

If Suzanne could have connected the emotional dots, she would not have been surprised to learn about these problems. Here's where a what-if analysis is valuable (we'll talk more about this later in the chapter). Her analysis should have started by asking what causes anger. The answer is that anger often rises from a sense of injustice—a feeling that we are being treated unfairly. Suzanne knew Mary and George were angry, but she didn't have a clue as to why.

The next step of this emotional what-if analysis is to understand how anger grows and changes, even builds, over time. It can start out as a vague feeling of frustration and grow into dissatisfaction, resentment, and anger; if unchecked, it can turn into rage. Mary, a very sensitive person, performs a function that her boss, Suzanne, does not value. Such a lack of respect, although subtle, frustrated Mary. Months of such disrespect took its toll. George's need for recognition was strong, and without such recognition he felt increasingly unappreciated and devalued by Suzanne and the entire organization.

But it was not Suzanne's failure to identify her employees' feelings that was the issue. The problem stemmed from Suzanne's misdiagnosis of the cause of their feelings and the trajectory they would take over a period of time.

Suzanne has a limited understanding of emotion.

Len: Excellent Team Motivator

With degrees from Harvard, both an undergraduate degree and an M.B.A., Len had a successful career in investment banking. He was articulate, pleasant, and insightful. Len had a rich emotional vocabulary and could parse complex emotions into component parts. When dealing with important issues in his team of investment professionals, Len was quickly able to generate and then to evaluate different emotional scenarios.

In the previous fiscal year, his team had received one of the largest bonus pools in recent memory. However, it was now the year after the tech bubble had burst, and the current bonus pool was less than 10 percent of the pool from the height of the market. And yet his team was just as hardworking and as dedicated as the year before. In many cases, group members logged even more hours as they chased fewer and smaller deals. The formula was being written for a huge morale problem: work harder, earn much less money, and perhaps lose your job.

Len knew that springing the news of a tiny bonus pool on his team at year's end was guaranteed to create a mutiny among his staff. At the same time, if he simply let everyone know that no matter how hard they worked, they'd be making a lot less money, there would be a major, negative effect on productivity. He had to reason his way through this complex motivational issue.

Len recognized that people wanted to be treated honestly and fairly. So the first decision he made was to let his people know about the bonus pool situation. He shared the news with the entire group and followed up with each person individually. He managed their expectations and noted that as the economy turned around, they'd bring in more deals and, he hoped, increase the size of the pool. He then reserved a small portion of the pool for an incentive bonus to reward those employees who went above and beyond expectations. The criteria for such rewards were clearly spelled out and understood by everyone in the department. Even with his belt-tightened expense budget, Len managed to eke out a few dollars to hold recognition lunches for each employee; he would take his direct reports, as well as their reports, to lunch as a way of thanking them for their dedication and hard work.

As the economy came back and organizations began hiring again, Len's group had the highest retention rate in the bank and, in the next year, one of the most productive teams. Such outcomes were due to many factors, but one was Len's sophisticated understanding of emotions.

What Is Understanding Emotions?

Where does happiness come from? What about joy? Is joy the same as happiness, or is it qualitatively different? If excitement gets out of control, what happens to that person's emotions?

The ability to understand emotions is the most cognitive, or thinking-related, of the four skills of emotional intelligence. It involves a great deal of knowledge about emotions, as well as the ability to understand what causes emotions, what the relationships among various emotions are, how emotions transition from one stage to another, and how to put all this into language.

Considering these skills suggests an idea that many people find objectionable: there may be one correct way to feel. One of the premises of emotional intelligence is that there are indeed more and less likely ways to feel, given a certain event. There are times when one's feelings will follow a certain trajectory; our responses to events are influenced by emotional rules as well as by our interpretation of events and our past emotional history. But we reject the idea that there is necessarily a correct way to feel, per se.

A New Vocabulary

All areas of knowledge have their own vocabulary. The language spoken by IT managers may not be readily understood by the people in marketing, and a sales manager's vocabulary probably differs from the vocabulary of a finance manager. The specific words these managers know and use can be hard to understand if you don't have the same experience or training they have. People who lack the language of sales, marketing, finance, or programming will struggle to understand the nuances of those fields; the same is true for emotions. There is a vocabulary of emotions that you need to possess in order to engage in sophisticated reasoning about emotions.

How many emotion words do you need? Is there is a finite number of human feelings, or is each person unique, experiencing his or her own blend of emotions? There exist a wide variety of individual experiences of emotions, but the basic emotions are almost universally experienced by human beings.[1] In fact, Darwin, in *The Expression of Emotion in Man and Animals,* makes a forceful case for the existence of basic, universally experienced emotions, not just in people but in other species as well.

A century later, psychologist Paul Ekman described a theory of emotion that includes a set of basic human emotions such as anger, fear, happiness, sadness, surprise, and disgust.[2] Other researchers have their own models, with perhaps one of the more comprehensive emotions model being devised by Robert Plutchik.[3] A few lists of basic emotions, as described by Plutchik, Ekman, Tomkins, and Izard, are shown in Exhibit 5.2.[4]

Exhibit 5.2. Basic Emotions.

Plutchik	Ekman	Tomkins	Izard
Joy	Happiness	Enjoyment	Joy
Acceptance			
Fear	Fear	Fear	Fear
Surprise	Surprise	Surprise	Surprise
Sadness	Sadness	Distress	Distress
Disgust	Disgust	Disgust	
Anger	Anger	Anger	Anger
Anticipation		Interest	
		Shame	
		Contempt	Contempt

So what would a new vocabulary sound like? Something like this: "How are you doing?" you might ask. Rather than answer with an "okay" or a "fine," individuals who understand emotions distinguish among different and more subtle feelings and reply, "excited and expectant." The understanding of emotions, whether one's own or those of another person, can be quite sophisticated; this person understands how he or she feels.

There may be only shades of difference among emotion terms. The exact word can convey a precise emotional meaning. Consider the difference between envy and jealousy. What about irritation, anger, and rage? Am I annoyed or frustrated or angry? The words are different, and the meaning of each emotion term is different. To convey emotion accurately requires us to have a rich emotional vocabulary and to use it effectively. Our communications improve when we provide the other person with more precise information about our feeling states.

Emotional Cause and Effect

Emotions can be thought of as mathematical equations of the form "if X then Y" or, more precisely, "if event X then emotion Y." We've made the point repeatedly that emotions contain information or data about ourselves in relation to our environment. What is that information? The information in a feeling tells us about the event that gives rise to that feeling.[5]

Our ability to connect emotions to various events provides us with this emotional linkage of cause and effect. If we hear that a colleague has lost a valuable account, we may guess that he is feeling sad. If we later hear that he lost the account because one of his fellow sales people knowingly stole the account away, then we may guess that our colleague is feeling angry.

Emotional Complexity

Emotions are complex, and so are our feelings. Some emotions consist of combinations of simpler emotions. The emotion of contempt, for example, includes elements of disgust, anger, and even happiness. Situations can also give rise to complex or multiple emotions that may seem contradictory. Can you feel love and anger at the same time? Absolutely! Just ask any young lover whether he or she has been angry with a loved one. Can you feel both surprised and sad simultaneously? Just consider your own reaction if you received some unexpected bad news.

Indeed, some emotion theorists, including Plutchik, explicitly recognize the existence of emotional blends and the similarity of various emotions. And some individuals are more aware of this kind of emotional complexity than others.[6]

Emotional Progressions

Emotions by their nature change, develop, and progress. They are usually not static; instead, they follow a certain course as the feeling lessens or intensifies. This knowledge of emotional changes, and of their rules, represents a sophisticated understanding of emotion systems.

We can perform another type of emotional simulation (or what-if), whereby we predict the emotional future. Take a person who feels a certain way because of a given event. Because emotions arise from certain causes, if the cause of that emotion continues and intensifies, we should be able to predict how the person's feelings will change. For example, if you are feeling *content,* and the feeling grows, you will next feel *happy.*

Why Understanding Emotions Is Important

Emotions convey meaning. It's as simple as that. If we wish to understand ourselves and one another fully, we must have a sophisticated emotional knowledge base. Understanding emotions provides us with information about what makes people tick.

If we understand the causes of emotions, then we have learned something very important about a situation: we can gain insight into the causes of a problem. If we understand the ebb and flow of emotions, then we know something about the future: we can predict, perhaps with some accuracy, how the person will feel next, if certain events unfold in certain ways.

Our emotional vocabulary gives us a means of communicating this information to other people and provides us with an emotional language and reality.[7]

Figuring Out What Makes Someone Tick

There are huge differences in people as to why they feel a certain way. Consider the emotion of joy. Joy comes from gaining something valued, but what an individual person finds of value varies. At the same time, emotions obey rules, and if you understand these rules, you can understand people a whole lot better.

Let's say this morning your boss rushed into the office a few minutes later than normal. It's unusual for her to be late, and she seems a bit distracted. A colleague nudges you and whispers, "The boss is not in a good mood today, I can tell you that." You conclude just the opposite, because you understand that your baseball-loving boss is late because she took an out-of-town client to a baseball game last night. You'd figure that there is a good chance that she'd be feeling happy this morning, having engaged in an activity that she enjoys. You also know that it was a well-played, close game and that her team won. Your conclusion? The boss is tired but feeling quite content and happy.

Understanding Complexity

We all experience "mixed emotions" at times. What, exactly, do we mean by emotions being mixed? Mixed emotions are two or more emotions that are usually seen as contradictory, at least to some degree, with one another or in opposition to one another, such as happiness and sadness.

One of our clients, a foreign equities trader, was known for her brash, aggressive style. "Typical trader mentality" was how most of her colleagues viewed her, and to some extent they were correct. She was quite successful in this male-dominated environment. On the trading floor, she could scream as loud as her male counterparts, and she was a gung-ho, take-no-prisoners Wall Street warrior.

But Eva, like many such people, was more complex than that and did not quite fit the stereotype. Our first meeting with her was in a conference room off the trading floor. Eva expressed ambivalence regarding her role, was contemplative and thoughtful, and seemed both energized and excited by the nature of her work. But she was unhappy about the personal sacrifices she was making. She often seemed both happy and sad, energized and low-key. Eva is certainly not unique in this respect, and our ability to understand emotional complexity provides added insight into ourselves and others.

Predicting the Future with Emotional What-If Analyses

We've mentioned emotional what-if analysis several times. Now let's look at it more closely. What-if planning is critically important, and it doesn't matter whether you're in marketing, strategic planning, research, production, finance, operations, or technology. New products are usually developed only after you run your focus groups, understand the market, analyze the competition, and forecast market trends. Some people are better at this kind of what-if planning and forecasting than others, although even the best of them still can be off by a significant margin.

We can also do what-if planning and forecasting with people and emotions. We've talked about how emotions follow certain rules. These rules give us the data we need to do fairly accurate emotional forecasting. Consider a performance evaluation meeting. It is the end of the year, and you plan to give two of your employees negative feedback about their performance, a low rating, and no raise. Here's your emotionally intelligent manager question: *How will each of the employees feel?* It's a tough question to answer, so let's make it easier: How likely is it that the people will feel happy, excited, and joyous? How likely is it that they will feel sad, angry, or surprised?

Let's give you some more data to work with. The first employee has been avoiding you for some time, and you suspect that she realizes that her performance has been sub-par. The second employee is harder to read, but he seems to believe that he's had a good year, certainly not a poor one. The feedback you will give is almost identical in terms of performance. Emotional what-if analysis provides the tool you need to be able to make certain emotional predictions. Your analyses tell you that the first employee is less likely to feel surprised than is the second employee. Your knowledge of how emotions change over time also allows you to predict successfully that the first employee may become sad later on and that the second employee's surprise could turn to anger at some point. This knowledge can help you better prepare for the feedback sessions, as well as your later actions.

◆ ◆ ◆

Emotions aren't completely predictable, of course, but at times they are more predictable than the value of a company's stock. There may come a time when we train people to be mood analysts rather than equity analysts.

The first three steps of the Emotional Blueprint prepare you to take action. In the next chapter, we show you what to do with the data you have acquired from emotions.

CHAPTER 6

Do It with Feeling
Managing Emotions

We're now at step four of our model: managing emotions—that is, having the ability to incorporate one's feelings and the feelings of others into thinking. This is a fundamentally important part of emotional intelligence. In fact, it is likely what came to your mind when you heard about the idea of emotional intelligence the first time.

What are the attributes of someone who can manage emotions—their own and those of others? Manager A in Exhibit 6.1 is skillful at managing emotions, whereas Manager B lacks the ability.

Exhibit 6.1. Managing Emotions.

Column A: Skillful	Column B: Not Skillful
Emotions focus attention, inform decision making, and energize adaptive behavior	Emotions are distracting and derail adaptive behavior
Can "psych up," calm down, or maintain a mood, as desirable	Is a slave to passions
Can cheer others up, calm others down, or manage others' feelings appropriately	Has no intentional impact on others' feelings; has unintentional impact on others' feelings
Is open to one's feelings and the feelings of others	Shuts off feelings
Leads a rich emotional life	Leads an emotionally impoverished life
Inspires other people	Cannot connect with other people

Consider two people we know who reflect the profiles of Managers A and B. Avery, an engineering project manager, is best described by the Manager B list, whereas Cory, a product manager, is more like Manager A.

What Does Managing Emotions Look Like?

Avery: A Disabler

Enabling people to act is a core leadership function, but Avery seemed to be a master at *disabling* those on his team. Avery was intellectually gifted, and he knew it. His analytical skills were superb, and he could run intellectual rings around most people. He loved crossword puzzles, chess, and Scrabble, and he enjoyed taunting others who unwittingly accepted his challenge to play these games with him.

His taunts and public humiliations of others came at the most unlikely times. Avery's sense of superiority would bubble over into arrogance and spite during presentations and team meetings, although rarely when his boss was in the room. It appeared that Avery could keep himself in line on such occasions, but his real self emerged during his one-on-ones and team interactions. He wasn't subtle, either. On one occasion, Avery angrily stood up during a presentation that one of his team members was delivering and started to yell at him about how stupid the presentation was. "This is a waste of my time!" he fumed.

During an unexpected downsizing, his HR contact suggested that Avery should deal compassionately with those losing their jobs. Avery just looked at the HR person and said, "Why would I do that? They're fired, gone. It's done, and it doesn't matter what I say." "Well then," the HR person wondered, "what about supporting the staff who survived the downsizing?" With a look of disdain, Avery replied, "They should feel lucky they even have a job."

Generally, it seemed that Avery lashed out in anger at those who were least able to defend themselves. He was, in a word, a bully. Avery's ability to manage emotions was low—very low.

Cory: An Enabler

Now consider the product manager, Cory. Cory was charged with guiding a new product out the door and into the hands of the direct-sales force. But standing in her way was the director of the service organization, who was responsible for installing and maintaining the new product in customers' offices. Cory spent many an hour with Will, the customer service director, trying to understand his issues, needs, and ideas. There was clearly a lot of negativity toward the new product, as there was toward anything new and different. Over a period of several months, Cory worked with Will, listening to Will's concerns and making appropriate changes to the product schedule to meet the needs of the service staff. Finally, Will agreed to support the plan. Cory knew that Will had not fully bought into it, but for now it was the best she could do.

It was therefore not a big a surprise to Cory when Will brought up the product plan during his quarterly update to the division's president. Will indicated that service had never seen the need for the new product and was "troubled" by the product plan. Cory was angry. She had reached an agreement with Will, and he had clearly violated the agreement. Not only that, but he had done so in front of the president, knowing full well that this review session was just that—a review session and not a working meeting for discussion.

The division president nodded and took a few notes, and Will was ready to go to the next agenda item when Cory stood up. Her anger guided and motivated her but did not blind her. Will had a panicked look on his face as he realized that Cory was calling his bluff. But Cory did not slam Will. Instead, she said, "Excuse me. Will and I have been working through these issues for more than two months now. We seem to resolve each issue as it arises, but there is still a fear in the service group. It's partly a workload issue, but it's also about having different expectations for the service engineers. I don't think we as an organization have addressed this other issue. If we don't, there is no way for our product to succeed. Not only that, there is no way that any of the other new products in the pipeline will make it either. It's all the same technology and the same service issue. I'm surprised by Will's comments, as service and marketing have come to an agreement over these issues. So, Will, perhaps you want to clarify just what it is that service has agreed to?" Cory gave Will a hard stare, and she remained standing until Will reluctantly got up to speak.

Will was still flustered, and it took him a moment to find his voice. When he did, he simply looked at the group, noting, "Yeah, that's about it. My guys are good people, but this is different. I'm concerned about our capabilities. We're going flat out now, and then we're expected to also learn this new technology." Will paused, watching as Cory prepared to get up and call his bluff again, but Will jumped in with one last statement: "And, yeah, service has agreed to support this plan. So, we're okay to go ahead." Then Cory stood and voiced her support as well and reminded the president that the product launch plan called for additional service training, which the board had put on hold temporarily.

The president pondered all of this for a moment, and then he promised to go before the board and get that training funding fast-tracked. "Does that give you the time and resources you need?" he asked, looking both at Will and Cory. To which, they simultaneously answered, "Yes!"

Cory's quick thinking represents an impressive demonstration of managing emotions successfully. Most people would have either lashed out, stalked off angrily, or slunk into the chair, wounded and hurt. Cory was not happy to be attacked this way, but she had a choice—to meet fire with fire or to manage the situation so that the product could move on.

Cory's ability to manage emotions, both her own and those of others, is very strong.

What Is Managing Emotions?

This chapter explains the keystone of emotional intelligence: the ability to manage emotions. This ability does not mean that you never feel emotions or act emotionally but that your emotions are integrated into your decisions and into your behavior in a way that enhances your life and the lives of those around you.

People with a strong ability to manage emotions can be passionate, but they also have good emotional self-control, tend to be even-tempered, think clearly when they are experiencing strong feelings, make decisions based on their hearts and their heads, and generally reflect on their emotions often. At the same time, individuals who are not especially skilled in emotional management often are seen by others as having a bad temper, losing control, and taking their feelings out on others. They sometimes seem blinded by their feelings, doing stupid things by acting on gut impulse rather than thinking things through. Paradoxically, they don't try very hard to reflect on these feelings.

There is another type of manager who lacks the ability to manage emotions. This is the cold, logical, analytical manager who is driven only by the facts, at least the facts as he defines them. This emotionally unintelligent manager tries, in vain, to make so-called objective and unemotional decisions, and in doing so, fails to see the forest for the trees.

The emotionally intelligent manager leverages the data of emotions and the wisdom in feelings while recognizing that moods arise for unknown reasons. Whereas acting with our emotions is usually the smart choice, acting out with our moods isn't usually a good idea. Emotions signal that something important is going on or is about to happen. But they also bring feelings and thoughts that we may not want to experience. How we deal with emotional events makes a big difference in how successful we are in achieving our objectives, even in how we remember and process information.

Consider an experiment by Jane Richards and James Gross at Stanford University in which these researchers showed an upsetting film to people. Some were told to suppress the expression of their emotions, and some were not given any special instructions. After the film, everyone was given a memory test about details in the film. Those who tried to suppress their emotions remembered *less* about the movie than did the people who were not given any special instructions.[1]

In another experiment, people viewed upsetting slides. Some people were asked to suppress their emotional reaction, and others were asked to try to make the experience a positive one. Both groups looked at the slides the same amount of time; those asked to hide their feelings did not look away. The people who tried to see the experience as a positive one reported less negative emotions than the others. The most fascinating finding was that those people who were asked to suppress their reaction remembered less verbal information about the slides (such as what people said) than the others did but that there were no differences in their nonverbal memory (such as describing what was in a particular scene). This may mean that we talk to ourselves when we try to suppress our emotional expressions. We monitor how we feel, think about how we might look, match the two, and then make any necessary corrections to our expression.[2]

What this research tells us is that if we always try to suppress our emotions, we may not remember as much information about an upsetting or emotional event. If we suppress our feelings, memory for painful or emotional encounters suffers. In fact, it is hypothesized that men may remember less about social interactions than women because men, in general, tend to suppress their emotions more than women do.

Welcoming Emotion

Emotions are not always welcome. There are many instances when we try to suppress emotional reactions. This kind of suppression can make sense at times, because we lack the resources to process the feeling, and we need to ignore the emotions and the information contained in them. If this suppression becomes habitual, however, we lose the information value of our emotions.

At other times, we have to allow ourselves to *feel* a feeling, even to welcome the emotion that might be unexpected or uncomfortable. It takes a good deal of energy *not* to feel, and this energy—mental energy—gets siphoned away from problem solving, decision making, and being aware. Imagine trying to mourn the death of a loved one by trying hard not to feel sad. It just doesn't work.

Remaining open to feelings can be problematic for positive as well as negative emotions. Some people are uncomfortable with happiness, or at least with the extreme form of happiness—joy. They may be afraid that they will lose control and in a burst of enthusiasm expose themselves to ridicule. In some cultures, for example in Asian countries like Japan, experiencing too much joy, especially if it is due to one's accomplishments, is seen as a bit selfish and embarrassing. Sometimes people from these cultures cover up a joyful facial expression with their hands or try not to look too happy. Similarly, in many parts of the world it is considered bad luck to arouse the envy of other people by being too happy about one's good fortune. One doesn't want to tempt the "evil eye." In such cultures, the regulation of positive feelings may be especially important, and people may develop all kinds of strategies in order to be effective in doing so. Americans, if they are outside the office, do not seem especially troubled about experiencing "too much" joy, however.[3]

Not Being Used by Emotions

Emotion management includes the ability to control overwhelm-ing emotion when the feelings threaten to hurt us, or others, phys-ically, mentally, or emotionally. We also learn not to express certain emotions when doing so would be inappropriate. Many times, it is a more intelligent decision to smile, even though we are sad, or to let pass a slight or an insult.

Emotions act as a signaling system, yet if we always act on those signals, we can react impulsively and not blend emotion and thought. Perhaps the emotion and its source need to be con-firmed, or we need to ensure that our perceptions of the emotion-causing event were correct. The familiar strategy of just waiting a moment—counting to ten—can often make a big difference in whether the response we make is effective.

But there will be times when "he who hesitates is lost." If we stop and reflect on the unreasonableness of our fear and see that it is unnecessary to flee, we may end up being trapped on a sinking ship or cornered by a threatening adversary. Similarly, if we don't trust the happiness we feel and let an opportunity pass us by, we may come to regret not acting on our passion. As we mentioned earlier, in the workplace the emotion most often *not* acted on is joy.[4]

For many years, psychologists debated whether venting one's feelings—for example, expressing anger cathartically such as by yelling and screaming—helps one manage such feelings. The ver-dict is now in: catharsis does not seem to help.[5] The more one vents, the worse one tends to feel (at least until exhaustion takes over). Given these findings, we argue that emotional management is nei-ther suppressing one's feelings nor venting them. Effective emo-tion management is not a question of whether we should strive to control our feelings but how we can intelligently engage and dis-engage from them.

Letting Emotions Motivate and Inspire

We shouldn't forget the lesson that an emotion teaches us. Just as an emotion directs our attention to an event, it can motivate and inspire us. As an emotion lingers but weakens over time, we can draw on it for insight and energy. As our rage cools to anger, the feeling can be harnessed to take a stand against injustice. Or we can use the feeling to communicate the injustice to others who are not in an angry state at the time.

Emotions are not passive. They have an *action* component or tendency. They motivate our behavior. In fact, some emotion theorists, such as Nico Frijda at the University of Amsterdam, believe that the tendency for emotions to impel us into action (running away when afraid or accepting help from others when sad) is the primary reason we have evolved an emotion system.[6]

Finding Out What's Going On

The first step in managing emotions is to be aware of them and accept them. Emotional awareness is the building block of successful emotion regulation, but we need more than simply to be aware of our own and others' feelings. We require a bit of sophisticated processing of the emotions we experience.

How am I feeling? is an important first question to ask oneself, but to that we would add:

- Am I clear about my feelings?
- How strong is this feeling?
- How much influence does this feeling seem to have on my thoughts right now?
- Is this an emotion that I often experience?
- Is it unusual for me to feel this way?

These are the automatic questions that people who are sophisticated and skillful in processing their emotions ask themselves. They associate a current feeling with a larger picture of identity and reality. They relate emotions to a sophisticated sense of oneself. The questions also help to filter out the "noise" of a mood from the signal of an emotion.

Integrating Feelings

Feeling bad can be good, and feeling good can be bad. It all depends on the situation, the people involved, and our goal. Sometimes it makes sense to keep a bad mood intact, whereas at other times it makes more sense to snap out of it and feel happy or neutral. As Aristotle said, "Anyone can become angry—that is easy. But to be angry with the right person, to the right degree, at the right time, for the right purpose, and in the right way—that is not easy."[7]

We need to make intelligent choices about our emotions. To do so means that we need to integrate emotions and thought into all that we do. This requires us to be balanced and fair with our emotions—to neither push them down below the surface of awareness nor to elevate them so that they are exaggerated in importance. To do either means that we are being too rational or too emotional. Emotional balance is the goal: passion with reason.[8]

This is not to imply that we should never experience, or act, on strong emotion. In fact, many times this is the intelligent choice. Feeling joyful, we can sing, dance, and celebrate a wonderful event. That joy can be expressed to its fullest, such as at the birth of a child or the winning of a major contract. In the face of a violent physical assault, our anger rises and intensifies, motivating us to defend ourselves against the assault. Often we should defend ourselves against an unfair verbal attack; not to do so can spell disaster.

Why Is Managing Emotions Important?

Successfully managing emotions means that our conduct is guided by both our thoughts and our feelings. This ability allows us to integrate cognition and affect to generate effective solutions. The idea that there is passion on the one hand and reason on the other represents a false dichotomy that may encourage us in the mistaken belief that somehow our feelings are neither rational nor informative. Without the ability to integrate thinking and feeling, we may analyze problems in painstaking detail and pride ourselves on being a calm and unemotional person. But we miss important sources of information that are signaled by our feelings. Or we may be awash in emotion, becoming overwhelmed with feeling and flailing around looking for a way out.

The ability to integrate balances heart and mind. It helps us recognize that emotions contain powerful and important information and that decision making cannot succeed in the absence of emotion. As Damasio demonstrated through the study of patients with various kinds of brain damage, when the brain centers involved in emotion are not functional, it is nearly impossible to make good, "rational" decisions.[9] The ability to regulate your own mood and that of others may be part of what makes good managers great leaders.

But what happens when we fail to regulate our emotions? An example may be found in the failure of so many of our New Year's resolutions. It seems that the deck is stacked against us in this battle, especially when we get emotionally upset. Immediate emotional regulation (making ourselves feel better in the short term) is much more important to us than is impulse control (achieving our long-term goals). Even if we are extremely committed to achieving some important but long-term goal by controlling our impulses, we will likely give up on our resolutions when we are upset as a way to stop feeling upset. Our bid to control impulses fails because we find that feeling good, or not feeling bad, is much more important to us than achieving some distant, far-off goal such as going back to school for an advanced degree, not yelling at customer service, or revising next year's budget.

In a set of classic experiments, Columbia University psychologist Walter Mischel found that children who were asked to remember a sad event in their lives were later less able to resist the temptation to play with a forbidden toy than were other children.[10] Their sorrow made it hard to delay immediate gratification.

In another experiment by Roy Baumeister and colleagues, some people were given a pill and told that it made their mood unchangeable, whereas others were not given the pill. Each group then experienced a stressor in the laboratory. The group with the mood-freezing pill was less likely to give in to their impulses.[11] This means that you turn to the refrigerator or a cigarette only if you believe it's going to help you feel better. Of course, the mood-freezing pill might have also changed the subject's physiology and body chemistry. The problem with this hypothesis is that there is no such thing as a mood-freezing pill—the pill was just a placebo and had no noticeable physiological effects. The effects were all in people's minds.

When we feel that our moods are fairly set and stable, we continue attending to the difficult or boring task at hand, rather than taking a snack break or hanging out at the water cooler chatting with colleagues. When we experience emotional distress, however, we are more likely to give in to our impulses. In the short run, this works fine; eating or drinking makes us feel better. In the long run, though, giving in to these impulses is not adaptive, and we end up feeling worse than we did before. Our negative mood returns, and it is now accompanied by feelings of guilt.

You can see a classic, real-world experiment, unfortunately, almost anytime at your neighborhood pub. Most people believe that drinking alcohol enhances their mood and lowers anxiety. If you are feeling upset, angry, or depressed, having a drink to calm yourself or to get out of that funk may work, but only for a short time. After another drink or two, however, you will likely feel even worse than when you started. Alcohol may elevate your mood, but after a few drinks it does just the opposite, and you end up feeling worse. Pharmacologically, alcohol is a depressant.

Similarly, when people try to lose weight and are feeling a bit depressed, that piece of chocolate cake in the refrigerator looks awfully good. Eating makes us feel good, and eating chocolate can make us feel *really* good. That is, until we realize that we blew our diet—again! Food is no substitute for good emotion management skills.

Aggression is another area where impulse control loses out to affect regulation. If we experimentally create a bad or negative mood in someone, that person is more likely to become aggressive as a means of trying to feel better. You are even more likely to lose your cool in such a situation if you believe that blowing your top and venting your anger will make you feel better. In fact, June Tangney, a psychologist at George Mason University, has shown that feeling shame is one of the great instigators of subsequent rage.[12] Reflect on that before you publically embarrass a coworker!

Our desire to get out of a bad mood can also influence long-term investment strategies. Diane Tice and her colleagues had students participate in an investment simulation game in which a long-term strategy would result in higher winnings than a short-term strategy to maximize profits. Tice found that people in a sad mood were more likely to cash in earlier than were people in a positive or neutral mood, presumably because those in a sad mood wanted to feel better, and making money—in the short term—was the way to do it.[13]

Procrastination is another dysfunctional affect-regulation tool. Working on our long-term goals often means engaging in tasks that are not much fun. We also may worry about our ability to succeed. The result is that we procrastinate by engaging in some enjoyable activity. When we are in a bad mood, we procrastinate even more, since doing something fun is one way to make ourselves feel better. A sad marketing manager, given the choice between preparing routine reports or hanging out with his coworkers during lunch, will likely opt for the long lunch. If we are feeling sad and we are at the office, we might spend time sharpening our pencils or grabbing a candy bar out of the vending machine rather than working on the marketing presentation.

◆ ◆ ◆

If we can manage our emotions, that is, blend emotion and thought, we increase the chances that our decisions will be more effective and our lives more adaptive. This is the challenge of emotion management—neither to suppress feelings nor to vent them but to reflect on them, integrate them with our thinking, and use them as a source of information and an inspiration for intelligent decision making.

In the next chapter we tell you how we measure these four emotional abilities, and then we help you enhance your skills.

CHAPTER 7

Measuring Emotional Skills

Do people know how smart they are? It's easy enough to find out. First, teach a group of people what IQ scores represent and then have them estimate their own IQ. Next, give them an IQ test and see how closely the two numbers match. What would you think the match is? Are people generally accurate or inaccurate estimators of their intelligence?

Research by a number of scientists indicates that we are not terribly good at estimating our intellectual skills. The correlation between estimated and actual IQ ranges from .15 to about .30.[1] (Correlations can range from 1.00, indicating a perfect relationship, to .00, indicating no relationship at all. There are also *negative* correlations, meaning that a correlation of −1.00 shows a perfectly negative relationship between two things: as one goes up, the other goes down.) A correlation between .15 and .30 suggests that people have some understanding of how smart they are, but not very much.

If this self-estimating method does not work, then you could ask someone else to help you out. Ask an observer to rate your IQ, and perhaps the result will be more accurate. Perhaps. In studies in which teachers evaluated the IQ of their students, the correlation increased to about .50—a great improvement but with a lot of room for error.[2] Clearly, just asking people to rate their own or others' skills doesn't produce very satisfactory results.

How to Measure Skills

If you can't ask people how smart they are, and you can't ask others how smart you are, how can we find out whether you are smart or not? Well, what if we wanted to know how fast you could type? In this case, we would probably administer a typing test; you'd be given a few pages and asked to type them up. We would count the number of words you typed correctly, and that would be your typing skill, or typing speed. Next, by giving a typing test to a large and representative sample of people, we would be able to gauge your typing ability relative to other people's ability. We could, in effect, compute your Typing Quotient, or TQ.

Emotional skills can also be measured in an objective way through the use of ability, performance, or knowledge tests. Such tests would ask a series of questions like these:

- What is the cause of sadness?
- What is an effective strategy for calming an angry customer?

This is more or less what the Mayer, Salovey, Caruso Emotional Intelligence Test (the MSCEIT) does.[3] The MSCEIT (pronounced mess-keet) asks people to solve emotional problems, and the correctness of the answers is evaluated. In turn, a person's scores are compared to a large, normative database (from the general public or from emotions experts) to compute a sort of emotional skill quotient. Although we could call this score an EQ, we prefer to call the scores an emotional intelligence quotient or EI score. The term EQ is often used to refer to the non-ability-based approaches to assessing emotional intelligence.

Right and Wrong Answers

One concern that people raise about an ability approach to testing emotional intelligence is that intelligence tests assume that there are right and wrong answers. Yet, how can a feeling be correct or incorrect?

Take the example of assessing how accurate a person is in identifying the emotions of other people. Consider a person who has a huge smile on her face. Her eyes are twinkling, her mouth is up-turned in a big smile, and she is laughing. How is this person feeling? If you were to say "angry" because you felt that it is possible that the person is angry, you would most likely be wrong.

Not all emotional intelligence test items can be scored in this manner, but many certainly can be.

Sample Measurements

Try your hand at a few sample ability items from an emotional intelligence test. These sample items won't give you an estimate of your actual skill level, but they will give you a feel for the way scientists measure emotional skills.

Measuring Your Ability to Read People

The ability to identify emotions means that you are able to gauge accurately how another person feels. Figure 7.1 shows one way we can test your ability to do so.

What's the Answer?

An initial look at this face leads most of us to say that she is feeling happy. After all, that's quite a smile! She must be happy, perhaps excited. It's a fairly easy task to cross out some emotions. We can quickly dispense with sadness and disgust.

Let's make this a bit harder. Look at the face again. Now ask whether she *really* feels happy or not. Is she smiling out of happiness? Is it a *real* smile?

When we are asked a follow-up question about the genuineness of her emotional expression, we need to go back and take a longer, more critical second look. It is this analysis that requires our critical emotional skills—those that do not merely identify surface emotion in others but go deeper as we compare different features of her face. We ask what a real smile consists of and whether our target person displays these components.[4] In this example, the smile is mirrored by her eyes. Hers is probably a real smile, not a posed smile. (Happiness, and perhaps Excitement, would be the best responses.)

Figure 7.1. Identifying Emotion: Sample Item.

Look at this face and indicate how the young woman is feeling. Is she feeling any of these emotions?

Sadness

Happiness

Anger

Disgust

Surprise

Excitement

Photograph by Ethan Spector.

Measuring Your Ability to Get in the Right Mood

The next EI test question is about feelings and whether they matter. Do you know how feelings change the way we think, plan, and decide? Try the sample question in Exhibit 7.1.

What's the Answer?

Down or negative moods such as sadness focus our attention. We attend more carefully and critically to details. We easily seek and find errors and problems. Being in a sad mood can be helpful if our task is to proof a document such as a budget.

Exhibit 7.1. How Sadness Influences Thinking.

Imagine that you are feeling somewhat down (sad) right now. Which of the following tasks would you best accomplish in such a mood?

1. Writing a thank-you note
2. Proofing a budget
3. Calling a friend to wish her happy birthday

Note that we are not talking about depression, when a person finds it hard to function or to care about what he or she is doing. This ability helps us to match feelings with thinking tasks.

Measuring Your Ability to Predict the Emotional Future

Understanding emotions is the ability to recognize the causes of emotions, how emotions change, and how complex emotions are combined from two or more simple emotions. One way to estimate a person's level of skill in this area is to ask emotional vocabulary questions, such as the one in Exhibit 7.2.

What's the Answer?

Why do people feel sorrow? They feel sorrow when they experience a loss, whether a death, a loss of an idea, a chance, or a dream. They are disappointed about not getting something they had hoped for. Disappointment in turn can lead to frustration, a subtle form of anger. It is when we realize that the loss is unavoidable and come to accept the loss that our disappointment merges into a feeling of sadness. This is a very sophisticated form of reasoning. (Option "c" is the best response.)

Measuring Your Ability to Do It with Feeling

How should emotions be managed? Is there a better or worse way to help others? The test sample in Exhibit 7.3 attempts to measure your ability to manage emotions effectively.

Exhibit 7.2. Emotion Vocabulary.

Sorrow most closely combines which two feelings? Choose the best option:

    a. Anger and surprise

    b. Fear and anger

    c. Disappointment and acceptance

    d. Remorse and joy

Exhibit 7.3. Effective Emotion Management Strategies.

One of your colleagues at work looks upset and asks if you will eat lunch with him. At the cafeteria, he motions for you to sit away from the other diners. After a few minutes of slow conversation, he says that he wants to talk to you about what's on his mind. He tells you that he lied on his résumé about having a college degree. Without the degree, he wouldn't have gotten the job. Which of the following would be most likely to result in having your colleague immediately feel better about the situation?

1. Ask him how he feels about it so you can understand what's going on. Offer to help him, but don't push yourself on him if he really doesn't want your help.

2. Have him share all the possible negative consequences of his act. Get him to work through what the worst outcome could be so he realizes that the situation may not be as bad as he thinks.

3. Quickly change the subject and do not deal with his issue right now. Getting his mind off the problem is the best thing to do.

What's the Answer?

Perhaps none of these options really grabs you. Although we might believe that suppressing the issue—not thinking about it—can have immediate positive results, it may be one of the ways to cause your colleague greater distress. Telling someone *not* to think about an issue can focus even more attention on the problem.[5] Entering into imaginary, negative outcomes may heighten his or her worry and concern. Talking it through in a supportive manner may be the best option (Answer 1).

Deciding on the most effective solution in such a problem depends in large measure on the goal. You must start with identifying what your objective is in the situation, and then you can weigh various alternatives. In many cases, the emotionally intelligent alternative is the one in which the underlying emotions are processed and can inform your thinking and reasoning. As uncomfortable as this may feel, it is necessary. Our thinking can lead us down all sorts of dead-end paths, whereas clear emotional data hold the key.

The Real Deal

Developing a scientifically valid test takes a lot more work than just writing some test questions. When we developed the MSCEIT, we had thousands of people answer the questions; we revised many questions and analyzed each of them to make sure they "worked." After all, not all emotion problems have good answers. We also worked hard to make sure that the results of the MSCEIT were reliable, that is, they are stable estimates of emotional intelligence. The next step was to find out whether the MSCEIT really measures what it is supposed to measure (it does) and to find out what it relates to (that's what we cover in this book).

◆ ◆ ◆

The brief examples in this chapter can help you better understand how scientists have attempted to objectively measure these intellectual skills. The actual MSCEIT has 141 items and takes about forty-five minutes to administer. Your scores are compared to a normative database of five thousand people. If you are interested in the MSCEIT, we have placed more detailed technical information about it at a Web site: www.emotionaliq.org.

The next part of this book provides hands-on skill building for each of the four emotional intelligence abilities.

PART 3

Develop Your Emotional Skills

If emotional intelligence is really just that, a kind of intelligence, then how can you hope to become *more* emotionally intelligent? After all, many researchers claim that your IQ is what it is, and is relatively fixed throughout your life. Does the same hold for your emotional intelligence quotient?

The answer is that we don't know for sure, but we do know that people can acquire skills and knowledge. So, for example, emotional intelligence, as measured by the MSCEIT, is higher among middle-aged adults than among young adults. We are optimistic that the skills comprising emotional intelligence can be improved. After all, it is one purpose of this book to help you develop your emotional knowledge further and to enhance your emotional skills. Skill development in this area can start with knowledge. To truly develop these skills, you have to go well beyond simply reading this book into the realm of action. We'll provide the knowledge you need to develop your emotional intelligence skills, and we'll guide your actions. The rest, and the most critical part of development, is up to you.

CHAPTER 8

Read People Correctly
Improving Your Ability to Identify Emotions

We have discussed the ability to identify emotions (step one of the model) as part of emotional intelligence, including emotions in one's own feelings and in the faces, bodies, and voices of other people. This ability also includes the accurate expression of emotion so you can communicate effectively with others.

The purpose of this chapter is to present some exercises that might help you learn to identify emotions better. You obviously have some skill in this area already. When facial expressions are clear—your child smiling with joy while unwrapping a birthday present, for example—it isn't hard to identify the emotions they reflect. But sometimes identifying feelings can be trickier. Not all facial expressions come about honestly, for example.

We will focus especially on helping you develop your abilities to read people better. Without solid and accurate emotional information, the rest of your decision making and thinking with and about emotions is faulty. Computer programmers have a saying: "Garbage in, garbage out," and this idea also applies to emotional intelligence. If emotions aren't identified correctly, they can't be used, understood, and managed. However, before one can read other people, one has to be aware of one's own feeling. It is a rare person whose skills in understanding others do not begin with understanding oneself.

Becoming Aware of Your Own Feelings and Emotions

Do you know how you feel? A silly question, perhaps, but we need to ask you anyway. Many of us block out our feelings, at least part of the time. Emotional intelligence requires us to have access to our emotions, if not all the time then certainly at critical moments.

Take the short quiz in Exhibit 8.1 to help you start thinking about your own level of emotional awareness.

The more YY's and Y's you circled, the greater your emotional awareness might be. Becoming more aware of emotionality in yourself will help you identify the emotions of other people. Beyond just saying that you need to be aware of various emotional clues, it also helps if you actively begin to process emotional information.

For those of you who found that you are not very aware of your emotions, moods, and feelings, a mood journal is a useful tool for raising personal emotional awareness. You can use any format that makes sense to you, but we recommend that you use some form of a rating scale several times a day, for several emotion terms.

Here is an example of a mood scale that you might find of value in keeping a mood journal. This mood scale is organized around positive and negative affect, a convenient way of thinking about moods.[1] Ask yourself this set of questions several times each day (for example in the morning, afternoon, and evening). Rate each feeling listed in Exhibit 8.2 as quickly as you can.

Exhibit 8.1. Becoming Aware of Your Own Feelings.

	NO!	No	Yes	YES!
It's important to think about feelings.	NN	N	Y	YY
Emotions should be felt and noticed.	NN	N	Y	YY
I pay attention to how I am feeling.	NN	N	Y	YY
I usually make sense of how I am feeling.	NN	N	Y	YY
My feelings are clear.	NN	N	Y	YY
I know how I am feeling.	NN	N	Y	YY

Exhibit 8.2. Mood Scale.

Feeling	Definitely do *not* feel			Maybe, maybe not			Definitely feel		
Lively	1	2	3	4	5	6	7	8	9
Excited	1	2	3	4	5	6	7	8	9
Gloomy	1	2	3	4	5	6	7	8	9
Tired	1	2	3	4	5	6	7	8	9
Caring	1	2	3	4	5	6	7	8	9
Content	1	2	3	4	5	6	7	8	9
Down/blue	1	2	3	4	5	6	7	8	9
Jittery	1	2	3	4	5	6	7	8	9
Drowsy	1	2	3	4	5	6	7	8	9
Grouchy	1	2	3	4	5	6	7	8	9
Peppy	1	2	3	4	5	6	7	8	9
Nervous	1	2	3	4	5	6	7	8	9
Calm	1	2	3	4	5	6	7	8	9
Friendly	1	2	3	4	5	6	7	8	9
Fed Up	1	2	3	4	5	6	7	8	9
Active	1	2	3	4	5	6	7	8	9

An alternative way to represent feelings adds a bit more complexity (see Exhibit 8.3). This is also a useful way of characterizing how you are feeling at any given time.

Your mood journal, using the scales shown, can be expanded into an emotional diary. This requires a bit more work, but it is a good way to become more in touch with your emotional experiences. It is helpful to list your emotions at some points in your day, along with the events that occurred just prior to listing them. This emotional diary can help you see patterns in your emotional life, how external events influence you, what bothers you, what sets you off, and what brings you pleasure.

Here's a suggested format for an emotional diary:

Exhibit 8.3. Emotion Scale.

Emotion	Definitely do *not* feel			Maybe, maybe not			Definitely feel		
Lively	1	2	3	4	5	6	7	8	9
Happy	1	2	3	4	5	6	7	8	9
Sad	1	2	3	4	5	6	7	8	9
Angry	1	2	3	4	5	6	7	8	9
Anticipating	1	2	3	4	5	6	7	8	9
Fearful	1	2	3	4	5	6	7	8	9
Surprised	1	2	3	4	5	6	7	8	9
Accepting	1	2	3	4	5	6	7	8	9
Disgusted	1	2	3	4	5	6	7	8	9
Jealous	1	2	3	4	5	6	7	8	9
Ashamed	1	2	3	4	5	6	7	8	9

Emotional Diary Entry
Date:
Time:
Place:
People involved:
Event:
Events *preceding* emotion:
Emotions felt:

Don't try to analyze the event in this part of the diary. Just keep a list. Then feel free to write about the event—how it made you feel and how you responded. There has been a good deal of research on moods and biological rhythms or cycles. For instance, some people say they are "morning people"; others label themselves "night owls." There may be something to these labels, as we all tend to cycle up and down during the day.[2]

Once you've collected enough emotional data, go back through the diary and try to determine whether you, too, have natural mood cycles. For some people, food has a major impact on their emotions. The "sugar high" we hear about is a real phenomenon for many of us. A big meal may make us drowsy or bring our mood down. Lack of sleep influences emotions as well. Perhaps you will find that those unproductive afternoon meetings are not due to the meetings themselves, but to how you feel![3]

Becoming Aware of Your Emotional Expressions

Unless you are playing high-stakes poker, it can be vitally important to be able to express your feelings in nonverbal ways. Remember that emotions contain information. In order to facilitate communication, it seems that it would be important to be able to match your words with appropriate facial expressions. Getting your message across and being understood require thinking *and* feeling.

Consider the list of discrete emotions described and the ones you used in your emotions journal. Now stand in front of a mirror. Repeat each emotion word, and watch your face in the mirror as you do so. Examine your facial expression as you pronounce the word a few times. Try to say the emotion word with *feeling*. If you are on the word *happy,* say the word in a happy manner. To help you do this, think about a time in your life when you were very, very happy. Continue with other emotion words from the list. The point of this exercise is to help you become aware of the way your face looks when you are expressing certain feelings and emotions.

Most of us are not aware of the impact we have on people. We are often surprised when we hear our voice on a recording, see our photograph, or, even more so, watch ourselves on video. If we are shy, we may feel extremely uncomfortable with some of these exercises. We may feel embarrassed or awkward when we smile at someone, ask personal questions, or in any way deviate from our typical behavior. If we are shy and we do these things, we can often feel that we are coming on too strong.

Yet shy individuals often are overly focused on how they think others are responding to their behavior. They think they are acting in a silly or too-informal a manner. They're not, but they perceive it that way. Looking in the mirror is an excellent way to learn how you come across to others. After you've watched yourself while pronouncing the emotion words for a while, pretend to greet someone as you watch yourself in a mirror. Next, try smiling more; show interest in the other (imagined) person. How does it look? Too obvious? Not obvious enough?

You can make this exercise especially helpful if you have access to a video camera. Set up the camera in your home or office and reenact an interview or an initial meeting with someone (you may want to ask someone else to play the role of this other person). Watch the video on your own, and share it later with a family member, friend, or a colleague. Are you happy with your presentation style?

If you feel that your emotional expressions do not seem genuine or they make you self-conscious, you may want to try your hand at a game of emotional charades. The basic rules of emotional charades are outlined here, but there are many alternative ways to play the game. The main thing is to practice expressing emotions. So here goes:

- Make a deck of "emotion scenario cards" (examples are listed).
- Gather together a group of friends or other interesting people.
- Have the group face a "stage"—a couch or open floor area, for example.
- Ask one person to select an emotion scenario card from the deck.
- Ask the person to read the card silently and try to get into the emotion (allow fifteen seconds or so, not much more).
- Ask the person to act out the emotion nonverbally, without making any sort of vocalizations but expressing the emotion listed on the card using facial expressions, body language, and other nonverbal cues only (allow up to thirty seconds).
- Ask the observers to rate the actor on:
  The emotion being expressed
  The genuineness of the emotion
- Have the actor read the emotion scenario card, and ask the group to write down the emotions that the actor *should* have conveyed.
- Ask the group to discuss and agree on the key emotions in the emotion card.
- Ask all observers to share their ratings with the group.

At the end of the game, ask the highest-scoring people these questions:

- What is a phony emotion and how do you know?
- What are the keys to understanding nonverbal expressions?
- What about facial expression?
- Did you pay attention to body language, such as posture?

Here are some example emotion scenario cards to get you started:

The client presentation went quite well. Your boss did a great job, and the clients loved the idea and the proposal. At the conclusion of the meeting, your boss turns to you and says, in front of everyone, that you put the presentation together and you were the originator of the great idea that the client loved. You are beaming inside.

Just what you don't need: they changed their minds—*again!* It is not the first time. But tonight you wanted to leave at a reasonable hour because you have a date. Make that *had* a date. You'll have to call and cancel and explain why, but no way this lame excuse will be accepted. You are really frustrated.

It's time for your performance review. You've done a reasonably good job the last six months. Most of the projects have gone well. There were one or two rough spots, but you made up for it with extra work and a bit of ingenuity. Your boss is reviewing your accomplishments and says that you were an average performer and that you need to work on your organization and time management skills. "Maybe," she says "you'll get that promotion next year if you pull this all together." What a disappointment! Maybe you deserved it, but you are quite unhappy.

What a crummy day. You wanted to leave early since it's your birthday. Not that it matters much, because you don't have any plans. Anyway, it's just a birthday, no big deal. You hear a noise in the conference room and walk in. All of a sudden, every light in the darkened room turns on, and the entire department yells, "Surprise! Happy Birthday!" There's a cake, candles, signs, and gifts. What a surprise!

A perfect day! It's your vacation, and you are lying on the most gorgeous beach you have ever seen. You left the office in great shape—no backlog when you return—and you still have ten days left. The sun warms you, a gentle breeze blows, and the waves lap at the peaceful shore. You are relaxed, calm, and ever so content. All is right with the world.

The job interview with the department manager, Joe, went quite well, and you are really pleased with your performance. The next day, you call a friend who works for the person with whom you interviewed. She hesitates when she hears it's you on the phone, and after a brief pause says, "I'm really sorry that the interview went badly for you. Joe told me all about it."

Becoming Aware of the Feelings and Emotions of Others

Now that you have logged your own emotions, played emotional charades, and generally have become better at being aware of your own feelings, we can begin to focus on other people. What are the people around you feeling? How do you figure this out?

Accurately identifying emotions starts with the basics: awareness. Many people we've worked with are just awful at recognizing other people's emotions because they simply don't look for them. It's not that they are unable to figure out how someone is feeling; it's that they don't know to look for the valuable clues in the faces of people they meet.

The first step, then, in identifying emotions is simply to pay attention to the world around you. Just follow the method of Sherlock Holmes, the great fictional detective, who believed in the powers of observation and deductive reasoning. Holmes could find clues that others overlooked, in part because he was actively looking for them.

There are three main sorts of emotional clues that you can look for to help you identify others' emotions accurately. What are they? Accurate emotional identification includes: (1) people's facial expressions, (2) the pitch, rhythm, and tone of people's voices, and (3) the feelings conveyed by the posture of someone's body. Let's consider each of these in turn.

Face Off: Others' Facial Expressions

When people look at you directly as they talk or listen, it usually means they like you. They will tend to feel more interest in you and be more willing to cooperate with you. If people don't like each other, or if they disagree with each other, they tend not to make as much eye contact. When meeting someone for the first time, if the other person both looks directly at you and is smiling, that likely means the person has positive feelings toward you.

Of course, directly gazing at someone can lead to an unwavering stare. For most people, this is awfully disconcerting, and it should be. An unwavering gaze has been thought to be a sign of threatening and dominant behavior among certain primates. This probably applies to encounters with people as well.

Listening to Emotions: Voice Pitch and Tones

Klaus Scherer, one of the pioneering figures in emotions research, has examined ways in which a person's tone of voice contains valuable emotional information.[4] Although such voice tones vary from person to person and certainly across cultures, consider the voice tones and their typical meaning, as listed in Exhibit 8.4, when trying to accurately determine a person's emotions.

However, as with any such technique, it is important to modify your knowledge base and decision rules as you gather more data. For instance, individuals have their own vocal styles. That is why it is important to process the relative changes in vocalization so that you can calibrate your awareness to different individuals.

Looking Beyond the Face: Body Language

You also can develop your ability to read nonverbal emotional cues in someone's body posture. Whether engaged in conversation or

Exhibit 8.4. Speech and Emotion.

Tone	Meaning
Monotone	Boredom
Slow speed and pitch	Depression
High speed, emphatic pitch	Enthusiasm
Ascending tone	Surprise
Abrupt speech	Defensiveness
Terse, loud tone	Anger
High pitch, drawn-out speech	Disbelief

observing someone, you can pick up clues to the person's feelings by examining their nonverbal behavior. The chart in Exhibit 8.5 illustrates aspects of nonverbal behavior and what the behavior may suggest emotionally.

Analyzing the face, voice, and body posture of your friends, family members, and associates at work may be just a little uncomfortable, especially at first. So we suggest practicing these skills by watching movies, an exercise suggested to us by Dr. Amy Van Buren. Pick up a movie at the local video store or library. It is best to get a movie you haven't seen before. Scan through the movie and stop at any point where there are people talking. Watch the movie but turn the sound off completely. Watch the scene unfold for thirty seconds to one minute. If there are several characters, try to focus on one or two main characters.

At the end of the scene, stop the movie and write down how each of the two main characters in the scene feels using the Emotions Checklist shown in Exhibit 8.6. This can be a very difficult task, as all you have to go on are the visual cues and little context. After you have rated each of the two main characters' emotions, rewind the video to the start of the scene you just analyzed and replay it. This time, however, turn the sound on. As you watch the scene unfold again, keep your Emotions Checklist in front of you and record the emotions expressed by each of the two main characters.

Turn the movie off and look at your emotion ratings. How similar are they? Were there emotions that you were able to identify correctly just from the nonverbal cues? Were there others that you needed vocal cues as well in order to get them right? It is very in-

Exhibit 8.5. Nonverbal Cues.

Nonverbal Cue	What It Looks Like	What It Suggests
Orientation	Facing toward you	Interest
	Turned slightly away	Closed off
Arms	Arms open	Openness
	Arms folded	Defensiveness
Posture	Leaning forward	Interest
	Leaning away from you	Rejection

structive to review the emotions you identify well and those you have some trouble identifying. Ask yourself what clues you might have underemphasized or overemphasized. What did you miss? And of course, which clues were you really good at noticing?

Exhibit 8.6. Emotions Checklist for Movies.

Emotion Checklist: No = Not Present; Yes = Present				
	Character 1		Character 2	
	Silent	Sound	Silent	Sound
Happy				
Sad				
Angry				
Anticipating				
Fearful				
Surprised				
Accepting				
Disgusted				
Jealous				
Ashamed				

Because the need to assess how people feel often occurs in public settings (and rarely while watching movies), it is a good idea to practice this skill in such a setting. Take care not to alarm unsuspecting people by staring at them, however. Use the people-watching form shown next or one similar to it that you make up on your own. Look for a "target" person, and observe him or her quietly and from a bit of a distance for a few minutes. Try to complete the people-watching form shown in Exhibit 8.7 as best as you can. If you are really brave, approach the person you were watching, extend a greeting, and ask how he or she is feeling. Compare the person's verbal responses with those you recorded on the form, and compare the emotions you thought the target was experiencing with those described to you. Of course, if your targets are not interested in talking to you, we do not advise that you continue this exercise with them.

It's fun and instructive to do this with another person. Both of you agree on a person to observe and evaluate, but don't share your responses and ratings until after you've completed them. Then compare your ratings and discuss them.

We think it is especially important to learn to read facial expressions of emotion. Decoding the various clues in faces is not easy. A very well-regarded system of coding facial expressions, developed by Paul Ekman, examines dozens and dozens of discrete

Exhibit 8.7. People-Watching Rating Form.

Setting	
Physical Description	
Gender	
Salient Characteristics	
Nonverbal Cues	
Facial Expression	
Posture	
Verbal Cues	
Emotion Words	
Tone	
Likely Emotion(s)	
Reported Emotion(s)	

facial movements.[5] Computers are being trained to do this as well. You don't have to be a computer scientist to enhance your ability to recognize emotional expressions in faces, nor must you analyze dozens of facial clues to determine how someone is feeling. If you focus on a few key principles of emotional expression, you can greatly increase your accuracy of decoding emotions.

Take a look at the table in Exhibit 8.8. It shows you the major facial clues for six primary emotions. Focusing on the mouth, eyes, and nose is an especially effective way to ascertain what another person is feeling.

It's not the real thing, but we'll share a schematic view of these features with you in Figures 8.1 and 8.2. It's basic but a great start to picking up the visual cues of emotions.

Exhibit 8.8. Facing Emotions.

Emotion	Mouth	Eyes	Nose	Other Features
Happy	Smile	Crow's feet		Can be active
Sad	Frown	Lowered brows		Low energy
Afraid	Grimace	Fast blink		
Angry	Compressed lips	Narrowed	Flared	
Disgusted	Curled lip		Wrinkled	Tongue sticks out
Surprised	Open mouth	Wide open		Movement halted

Liar, Liar

Of course, one challenge is differentiating true from false feelings. How do we know if the person we are observing really is feeling an emotion or just acting like he or she is? Smiling, for example, is not always a valid indicator of happiness. Often a smile is voluntary, or forced, in order to mask underlying, negative feelings. A true smile involves both the muscles around the corners of lips—pulling them up—as well as those near the eyes, creating crinkles or crow's feet near the corners of the eyes. A smiling mouth with no eye crinkles is not a real smile. A false smile also comes on too quickly, and the lips may appear to be more stretched sideways than curled upward.[6]

Figure 8.1. How to Decode Emotions in Faces.

Standard Facial Features   Where to Look

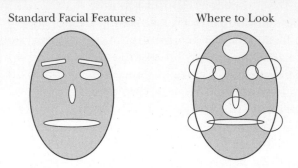

Figure 8.2. Basic Emotional Expressions.

Surprise   Fear   Disgust

Anger   Sadness   Happiness

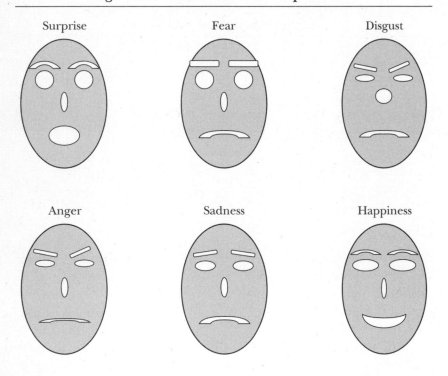

Sometimes these false smiles are clues to deceit or lies.[7] How can you catch an emotional liar? It depends on the nature of the lie or the situation. Strategies will differ, depending on whether the lie is a "white lie" and does not involve strong emotion or whether it is a high-stakes lie and thus generates stronger emotions. Let's take a look at the low-stakes lie and liar. Consider this low-stakes lie communicated by a ten-year-old boy:

Father: Did you brush your teeth before getting into bed?
   Son: Yes Dad, I did. Good night.

The boy was reliable and very motivated, so the father never doubted the statement—until a dental check-up revealed several cavities and the need for a minor root canal. (In fairness to the boy, the dentist said that the root canal was not due to poor dental hygiene, but it's a good story.) Now, the nightly question became less routine and took on greater importance.

When strong emotions are not generated in a situation that involves lying, then you need to catch a liar using clues that do not involve overt emotional displays. In the tooth-brushing situation, one might especially focus on speech. Did the boy pause in his responses? Take a long time to say something? Make errors of speech? Say anything inconsistent?

Alternatively, consider a situation in which you have a new sales person. You find a major error on a large order and call him into your office. He claims that he entered the order correctly into the system but that one of the administrative people must have messed it up. He goes on to say that the admin person appeared to be bored and tired at the time he handed the order entry form to him last Friday afternoon. He apologizes for not checking the order and says that he will be more careful next time.

You know the admin person well and are surprised to hear about this lapse. But something is bugging you about the story, only you can't quite put your finger on what it is. Certainly, if the sales person is at fault, it could be grounds for dismissal under the conditions of the probationary period of his contract. But he seemed so sure! How can you hope to figure out if he is telling the truth or unfairly pinning the blame on someone else?

In this case, the stakes are much higher than in the tooth-brushing incident. Lie detection strategies change when the lie is a big one. Big lies may be accompanied by more obvious emotional overtones. Now the way to catch a liar is to ignore the little clues of inconsistency in speech patterns and associated verbal clues. Instead, you need to focus on several aspects of the person, including nonverbal and verbal cues and, most important, subtle facial expressions.

When it's a big lie, as in the sales example, we are more likely to experience strong emotions. If we are attuned to the person's emotional displays, we stand a better chance of detecting the lie. The basic strategy is to look for negative emotional displays. Liars, when the stakes are high, are much more likely to feel strong negative emotions and to display them. People telling the truth usually do not feel strong negative emotions at all. Sometimes the liar attempts to cover up these negative feelings by smiling, but the smile will look false, as described earlier.

The Advanced Course: Putting It All Together

In order to be truly effective at reading emotions in yourself and in other people, you should try to integrate all of the skills we have discussed in this chapter. Here is a guide to help you synthesize your emotion-identification competencies:

1. Pay attention: attend to and accurately identify *your* emotions and moods, and look and listen to the person
2. Process the verbal information:
    Emotion words used
    Tone used
    Speed and pitch of words
3. Process the nonverbal information:
    Facial expressions
    Eyes and mouth
    Posture
    Gestures (interpreted in context)
    Words, tone, and situation, as they relate to gestures

4. Look for consistency or inconsistency:
   Match between words and tone
   Match between expression, words, and tone
5. Analyze discrepancies, but be aware of the misleading nature
   of discrepancies:
   - People laugh when grieving
   - People may not wish to admit feelings
6. Become self-aware of:
   Your own emotional reactions
   Your personal reaction
   Your feelings
   - We sometimes mimic others' emotions
   - We may feel uncomfortable around certain emotional
     displays
7. Check it out:
   Use language such as "You seem" to confirm others' feelings
   Determine your awareness of feelings
   Provide an offer of encouragement to open up

   Lastly, it often helps to check out your observations with another observer.

◆ ◆ ◆

It's not easy, but we believe that with practice and feedback you can improve your accuracy of emotion identification. And once you have good data, you are ready for the next step.

CHAPTER 9

Get in the Right Mood
Improving Your Ability to Use Emotions

There are strong links between emotions and thinking. We all know that there are times when emotions can assist our thinking and other times when they interfere with our work. Part of becoming an emotionally intelligent manager is to be able to match the mood to the situation. Getting into the *right* mood generates a helpful mind-set that is one of the keys to creative thinking, empathy, and vision.

Sure, for some folks feelings don't enhance their thinking and instead really mess it up. That happens to all of us sometimes. But to some people, it happens a lot of the time. That's because they have an angry disposition or a joyful disposition, and their "normal" or baseline feeling is one of anger or joy (or some other feeling).

We cannot separate feelings and thinking. The question isn't just, *When* does emotion assist thinking? The question is also, *Which* emotions enhance our thinking process? In this chapter, we help you learn how emotions influence our thinking and then teach you how to get into the right mood for a given situation—the mood that helps you get to your objective.

How Feeling Affects Thinking

Emotions influence thought. Thinking cannot and does not occur without emotion. These are two fundamental principles underlying emotional intelligence. Let's take a closer look at how different emotions direct attention and kick-start thinking.

What Does Happiness Do for Us?

Happiness helps us generate new ideas and allows us to think in new ways and to see possibilities. Happiness is about having dreams and realizing them.[1]

We know that being happy actually helps us to be better at solving inductive reasoning problems, that is, problems in which you are given a general problem and need to generate possible solutions.[2] And creative problem solving is enhanced if we are in a happy mood.[3] Happy moods result in:

- More novel and creative solutions
- Going beyond specific information
- Thinking outside the box
- Generating many ideas

Happy people often remember events in their distant past as being pleasant.[4] Being in a happy mood can also make people feel more giving, charitable, and friendly. Work by Alice Isen has found, as we noted earlier, that inducing a positive mood enhances people's decision-making abilities.[5] This means that an "up" mood is key to successful brainstorming, generating new ideas, and expanding your list of alternatives.

People who are in a positive or happy mood tend to rely on general knowledge structures. Happy people tend to cluster information more than people in a negative or sad mood. They rely more on generalized plans and processes (or schemas) than on details.[6]

What this means is that big-picture thinking may be enhanced when you are feeling happy. If you are discussing a vision that you have for a new product, for instance, and you are in a happy mood while a colleague is feeling sad, you will not be on the same wavelength. You clearly have the long term and the big picture in mind, and your colleague is seeing details and not connecting the dots.

However, there is a downside to happy moods. They often result in a greater number of problem-solving errors.[7] The difficulty with a happy mood is that it signals that we have done well and succeeded in our task. We may, as a result, think that our job is complete, and we stop trying to solve the problem further.

What Does Fear Do for Us?

We become wary when we are fearful. Our senses can be heightened, and adrenaline pumps through our body. We are mobilized and ready to get the heck out of there! Fear motivates escape from danger. When fear becomes intense, we can become paralyzed by it and immobilized.[8]

Anyone who has ever had a job probably knows that fear is no stranger at work, so why would anyone suggest that fear does something good for us? (Note that we're not endorsing the behavior of managers who use fear as a tactical weapon, intimidating people, bullying them, and getting their way.) Fear is not a great feeling, but mild fear may be just what the doctor should order when we need to consider what could go wrong with our sales forecast or our new-product strategy. Fear gives us a style of thinking where everything and everyone is suspect. Harnessed properly, fear allows us to revisit our old assumptions, and we see new things in the familiar.[9]

What Does Sadness Do for Us?

People in a sad mood will likely view the world in these ways:[10]

- Negative events have stable causes.
- Negative events are due to global issues.
- Negative events will continue.
- Negative events will likely happen to them.

This is a depressing view of the world and one that is difficult to live with, if it's your dominant mood. Yet sadness can help us solve a certain type of problem: deductive reasoning problems.[11] These are problems in which we need to focus on the details, look for something wrong in a set of facts that have already been provided for us. Bringing the mood of the group down a notch or two before they seal the deal may help them consider problems that they had previously ignored in their upbeat, brainstorming session.

Most coaches will tell you that their teams can potentially learn more from a loss than they can from a win. Losing can be instructive because it makes us somewhat disappointed and sad. We see where we went wrong and note problems we had not previously observed. At the same time, losing is instructive only if the feelings of sadness that it generates are used intelligently by the team's leader.

What Does Anger Do for Us?

If we consider the devastation wrought by anger, it would be hard to imagine that it has any place whatsoever in the development of a good manager or an effective leader. We've worked for angry people, and it's not a whole lot of fun. Problems with anger are all too common, and anger management or violence prevention programs have been implemented by many companies.

We are hesitant to suggest that anger has its place in the emotional tool-kit of the effective manager. But there are times when our feelings of injustice need to be roused, when we must protect our intellectual property, trademarks, copyrights, market intelligence, and human capital from the grasping hand of an unsavory competitor. If we are smart enough to be able to perceive others accurately, then there will be real and meaningful threats. The world is not a fair place; it is not completely populated by honest, law-abiding citizens.

When should we be angry? How about when retirees lose their life savings to a scam artist, when pension funds are picked clean by unscrupulous fund managers, when our boss promotes his good buddy over an obviously more qualified person?

What does anger do? Anger narrows our field of vision, our view of the world, and it focuses and targets our energy on a perceived threat.[12] It gives us the energy and the focus we sometimes need to right a wrong, not to right a perceived wrong but a legitimate injustice.

What Does Surprise Do for Us?

Darwin probably said it best: "As surprise is excited by something unexpected or unknown, we naturally desire, when startled, to perceive the cause as quickly as possible; and we consequently open our eyes fully so that the field of vision may be increased, and the eyeballs moved easily in any direction."[13]

Consider the case of a product manager who is convinced that nobody else will have the competitive advantages that his new product has. Scanning the daily industry news reports, he reads a press release about a new product with most of the features of his product, plus a few even more useful features, at a lower price. Surprise!

Surprise reorients our attention when something unexpected happens. We get into information-seeking mode when surprised. Our complacency is disturbed, and we're all ears, or perhaps it would be better to say all eyes.

The Influence of Emotion on Decision Making

The mood we are in even influences how we persuade others and how successful we are in changing the minds of others. When people in a sad mood are asked to develop persuasive messages, they typically come up with better-quality arguments and more persuasive messages than people in a happy mood.[14] A sad mood results in a more careful, systematic, and bottom-up approach. But if you are in a happy mood, you are probably going to generate a greater number of arguments, and these arguments are likely to be more creative and original.[15]

Emotions and Decision Making

One of the fascinating research findings in this area indicates that our moods influence our judgments and our decisions. People in a bad mood see things in a more negative light. They overestimate the occurrence of negative events and underestimate the frequency of positive events. In contrast, the judgments of those in a happy frame of mind result in the overestimation of positive events and underestimation of negative events.[16]

Select one of the mood-induction strategies described later in this chapter and discover this for yourself. For instance, try to generate a sad mood. Then consider how you feel about certain general questions:

- Will you get stuck in traffic on the way home from work?
- Will you get a good night's sleep?
- What is tomorrow's economic news going to be?

Next, generate a happy mood, as indicated in the exercises later in this chapter (see "How to Get Into the Right Mood"). Consider the questions here or similar questions such as:

- Will you have good weather tomorrow?
- Will your team meeting go well?
- Will you have a productive day at work?

Notice how you approach these questions in different moods. Moods are subtle, and the effects will not be strong, but moods do influence thinking. That is why it is critical to be aware of your emotions and to actively manage them as well.

If moods influence these small decisions and judgments, how do our emotions influence us as we consider major life decisions such as:

- Will you be successful?
- What does the future hold in store for you?
- Are you on a positive career path?

The decisions we make today, which appear to us to be so completely rational, are the result of both our rationality and our emotions. This is a great way to arrive at a good decision but only if we are aware of our emotions.

Idea Generation and Problem Solving

Emotions facilitate thought, but they can also act like a stick thrown into the spokes of a bicycle wheel. The key is to match the thinking style to the emotion. Consider the different steps involved in problem solving, as shown in Exhibit 9.1, with each step and each specific technique being enhanced and facilitated by different emotions.

The emotionally intelligent manager accurately identifies emotions, knows the rules of emotion and thinking, and makes sure there is a match between the current feeling and the current situation. If there isn't a good match, what do you do then?

How to Get into the Right Mood

Our message has been that changing how you feel may be a good idea or a bad idea, depending on the situation. Now that you understand how moods facilitate thinking, we'll turn to ways in which you can get into a certain mood.

**Exhibit 9.1. Generating Ideas, Solving
Problems, and Experiencing Emotions.**

Step or Process	What It Is	Helpful Ways to Feel
Idea Generation		
"Blue-Sky" Thinking	A feeling of having no restraints.	Happy
Brainstorming	Use associations that arise with certain objects.	Happy
Idea Evaluation		
Fault Seeking	Consider possible problems and what could go wrong.	Somewhat afraid
Goal Matching	Match the goals of the project to features of the idea.	Neutral mood
Idea Selection		
Checklist	Assign weight to each aspect of the goal and each idea.	Neutral mood
Implementation		
Group Consensus	Get buy-in from team.	Happy and interested
Develop Action Plan	Decide on specific steps, resources, timing, and responsible party.	Interested
Take Action	Begin implementation.	Happy and excited
Follow-Up	Monitor progress, make adjustments, stay on task, and achieve the desired outcome.	Negative mood to evaluate possible issues; happy and positive mood to stay motivated and to overcome obstacles

Feel the Feeling

How do you generate a mood? Actors have well-developed techniques to do so—not just any actors but those who have been schooled in *method acting*. Which method is that? Some say it's *the* method, and it's what many actors call the approach to acting developed by the Russian director Constantin Stanislavsky.[17]

Stanislavsky believed that actors must be properly inspired to play their part. Although he did not develop fixed rules of acting, he did discuss many ways in which actors could prepare, physically and mentally, for their part.

As you know, this is not a book on acting. It is a book on becoming a more effective manager and leader. Yet there will be times when the emotionally intelligent manager has to display some acting skills in order to direct, guide, and influence the actions of others. Franklin Roosevelt, a four-term U.S. president, was known to have said, "It is necessary for the President to be the nation's number one actor." When Howard Gardner, the educational psychologist, trained his sights on leadership, he concluded that leaders are storytellers—they communicate meaning through their words.[18] The emotionally intelligent manager may not become a Broadway star, but there will be times when a manager is cast into a role that is vitally important to a team's success.

The methods Stanislavsky suggested include these:

- Relax to focus attention.
- Enhance the powers of imagination.
- Recall memories of emotions experienced in the past.
- Link past emotional memories to specific sensory details of the emotion (such as taste, smell, texture).
- Learn how to re-create the emotions on stage as necessary for the character.
- Learn to believe that the stage is reality and believe as well in the imagined truth of the character and the scene.

If you are thinking that this stuff is not quite corporate, we can understand that. However, before you skip down to the next idea, recall another idea attributed to Stanislavsky: *there are no small parts;*

there are only small actors. These skills can help you to become a great actor on your stage.

First, you must relax. Relaxation allows you to become more open and flexible. Openness is key to mood change, and openness allows you to change your behavior and your style to help you get into a certain mood and frame of mind.

Second, enhance your imagination. Once you're in a more receptive state, you can use guided imagery and similar techniques to generate various moods and emotions. Although this may be fun and interesting, the goal is to be able to generate moods that we can use to think differently. We can then create new ideas, feel what someone else feels (empathy), or switch perspectives.

One of our favorite ways to generate a relaxed mood is to try to create a mental picture of an idyllic, peaceful day. Close your eyes and think to yourself: "I am lying in a meadow on a hillside in early autumn. The sky is a deep blue, and the clouds are soft wisps high above. It is warm but not humid, and there is a sweet smell of hay and grasses in the air. I can hear the call of the whippoorwills. Fat honeybees buzz lazily through the air."

What works for us may not work for you. But the general process should work for all of us and consists of these steps:

1. Find a quiet spot if possible. Then try to relax.
2. Come up with a scene that you find peaceful.
3. If you have trouble doing this, think about where you might like to be.
4. Look around and imagine what objects there would be around you.
5. For each object, notice its details: color, shape, size, and texture. Where is it placed in the scene?
6. Can you hear anything? Listen and create the sounds that the scene should have.
7. How do you feel?
8. Look around and notice as much as you can.

Here are other suggestions:

1. When there are gaps in the scene, put your energy into filling in the missing pieces.

2. Try to make your imagined scene as real as possible by adding as much detail as possible. Use all of your senses.
3. Where are you in the scene? Are you there at all? Are you seeing it with your own eyes, or is this a feeling of being above the scene. What is your perspective?
4. Of course, unrelated thoughts and sounds will enter your imagined world. When this happens, simply acknowledge the sound or intrusion and then go back to the imagined scene.

Experience the Feelings of Others

Leveraging your imagination requires an additional step: injecting the right sort of physical feelings into your imagination—feelings that map onto the emotion you are attempting to create.

First, you have to know what different emotions feel like. A feeling is a bodily sensation such as warmth, heart rate, or respiration. Although many people believe that each emotion is related to a specific set of physical sensations or feelings, research does not support this belief. Emotions are not all distinguishable by a unique set of feelings or sensations. Still, by linking feelings to emotions, we can provide a way to more easily and accurately access or generate emotions. Consider some basic emotions, as listed in Exhibit 9.2, and the possible feelings associated with each of them.

This is the starting point for developing your feeling side. You start by simply paying attention and enhancing your emotional

Exhibit 9.2. Emotions and Sensations.

Emotion	Breathing	Heart Rate	Muscles	Temperature	Location
Fear	Increases	Increases	Tense	Cold	Abdomen
Anger	Becomes more shallow	Increases	Jaws tense	Hot	Whole body
Sadness	Becomes deeper	Slows	Relax	Cold	Chest
Happiness	Slows	Increases slightly	Relax	Warm	Chest

awareness. Next, you identify the various sensations and feelings that accompany emotion.

Develop Your Emotional Imagination

How can you develop your emotional imagination? This exercise will help you develop this important skill—one you can apply as needed to help you get in the same mood as others, to create a sense of interest or urgency, or to enhance your thinking processes. You will first need to determine what sort of mood, or emotion, you wish to create; start by trying to understand how mood influences thinking. Then:

1. Select the emotion you want to generate, and then think of a time when you felt this emotion. If you can't think of a specific incident, maybe these questions will help you remember one.
   Sadness: you lost something of great value.
   Anger: you were treated unfairly.
   Fear: you were worried that something bad was going to happen.
   Surprise: something unexpected just occurred.
   Happiness: you get something you really wanted.
2. Retrieve an image of this situation. Consider what the situation was. Who was involved? Picture the scene in your imagination. If you have trouble doing this, try a different situation, one that is more recent or vivid, and is easily recollected.
3. Try to experience or feel the sensations that accompany emotions.
   Sadness. It is cold, and you are feeling chilled. You feel heavy and slow. You find it hard to move about, as if there are weights on your ankles. You are hunched over slightly. It seems dark all around you, and although you can distinguish shapes, you seem to be in a fog. You breathe in slowly and deeply, taking time to slowly exhale. As you breathe out, make a low moaning sound. Your eyes droop down and your mouth relaxes.
   Fear. It is perfectly still all about you; there is no movement of air. Something is going to happen, but you are not sure what it is or when it will happen. All your muscles are tense. You are standing motionless. Your heart is pounding, and your skin grows pale. Your mouth is dry.

Love. Warmth suffuses your body. You cannot help smiling. A glow emanates from you, and you are sure that anyone who looks at you just knows that you are full of joy and passion and hope. Your heart beats just a little faster. The world is colored brightly.

Anger. Your jaws are clenched, and you are staring at the other person with a fixed gaze. You clench and unclench your hands and pound one hand into the other. You feel warm, and your heart begins to beat faster. A frown pulls the corners of your mouth down, and your mouth tenses up, as do your shoulders.

Happiness. You are feeling nice and warm—not hot, but safe, satisfied, content, and protected. Your body seems like it is floating, just as if you were in a warm spring-fed hot tub. You are laughing and smiling. Every now and then you shout out. You move about excitedly and feel like dancing around.

4. Intensify the visuals and the physical sensations as necessary. Intensifying the image may help you experience the physical sensations of different emotions. Take the image and replay it in your imagination in slow motion. With each frame of the scene, go through the sensations one at a time. Try to increase the overall vividness and intensity of the feelings.

5. End on a positive note. If the image is one of anger, sadness, or fear (or other negative emotion), it is important to end this exercise on a different note. Imagine a peaceful scene in which you are relaxed and happy. Intensify this image and the feelings until the sensations are suffused throughout your body.

Make It Personal

If you want to be able to change the way you feel so you can change the way you think, you'll need to practice these techniques quite a bit. But you will also need to develop your own method of integrating enough of these techniques into an everyday routine. It would not be advisable to have to engage in some sort of meditative trance just before you begin a sales meeting, for instance. Instead, look for ways to relax quickly, imagine a well-rehearsed scene, and get into character.

Perhaps you're really into music and art. You might select a happy tune and a happy painting to carry around in your head.

Think of the artwork, and play the tune in your head to generate a happy mood. You can even write down happy statements (we show you how to do this next), personal memories, or whatever works for you. The best images are those you find meaningful and rich. The list of scenarios described next can help if you are stuck or if you want to explore some other ideas.

- You win an award for Manager of the Year.
- Your boss surprises you with a well-deserved but generous raise and promotion.
- You've successfully completed an incredibly challenging assignment to the acclaim of all.
- You're invited to speak in front of an international convention of colleagues, and the speech is greeted with thunderous applause.
- You are laughing very hard.

Changing Moods Quickly

One of the most effective strategies for altering your mood is simply to repeat certain sorts of statements. It is a subtle effect, but it has been shown to be effective in changing a mood.

If you're looking for a quick mood picker-upper, all you need to do is to read the statements that follow. Ideally, you would say them out loud. Of course, this can cause problems if you are in a crowded elevator at the time. So if you determine that saying the statements out loud is not for you at that moment, just repeat them silently to yourself.[19]

- I am feeling really good today.
- I am very happy.
- Things are looking up.
- This is a great day.
- I am feeling good.
- I feel really up.
- I am bursting with joy.

If you were already bursting with joy but you're headed into a meeting where you need to terminate several employees, you might want to bring the volume down a notch or two. The self-statements you'll want to employ in this case should reflect the mood you're trying to establish.

Snapping Out of It

There are times when we *should* feel sad. A major disappointment likely leads us to feel sad and down. Such sadness is a sign to ourselves, and to others, that we need to be comforted, that we are in need of support.

But there are other times when we must put sadness aside, when it is preventing us from moving forward and taking action. History is full of stories of individuals who have faced enormous hardship and suffering. But history is also replete with stories of those who have not only survived incredible trauma but have emerged with renewed hope, strength, and courage. There are stories of individuals, but also of groups, who have been on the brink of destruction yet have blossomed in a new world. Whether it is the story of African slaves in the United States, survivors of the Holocaust, or residents of cities destroyed by natural disasters, stories of rebirth and hope can provide us with inspiration when we are feeling down.

Certainly, we don't mean to compare our own disappointments and crises with such horrific events as these. But it can be helpful to consider how others, and how we, have handled emotional conflicts. By creating a personal story of hope, we are then able to tap into our story in order to generate hope during times of personal despair. Try this exercise, taking the steps in order:

1. Remember an emotional conflict in which you were at your emotional best—a situation involving you and another person that was difficult and could have resulted in a very negative outcome but was resolved positively and effectively.
2. Recall who was involved.
3. Describe the situation in some detail.
4. Try to recall the events leading up to the situation.
5. Try to remember what each person, including yourself, did.

As you continue to reflect, consider what the resolution was, what you learned from the situation, and how you felt at the end of the emotional crisis. Take notes. Include positive, feeling words in your notes. Use your notes to create a short story of your own—one that evokes powerful memories of survival and of hope.

The story that results from the exercise becomes your means of generating a positive mood during tough and difficult times. Ideally, you would tell the story quickly with lots of energy and animation. Even if you just bring this story to mind, with its images and feelings, you will be able to get back on track toward a positive mood that is conducive to growth and development.[20]

It is stories like these that inspire us, and others. These are stories that emotionally intelligent leaders tell.

Summing Up

Every day we think and make decisions and judgments, and each of these thoughts, decisions, and judgments is made with emotion. This is not a choice we make; it's simply the way we're wired. By choosing to ignore the emotion component and trying to be coldly rational, we risk making a poor decision.

But you can choose to be smart about emotions. What if you could see the world and experience it as someone else does? Is that important? Does such a skill provide you with a unique opportunity to understand the other person? When dealing with a frustrated customer, the last thing you want is to have an angry person on your hands. Feeling what the customer feels establishes a rapport, a shared worldview. If you're in charge of a product development group that is making slow progress, it would be great to be able to create a sense of urgency. But you have to do so on the group members' own terms, at their level; to do so requires that you have a shared perspective.

◆ ◆ ◆

Getting in the right mood starts with accurate emotional identification. Then you need to tap your knowledge of how your feelings and thoughts work together as a team. And finally, you have to deliver that feeling. You're both the catcher giving the sign for a curveball or a fastball and the pitcher delivering the pitch with all of the finesse and skill you can muster.

We next turn to Understanding Emotions, the third step in our model.

CHAPTER 10

Predict the Emotional Future Accurately

Improving Your Ability to Understand Emotions

What if you are not very good at understanding why people feel the way they do, or you have a hard time explaining how emotions change, blend, and transition? Understanding emotions is, in many ways, the easiest set of the four emotional skills to acquire. Understanding emotions represents our emotional knowledge base, and it includes an appreciation of the language used to describe emotions and other feelings.

As we mentioned earlier, emotions have certain moves, just like in chess. And just like chess, emotional games can be played that vary in complexity from simplistic moves of individual pieces of a chessboard to games between grandmasters. Emotional grandmasters often are thinking several steps ahead and incorporating the entire emotional chessboard into their understanding of the game.

This chapter will help you become a grandmaster of emotions. It will not happen overnight, but by improving your emotional knowledge base and understanding emotional rules, you can begin to play more masterfully than ever before.

We'll start at the beginning by building your emotional knowledge and providing you with a vocabulary boost so you can better explain just what people feel. Then we'll help you predict the future—emotionally, that is.

Building Your Emotional Knowledge Base

"Howya doing? Fine, you say? I'm okay myself." That is our basic emotion vocabulary, and it is indeed basic. But you don't need to be a linguist to improve your emotional vocabulary, as most of us are starting out with some command of a feelings vocabulary; a little bit of knowledge will go a very long way.

A Vocabulary Primer

How many emotions are there, and how do we describe them? On the side of simplicity, we can use what are known as two-factor emotion models. One researcher, James Russell, developed a system in which emotions were arranged around a circle, with two major dimensions describing points in emotional space: pleasantness of the emotion (pleasant to unpleasant) and the energy level (calm to intensely aroused).[1] To help you develop your basic emotional vocabulary, we've created Figure 10.1. It plots emotions along two simple dimensions: feelings (positive to negative) and energy (high to low).

Now, when someone asks, "Howya doing?" you can reply, "I'm feeling pleasant and have a moderate amount of energy," or "I

Figure 10.1. Basic Emotional Vocabulary.

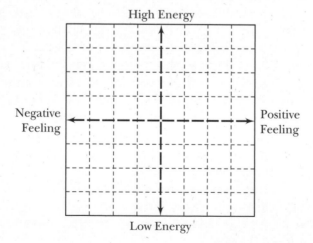

have a highly aroused, unpleasant feeling," awkward as such word-ing might seem in daily interactions. These statements describe your feeling rather than give it an exact word. If we connect these two dimensions of feelings to emotion terms in the first case, you might just say that you are "happy" and in the second "afraid." It's a start, but it's still fairly limited. We need more information.

Causes of Basic Emotions

We learn the meaning of many signals at an early age. Have you ever been to an ocean beach to swim in the surf? On days when the water is calm, with small waves breaking on shore, the life-guards fly green flags to mark the safe and guarded sections of the beach. They place red flags in areas off-limits to swimmers. When parents take a child to the beach for the first time, they often point at the flags and teach their child what the flags signal.

Emotions serve a similar function as these beach flags. Emo-tions warn us of possible danger or of good things to come. How-ever, emotions are usually more subtle than these brightly colored flags fluttering in the breeze, and, unfortunately, most parents do not explicitly teach their children how to interpret these emotional signals. We are left to learn them on our own, and some of us learn well, whereas others among us miss a few important lessons. No matter what our emotional training, we can all benefit from a review of what emotions mean and what they signal. We start our discussion with basic emotions: anger, happiness, fear, surprise, and sadness.

Anger

Anger is not necessarily a bad emotion to have. Anger arises out of a sense of wrong or injustice—a sense that someone is being un-fair to us or to others. Without anger, we would tolerate injustice, inequality, and prejudice.

However, anger can lead to destruction and violence, and what we believe is an injustice may be due to misperceptions. We can raise anger in others to create a senseless mob, ready to attack, seemingly devoid of a reason to do so or devoid of reasoning in general.

There is, then, an intelligent use of anger and an unintelligent use of anger. An unintelligent use or cause of anger is one in which our survival is not being threatened but we lose all ability to reason and to think—we are blind with anger. That is a powerful image: a blind rage. We are so angry that we do not see, and not seeing, we are wantonly destructive, lashing out at whatever and with whomever we come into contact.

A more intelligent use of anger grants us the power and the energy to confront an evil, to right a wrong. An intelligent use of anger is to use it as a force that stands up to a bully, that changes the world in order to make it a better place.

Anger does have a cost. The effects of anger on physical health are fairly well established.[2] Anger can erode our health in a number of ways, but we believe that there are times when we must pay such a price for our own long-term good and the good of our families and organizations. If anger takes a few hours off our lives, and it does so in the service of others, then this may be a trade-off that we are willing to make.

We will return to the topic of anger in the next chapter, when we help you acquire emotion management strategies and skills. In that chapter, we will show how to use anger intelligently.

Happiness

The ancient Stoics distrusted feelings of joy or delight, believing that such feelings were superfluous. Joy or happiness is not irrational, as these emotions move us to embrace others and approach them.

The achievement of a goal results in happiness, and happiness is a signal that we have done something good that we value. We are happy when our values are met, and happiness is a signal to pay attention to our life. Happiness tells us that we have achieved a goal and have been successful at something. We feel happy when we close a sale, make a great presentation, or get a terrific job offer. These feelings inspire and motivate us to try it again and repeat our success.

Fear

Worry, anxiety, and fear signal that something bad is happening or about to happen. These are the red flags of danger, and they have to be attended to. Fear is often future-directed; we anticipate that something bad is going to happen. There is a feeling of uncertainty as well. Fear signals that we might be missing something. The worry we have before a presentation may motivate a last-minute review, allowing us to discover that the LCD projector isn't working. Worrying about meeting quarterly sales can motivate us to make a few extra calls.

Anxiety represents persistent and generalized fear. Anxiety can feel like the gradual wearing down of our psyche. When we feel anxious in the absence of a potential threat, that is, when the anxiety is generalized, then we are no longer experiencing an emotion. Instead, we are anxious and may have what psychologists call an anxiety disorder. We'll talk more about these traits, or ways of seeing and experiencing the world, in the next chapter.

Surprise

When events do not unfold according to plan, we are surprised. Surprise warns us that our plans are not going to work because the unexpected has occurred. Surprise brings our attention to bear on a new problem.

Surprise serves a reorientation function. We drop whatever we were doing and thinking about, and pay attention to the source of the surprise. Eyes widened, we try to find out what's going on.

Sadness

Disappointment or loss results in sadness. When we do not achieve our goal, or when something we care about is taken away from us, we mourn its loss. Mourning allows us to grapple with the idea that we will not have the thing we wanted.

There is also an interpersonal aspect to sadness. When we are sad, we are not a threat to anyone else. Our sadness invites the support and assistance of other people, just at the critical time when we need it most.

Causes of Social Emotions

Social, or secondary, emotions are more culture-bound than the basic emotions are. Although we can understand fundamental causes for these social emotions, we also have to understand the norms of the group or society in order to figure out when these emotions occur.

Disgust

Disgust is a social emotion. It serves the purpose of keeping others in line. Disgust defines the limits of what we find acceptable behavior or behavior that is too far out to be tolerated. Given that there is a strong cultural component to disgust, it's important to recognize that what disgusts one person will not disgust another person.

Although disgust likely originated to keep us from eating things that might poison us, it has evolved into a complex emotion with multiple causes. An act that disgusts us is one that goes against our core beliefs of what is proper and improper. Disgust ensures that our societal values are held intact. When we are no longer disgusted by something, it is a sign that our values have changed. If our sense of disgust grows regarding an act, it is also a sign that our values have changed and that a behavior that once was acceptable is no longer.

Shame and Guilt

Shame indicates that you have not lived up to your personal ideals or values; in this way, it is similar to *guilt*. But there are a few important differences between these feelings.

Shame and guilt start out the same. You begin with a failure to achieve an objective or a moral standard of importance. For example, perhaps you promised one of your direct reports that you'd look into his pay raise for next year. The problem is, you didn't do it in time because you forgot. The result is that you feel *guilty* because you made a promise and you failed to keep it without a good reason. This failure was avoidable.

Both shame and guilt make us feel uncomfortable. And they should. They can serve as a reminder that we messed up and need to apologize to the person we let down, and to make sure we don't fail again. Shame and guilt can keep us on the right track.

Psychologist June Tangney, based on earlier work by Helen Block Lewis, argues that the fundamental difference between shame and guilt is one of attentional focus. In guilt, the emphasis is on the act: "Look what I *did*." But in shame, the emphasis is on my personal failing: "Look what *I* did."[3]

Embarrassment

Embarrassment is another one of the more complex emotions. It combines a number of simple emotions, including guilt and shame. In embarrassment, guilt is made public, and there is a bit of surprise at being found out when you've made a social blunder. We are embarrassed, then, when we realize that we have violated some social taboo or social norm. We understand this, expect to be punished for it, and seek to appease the other person through submission, namely, showing embarrassment.[4]

What possible purpose is served by feeling embarrassed, ashamed, or guilty? Such emotions make us feel terrible, and others around us may feel uncomfortable, too. However, embarrassment serves a very useful function by preventing fights and disagreements. If we accidentally say or do something to upset or to hurt another person, the other person may become angry with us. We know that anger can motivate fighting and, knowing that the fight could all be a horrible mistake, we need to show that our actions were in error and that we regret them and apologize for them. Embarrassment is a visible apology to the other person for messing up.

Consider not how you feel when you are embarrassed but how you *look*. You hunch over and look downward. Your shoulders are raised in a shrug; your lips form an awkward smile. You seem smaller somehow, weaker and less important.

It is much harder to stay mad at a person who shows embarrassment than otherwise. When we show embarrassment, we seem so sorry for what we did. So people who show signs of embarrassment may be less likely to be punished, whether they are children who have misbehaved or criminals who face a jury or judge for sentencing.

Reaching a Deeper Level of Understanding

You must use your analytical ability to understand yourself and other people. There are clues everywhere, but you have to know that they exist, know what to look for, and ask a lot of questions. And you must know how to leverage your what-if skills. (We talk more about these skills later in this chapter.)

Your emotional knowledge starts with the basic building blocks: understanding the root cause of emotions. Fine-tuning your knowledge must be based on your insight into group, organizational, cultural, and individual norms and values because what makes you happy may make someone else absolutely miserable.

Consider this example from our outplacement consulting practice. If you've been down the road of job loss yourself, you know that after the loss of a job, you're expected to be shocked at first, then sad, then angry. Former colleagues may tiptoe around the topic when they're with you, if they're with you at all. They speak to you as though someone's died.

However, the experience of losing a job can be turned into a moment of emotional insight. Consider this story:

> When I received a pink slip some years ago I was surprised. I knew something was up, but I didn't think it was me who'd get the axe. During the brief meeting with my boss when he told me that my position was being eliminated, I needed to exert all of the emotional control that I could muster. I didn't want him to see how I felt, which was quite happy. Happy to be fired? Not exactly. I had been feeling burnt-out and unfulfilled in the job for almost a year and had made plans to leave marketing and re-enter the business world as a psychologist. I was taking two counseling refresher courses, started to counsel on the side, and had begun to develop marketing materials. Being fired gave me the push I needed to take the plunge.

Consider another example, only this time an example regarding anger. One key to understanding anger at a deeper level is to realize that causes of anger vary a lot from person to person. Not everyone perceives unfairness or injustice, for example, in the same actions.

> A group of Harry's coworkers were very upset and angry when they heard the news that a newcomer to the group, Danielle, was promoted rather than Harry. They said, "Harry knows the place better than anybody," "This new person doesn't know anything," and "It's just a diversity thing—she's a woman, and a minority, that's why she got the big job." The group assembled in Harry's office to complain and commiserate, and were surprised when Harry said, "Guys, calm down. I'm not upset. This was the right person for the job. The boss and I had a long talk about it last week. Danielle has a great background."

The key is that you must get outside your own head and personal experience—to discern what another's experience might be—in order to be an emotionally intelligent manager.

Make It Personal

How do you determine people's emotional hot buttons? Why not start with your own feelings. For example, think about what upsets you. What events make you feel miserable and sad? Try to think about the last time you felt this way, following these steps:

1. Describe the event that made you feel this way.
2. Indicate what happened just before this event. How did you feel?
3. Indicate how you felt as the event unfolded or began.
4. Write down what you were hoping to happen or expecting to happen.
5. Indicate how you felt at the conclusion of the event that upset you.
6. Try to recall how your emotions changed after the upsetting event, and indicate how you felt until you remember a feeling that goes back to a neutral or slightly positive point.

You can ask yourself the same sort of questions about other emotions. If you are a keen observer of people, you can also unravel their personal demons, loves, and passions. Consider a time when a colleague was worried, and then trace back the events leading up to that observation of worry. Don't interpret the events personally, as you usually would; instead, think about whether it is possible that the colleague sees the world differently than you do.

Build Your Emotional Vocabulary

Once you understand the causes of various emotions, you're ready to learn the language of emotion and enhance your emotional vocabulary. You really need a rich vocabulary of emotion words to be an emotionally intelligent manager. Even if you are emotionally intelligent in three of the four ability areas, if you lack a sophisticated emotional vocabulary, then you may not be able to express your insights or communicate deeply with others.

We present a list of emotion terms in Exhibit 10.1 to help you develop your emotional vocabulary. For each common emotion term, we list a series of descriptors:

1. Least intense experience of that emotion
2. Middle-level intensity of emotion
3. Intense experience of that emotion

To use your emotional vocabulary, you first must be accurately aware of the emotion. Then you'll need to identify how intense the feeling is that you are experiencing. Finally, select the appropriate emotional word to describe and communicate the feeling as exactly as possible.

Language and words are powerful. Because emotions contain information and data, the emotionally intelligent manager must have a sophisticated emotional vocabulary in order to communicate with precision and effectiveness to others.

Why does this matter, and what does it have to do with management? It matters because it has a good deal to do with being an effective manager. Managers communicate with others, and the more effective the communication, the more effective the group. Does it matter whether you say that you are surprised by the team's recommendation, or shocked, or angry? You bet it does! A manager who simply indicates, "Your ideas are a bit surprising" is not communicating a lot of detail or information and certainly is not giving concrete feedback that the group can use as they review their proposed plan. Instead, what if this manager were to say, "I am surprised to hear that you need an extra six months to complete the project. I am upset that this is the first time I heard about this delay"? Would this emotional communication be heard differently by the team than the blasé comment, "Your ideas are a bit surprising"?

Predicting the Emotional Future

Emotions have rules, and they follow certain patterns and progressions. The ability to figure out emotional what-if situations—to determine what is going to happen next to us and to others emotionally—is one of the skills of emotional intelligence.

Emotional Progressions

What-if planning and analysis is a core managerial skill. Yet the most analytical of plans will fail if it does not incorporate *emotional* what-if analyses. You must consider how people will hear and

Exhibit 10.1. Emotional Vocabulary.

HAPPINESS

Serene
Happy
Joyous
Ecstatic

Related terms and phrases

Delight
Gladness
Euphoria
Satisfaction
Pleasure
Amusement
Spread cheer
Feel happy for another
Be positive
Share another's joy

ACCEPTANCE

Admire
Accept
Trust

Related terms and phrases

Embrace
Welcome
Feel confidence
Have faith
Cherish
Like
Love
Adore
Feel interest

ANTICIPATION

Interest
Anticipation
Vigilance

Exhibit 10.1. Emotional Vocabulary, Cont'd.

Related terms and phrases

Fascinate
Intrigue
Attract
Charm
Expect

SURPRISE

Distraction
Surprise
Amazement

Related terms and phrases

Wonder
Awe
Astonishment
Shock
Bewilderment
Disbelief
Incredulity
Stupefaction

ANGER

Annoyance
Anger
Rage

Related terms and phrases

Hatred
Irritation
Frustration
Malice
Ill-will
Fury
Indignation

DISGUST

Boredom
Loathing

Exhibit 10.1. Emotional Vocabulary, Cont'd.

Related terms and phrases

Revile
Be averse to
Dislike
Be amoral
Behave in a gross way

FEAR

Apprehension
Fear
Terror

Related terms and phrases

Dread
Jitters
Anxiety
Worry
Concern
Trepidation
Nervousness
Wariness
Edginess
Misgivings

SADNESS

Pensive
Sad
Grief-stricken

Related terms and phrases

Dejected
Unhappy
Sorrowful
Distressed
Anguished
Lonely
Blue
Down
"Bummed out"

respond to your plan. Will the plan and the way it is communicated make sense to your team, to the board of directors, to the customer? These plans must take account of how people are feeling, as a baseline, and then predict possible reactions to various aspects of your plan. It's not easy to do this, but because emotions do have rules, or patterns, it's possible.

Some emotional patterns seem to make more sense than others. Although we could create any number of scenarios to illustrate almost any emotional pattern or progression, some of these scenarios are just plain weird. For example, let's look at this emotional progression:

1. You are wondering.
2. You are surprised.
3. You are feeling shocked.

This emotional progression is complex, but I bet that you can come up with a story that follows it. Try it now. Write down a story that, as reasonably as possible, illustrates how you could feel each of these emotions, in order. Then read this story:

> I was sitting at my desk, *wondering* what the impact of our poor quarterly sales record would be on the company. I was *surprised* when my boss said that our sales group might be impacted by the poor financial results. But when I heard that my position was being terminated and that I was losing my job, I was *shocked.*

Was it easy to come up with your story? If you told your story to someone else, would that person think it made sense? Or possibly consider it to be a very bizarre series of emotional events?

What if we were to add to, and then jumble, this list of emotions? Would it be harder or easier to tell a story that made sense? Would the story be reasonable, or would it appear to be somewhat unusual? Try telling a story in which a person's emotions progress as follows:

1. Surprise
2. Wonder
3. Happiness
4. Shock
5. Sadness

Write these emotions on a piece of paper, and take a few minutes to tell a story about them—a story that makes as much sense as possible. Is it an easy task? Remember that this is not a creative-writing exercise; you have to tell a story that would make sense to you and to most other people. Sure, anything is possible, but the less an emotional progression follows the emotional rules, the less sense our story makes. It is difficult to tell a story following this emotional progression because the progression makes little emotional sense.

Progression of Negative Emotions

If emotions have rules, then it should be possible to ask which of the following two emotional progressions makes more sense. Read each set of emotion terms in Exhibit 10.2 and decide which is in the more sensible, emotionally intelligent order.

Exhibit 10.2. Emotional Jumble.

Getting Mad A

Mad

Irritable

Furious

Annoyed

Upset

Enraged

Angry

Frustrated

Getting Mad B

Irritable

Annoyed

Frustrated

Upset

Mad

Angry

Furious

Enraged

Emotion experts would likely say that *Getting Mad B* is a better illustration of how emotions work than *Getting Mad A*. We begin by being in a somewhat negative mood, not angry or upset but just a bit irritable. If that irritation continues and worsens, we become annoyed. When the annoying event continues, we become frustrated, as our plans are blocked and thwarted. Now this makes us feel upset, and the feelings build until we are mad. Turning our feelings toward someone else, we are angry at this person, and when that other person refuses to stop, we become furious. As the other person taunts us and we lose control, we become enraged.

It's important to be able to figure this out. If you know how emotions work and how they don't work, you can learn how to predict the future—at least how someone might feel if a certain event occurred, how a client will react to your proposal, or how you will feel if you take a new role.

Progression of Positive Emotions

Let's spend some time now on positive emotions. Consider the case of *joy*. What is the progression of emotions that leads to joy? Take the list of emotions in Exhibit 10.3, and try to put them in an order that makes sense emotionally. Your list should end with *joy*.

Although emotions have moves much like chess pieces, emotional moves are less precise than those in chess. There are a few ways to order the emotions leading to joy, but the order in Exhibit 10.4 begins with a positive neutral mood—calmness—and ends with an active, positive mood—joy, placing the scrambled emotion terms in an emotionally intelligent sequence.

Exhibit 10.3. Emotional Word Jumble for Joy.

Happy

Pleased

Joyous

Amused

Calm

Positive

Content

Exhibit 10.4. Calm to Joy.

Calm

Content

Pleased

Amused

Positive

Happy

Joyous

Try some other emotional jumbles, as shown in Exhibit 10.5. We don't want to sound like people are completely predictable. That's certainly not been our experience. But emotions follow a certain path, and they progress from one state to another. Emotions really make rational sense, and you can leverage your knowledge of emotional progressions to help you become a more emotionally intelligent manager. We began with a simple two-dimension approach to emotional vocabulary. To that, we have added several layers of knowledge and emotional sophistication.

◆ ◆ ◆

Emotions have rules. You can learn these rules and use this knowledge to help you better figure people out. Understanding the way in which emotions change and transition, as well as the underlying causes of emotions, gives you the ability to gaze into the future and to predict it with some degree of certainty. You won't be able to guess the lottery winners or someone's height and weight at a carnival side show, but you can learn to predict how a person will react to certain events and situations. This emotional what-if ability can help the emotionally intelligent manager to better strategize and plan better.

What do you do with your emotional insights and predictions? This is where the fourth step of our model—Managing Emotions— comes in. In the next chapter, we will describe strategies to help you become a better emotional manager.

Exhibit 10.5. More Emotional Jumbles.

Feeling Fear Jumble

Worried

Fearful

Edgy

Wary

Panicked

Nervous

Attentive

A Solution

Attentive

Edgy

Wary

Nervous

Worried

Fearful

Panicked

Sinking into Depression Jumble

Blue

Sorrowful

Down

Sad

Neutral

Despairing

Gloomy

A Solution

Neutral

Blue

Down

Gloomy

Exhibit 10.5. More Emotional Jumbles, Cont'd.

Sad

Despairing

Sorrowful

Love's Passion Jumble

Liking

Devoted

Passionate

Adoring

Loving

Trusting

Friendly

A Solution

Friendly

Liking

Trusting

Devoted

Adoring

Loving

Passionate

CHAPTER 11

Do It with Smart Feelings
Improving Your Ability to Manage Emotions

Do you feel especially intelligent when you get really emotional? Or are there times when our emotionally intelligent management approach simply doesn't work? We believe that because emotions and thinking are inextricably linked, it is impossible to avoid an emotion-based approach to decision making and problem solving. Nonetheless, sometimes our feelings, or those of others, need to be managed, and we focus on this issue here.

Remember that the emotions we feel signal us that a real issue or problem exists. Emotions direct our attention to what is important. Emotions contain information—one of our mantras throughout *The Emotionally Intelligent Manager.* Leveraging these data can give us the insight and direction we often need. But acting on impulse— on our gut—can lead to problems when the impulse is based on incorrect emotional data. It's when our data are sound and solid that we must attend to and act on our gut feelings. We usually end up regretting it when we don't, because we're failing to take account of important information.

If you tend to disparage emotions and close yourself off to them, it will take some effort to break these habits. Staying open to powerful feelings, whether negative or positive, brings critical information your way, but it can also bring sorrow and stress if not done with care. The following topics will help you do this by bringing you further along the emotion management curve in this chapter:

- What Doesn't Work and What Does
- Staying Open to Emotions
- Filter Out Moods, Filter In Emotions
- Emotion Management Basics
- Advanced Course: Managing Anger at Work

What Doesn't Work and What Does

Because the skills of emotion are usually not taught explicitly, all sorts of folk wisdom of varying quality and effectiveness surrounds the remedies for emotional distress. Some home remedies for emotions do work, of course, and others work for the wrong reasons. Let's take a quick look at a few of the emotion home remedies that we've all heard of, but that are not very effective.[1]

What Doesn't Work

The "eat, drink, and be merry" approach to stress relief does not work. But answer these questions, and decide for yourself.

Have you been traveling a lot? Possibly experiencing the after-effects of the latest organizational re-engineering effort? Are you being asked by management to work smarter, not harder, and don't have a clue how to do that? If so, you have a lot of company, and you are probably experiencing a lot of stress.

Common wisdom might suggest that you give yourself a break and do something enjoyable—possibly, have a beer. Actually, have a beer, some chocolate cake, and a cigarette, and you probably *will* feel a whole lot better. There's no doubt that giving in to our impulse to eat and drink often helps alleviate stress. It helps us forget about what was preying on our mind.

The problem with giving in to these impulses is that the strategy only works in the short term. The problem that caused the stress will still be there in the morning, only now, another day will have gone by and we haven't addressed it. We feel worse, and perhaps the problem has grown worse. The lesson is that we can pay a price for trying to feel good!

Let us emphasize that we are *not* recommending that you drink beer, smoke cigarettes, or eat chocolate to manage your moods.

That does not work, as Robert Thayer's research, to be discussed later in this chapter, reveals.

Similarly, escapist strategies that don't work very well include watching television and daydreaming. Sure, one might feel different emotions after distracting oneself in these ways, but such feelings are often short-lived. And because television viewing involves so little mental or physical effort, we can sometimes feel even more negative after engaging in it. Imagine how you would feel if, because you were in a bad mood, you spent mindless hours channel surfing in front of the TV set (or computer screen) rather than being engaged in a more productive and enjoyable task. You'd perhaps feel a bit guilty and irritable.

What Does Work

Just as music has a powerful emotional influence on us, so does writing. James Pennebaker's research shows that people who write about their feelings are able to lower their blood pressure and heart rate. Other researchers have discovered that writing about emotions has a positive impact on our immune system and how we cope with difficult situations. Even coping with job loss can be influenced by writing about our feelings and emotions.[2]

Writing About Emotions

It is not just the act of writing that has these beneficial effects; specifically, it's writing about our deepest feelings and emotions and integrating them with the thoughts we have about the situation that produced them. The best writing—the most emotionally healthful writing—has these elements. Such writing uses:

- Positive emotion words frequently
- Negative emotion words moderately
- Causal words and phrases like "caused me to" and "led me"
- Insight words and phrases like "understand" and "realize"

To write a healthy emotions journal, you should:

- Write for at least twenty minutes each day.
- Write without stopping.

- Keep on writing without thinking about what to say or how you want to say it; don't edit your thoughts or your written work.
- Include positive emotion words, as well as causal and insightful phrases.

What should you write about? It almost doesn't matter. You can write about any event that lets you explore your deepest emotions *and* thoughts.

Rather than keep a journal, you can write a letter to a friend or possibly an imaginary person. You don't need to actually send the letter. You can even write a newspaper article or a report—whatever works for you.

Exercising

Psychologists have found that exercise is an excellent way of restoring emotional balance. Robert Thayer believes that exercise is a key ingredient in the management of mood.[3] If you find that you often feel tense, angry, depressed, or just overwhelmed by your feelings, you might consider starting a regular exercise program. Try to do aerobic exercise at least three times a week for about twenty to thirty minutes a session. Excellent aerobic exercises include brisk walking, running, cycling, swimming, doing step-aerobics, and playing sports such as basketball, soccer, or field hockey.

Does this sound like too much for you to handle? Do you already exercise? Exercise does not always involve running ten miles. Even a simple, brisk walk around the block, up a few flights of stairs, or around the office can help restore your calm and provide you with more energy.

The easy way to get a boost of energy is to grab a cup of coffee, a Coke, or a candy bar. These things work, but they don't work for a long enough time. The biggest problem with a nonexercise solution to boosting energy is that after the effects of the caffeine and the sugar wear off, you are often in an even worse frame of mind.

Still don't believe it? Try it a few times. Take a five-minute brisk walk or climb the stairs rather than ride the elevator. It's really hard to exercise when you're tired, but it is the best way to energize yourself. (Of course, before you begin an exercise program, you should consult with your physician.)

Becoming an emotionally intelligent manager requires emotional awareness and the ability to stay open to emotions. We help you with that next.

Stay Open to Emotion

It helps to get a quick read on how accepting you are of emotion. What follows in Exhibit 11.1 is not a psychometrically sound test, but the questions and your reflective answers will help you begin to determine how open you are to experiencing emotion.[4]

Some people can't stand strong feelings. They overreact to them. One of the most significant scholars in the field of emotions research, Silvan Tomkins, described people's "affect-about-affect," or how we feel about our feelings.[5] Some people may be scared of their own anger, and others may feel disappointed or guilty that they have expressed or felt angry. Similarly, we have feelings about other powerful emotions as well.

If emotions contain valuable information, then being closed to this information can be harmful. In order to stay open to emotion, we can apply a behavior therapy technique known as *systematic desensitization* to our emotion experience. Systematic desensitization consists of several steps:[6]

1. Determine which emotions give you the most trouble.
2. Make a list of situations that result in the emotion.
3. Order the situations from least to most emotionally intense.
4. Learn to relax through, for example, progressive muscle relaxation exercises.
5. Generate a calm and pleasant mood and relax.

Exhibit 11.1. Do You Stay Open to Emotions?

I often think about my emotions.

It's best to experience my emotions to the fullest.

I pay a lot of attention to my feelings.

I feel at ease about my emotions.

I stay aware of my feelings, even when they are painful or negative.

6. Picture the least intense emotional situation.
7. As you find yourself tensing up, start to relax again and generate a calming mood.

Each time you are able to visualize the emotional scene and stay open to the emotion, you then move up the emotion-intensity ladder. Once you feel that you can remain open to the upsetting emotion, it's time to try it out in the real world; add actual behavior elements to your list of imagined events.

Consider a person who is optimistic, upbeat, and always happy. It's not a bad way to be, but what if this person—we'll call him John—runs away from negative feelings and thoughts? Won't John be missing valuable information?

John has determined that he does not feel comfortable with sadness. He then constructs an emotion hierarchy, listing events that may be mildly sad for him to events that evoke very strong feelings of sadness:

- He loses a poker hand.
- It rains on the weekend.
- He does not get a pay raise.
- A friend gets injured.
- A friend at work is fired.
- A relative dies.

John learns relaxation strategies and imagines the first scene. As he begins to close his feelings down and tries to push the sadness away, he remembers to relax and to stay open to the feeling of sadness or loss. It's pretty easy for him to do that because the emotion is fairly mild. With that success behind him, he later moves up the emotion hierarchy and imagines the next scenario. He repeats the process until he is able to stay open to all of his feelings.

John, or anyone else for that matter, will become quickly overwhelmed by trying to open up to strong feelings without a plan or preparation. So if you start down the path to greater openness, we want you to do so intelligently, by using an approach like the one we've just outlined.[7]

The key is—and we'll say it again—that emotions are data. Closing yourself off to your emotions and those of others closes you off to an important source of information. It's neither easy nor even advisable to move from being a rationality-embracing person to one who experiences the extremes of sorrow and joy. Making such a transition is just like learning to ride a bicycle: it helps to start by learning some of the basics—like how to change gears, for starters.

Change Emotional Gears

If you think you don't switch emotional gears, think again. We are fairly certain that you have had the experience of feeling a strong emotion and then almost immediately changing either the way you were feeling or the way you were acting. For example, do these or similar situations seem familiar?

- You are yelling at a colleague or a family member and the phone rings. You pick up the phone and say, calmly and pleasantly, "Hello."
- The team is discussing all the problems on a project that will delay the product launch by two months, something the president has said is unacceptable. Everyone on the team is very depressed. The president walks into the meeting room, ready to be briefed on the status of the project. You rise to begin the presentation.

What were your emotions at the time? How strong were they? Were you able to change gears? How did you do this?

You can practice the skill of changing emotional gears to help you in other situations. Here are some steps you can take:

1. Think of an emotionally charged situation.
2. Picture the situation, and picture yourself feeling the emotion.
3. Think of an interruption of that situation, such as a phone call, a knock on the door, someone calling your name or walking into the room.

How do you feel when this happens? What are you able to do to change the way you are acting?

Filter out Moods, Filter in Emotions

Emotions don't hurt our performance necessarily; thinking *must* include feeling. Although we've been driving this idea home in this book, you don't need to be a psychologist to realize that people know their feelings can truly mess things up for them. Our petty jealousies, unbridled anger, and baseless fears derail us and wreak havoc on our lives and the lives of those we touch. As we have pointed out, these problems are usually due to an inaccurate emotional appraisal of the situation or to the way we typically view the world.

As we've mentioned before, the typical way we feel is sometimes called a mood, as opposed to an emotion. Emotions are brief and attributable to some identifiable cause. Moods are the background noise and the diffuse feelings we have. Often the reasons we feel the way we do are unknown. Our interpretation of events is often based on our moods.

The impact of mood on feelings is illustrated in Figure 11.1. If you are starting out in a negative, or bad, mood, then little things will quickly get to you and annoy you. Soon you find yourself feeling angry, but you're not sure why. But start out in a fairly positive, or good, mood, and the same events don't upset you as easily. Eventually, you might feel angry, but it's going to take a lot to make you feel that way.

Figure 11.1. Example of How Mood Influences Feelings.

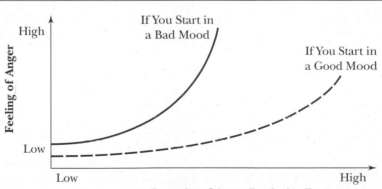

Mood Filtering

What if you are often in either a good or a bad mood? Some people do have typical ways of looking at the world and interpreting events, and they filter experience through their own mood lens. Such ways of behaving or viewing the world are sometimes called *personality* or *dispositional traits*. Some important dispositional traits are depression, anxiety, hostility, optimism, pleasantness, stress, and trust.

Take the example of depression. If you are depressed, then you may tend to exaggerate negative events and ascribe negative motives to certain events. You look on the dark side of things. You will be open to emotion but tend to be more aware of sad emotions and events. You'll take a neutral event and ascribe negative connotations to it. When you are depressed, you see depression in the world around you.

We've all heard about the importance of treating dispositional or personality trait problems of depression, anxiety, and hostility. These "irrational" emotions and thoughts are usually seen as negative and destructive. However, to manage emotion successfully, we should be aware of any tendency to minimize or maximize *any* type of emotion, not just sadness, anxiety, and anger.

For instance, the tendency to see things in a positive light and always to put a positive spin on events is one of the outcomes of being optimistic. Even though optimism has been linked to important and positive outcomes, in the context of emotion management, optimism can derail successful emotion management as much as depression can. When we are in a happy, expansive mood we can miss details. Our error-checking ability might be disabled. We can fail to recognize or to accept problems. Feeling positive and optimistic, we fend off criticisms of our marketing and advertising plan because we "just know that it will work." And if our judgment was based more on the optimistic feeling as background noise rather than a positive emotion based on real data, chances are we're going to have some explaining to do.

A related dispositional trait is that of agreeableness, or as we call it here, pleasantness—the tendency to get along with others, defer to people's wishes and needs, and be generally easygoing. Such a person is nonconfrontational and easy to be with. Often such people trust others and have faith in the goodness of others. It's difficult for a pleasant and trusting person to see and to admit that someone is, for lack of a better phrase, a real jerk. The impact of these and other traits is shown in Exhibit 11.2.

You can turn to Appendix 1 to help you better understand your moods, or dispositional traits. We've developed a special set of questions to help you figure out what sort of moods you may use to filter your experience. These questions help you discriminate the signal function of emotions from the noise of moods.

Exhibit 11.2. Traits and Their Impact.

Dispositional Trait	Impact
Depression	Experiences sadness
Anxiety	Experiences fear, surprise
Hostility	Experiences anger, disgust
Optimism	Experiences happiness
Pleasantness	Maximizes positive emotions; minimizes negative emotions
Stress	Exaggerates negative emotions
Trust	Fails to distinguish genuine from faked emotions

Emotion Filtering

However, when the feeling you have is based on an emotion—a feeling containing data—you still should not always act on it. The emotionally intelligent manager has to be clear about emotions and gauge how typical and influential these feelings are. Being clear requires that we neither minimize nor exaggerate the emotions. We also have to be clear about our openness to certain emotions and to determine whether we selectively filter out, or filter in, certain feelings.

We may "do" happiness well but have a tough time being open to feelings of anger. Or we may be quick to embrace a sad feeling but shy away from feelings of joy and happiness.

Positive and Negative Emotion Filtering

When certain emotions are less acceptable than others, we may filter out those unwanted feelings. We selectively attend to certain feelings and ignore others.

There are two general forms of emotional filtering: (1) positive emotion focus and (2) negative emotion focus.[8] We've heard about the power of positive thinking, but what about the power of a positive emotion focus? Without discounting the importance of optimism on health and other outcomes, positive thinking or a focus on positive emotions can lead to a lack of emotional awareness. This is especially true if we spend resources looking for positive emotions, leaving fewer resources available for the processing of negative emotions. Negative emotion focus works the same way, only in this case we are focusing on negative emotions.

Accepting Certain Emotions

Another way to view the emotional filtering process is to examine whether or not we allow only certain feelings to rise to the level of conscious acceptance and awareness. Some people may not filter out negative emotions in general, but they may find that they don't allow themselves to process anger. To them, anger is not an acceptable emotion to experience.

Although it may seem that the negative emotions are likely to be deemed unacceptable, it is common for people to see strong, positive emotions like joy as unacceptable or as unwelcome emotional guests in their daily work-life.

Overgeneralizing Emotion

Deciding how typical a feeling is can be made more difficult if we tend to believe that a single fleeting feeling is the harbinger of more to come. We become convinced that our feelings will intensify. We can also believe or convince ourselves that we are always feeling this way, and we become overwhelmed by the emotion.[9]

Jumping to Emotional Conclusions

When we believe that our current emotional state will have drastic consequences for ourselves, we jump to the conclusion, prematurely, that our feelings are incredibly influential and powerful.

The following exercise may create an experience of insight that will allow you to determine which emotional filters you tend to use.

Emotion Generalization Strategy

If you filter out certain emotions or overgeneralize certain emotions, this strategy may help you manage these emotions better.

1. Select an emotion that you might exaggerate.
2. Consider a recent situation in which this emotion was present.
3. Was it *reasonable* to feel this way? Consider the causes of emotions to help you to determine this. (See Exhibit 11.3.)
4. How strongly did you feel this way?
5. Consider the following:
   Did you have a warm feeling or cold?
   Were you tense or more relaxed?
   Did you have a light feeling or some sort of heavy, weighted-down feeling?
   Did you feel tired or energetic?
6. Do you often feel this way?

Exhibit 11.3. How We Feel.

The Event	We Feel
A threat	Fear
Obstacle in our way	Anger
A loss	Sadness
Distasteful behavior	Disgust
Unexpected event	Surprise
A gain of something valuable	Joy

7. What do you think about when feeling this way?
   Do you "catch" yourself when you feel this way?
8. Why do you feel this way? What causes the feeling? Identify what makes you feel this way.
   How did you interpret the event?
   Would someone else have interpreted the event in the same way?
   Is it possible that your view of the event was incorrect?
9. Evaluate alternative explanations for feeling this way. Ask whether is it reasonable.
10. Practice feeling this way:
    Before a situation, think about the likelihood of feeling _____.
    Visualize the provoking scenes.
    Relax and visualize your response.
    Then, enter the situation, ready for action.

Emotion Management Basics

The Emotionally Intelligent Manager is about integrating emotions and thought. But emotions can be processed and understood at many different levels. We may believe ourselves to be including and processing emotion in an intelligent manner when we are actually just including emotion at a surface level or in a cursory manner.

In most workplace settings, emotions are simply not business-like. This leads organizations to develop unwritten rules of emotions: which emotions are okay to recognize and which are not; which emotions are acceptable to express and which are not. The process of *normalizing* emotions, discussed by management researcher Blake Ashforth, can take a number of different forms, from active suppression of the emotion to reframing the emotion in a different light.[10]

Therefore, we need to have some way of differentiating various levels of emotional awareness and processing. Strategies can range from the nonemotional to the emotional; emotion is integrated into thought but at various levels of sophistication and processing. We will first turn to strategies in which emotion is kept at bay and defended against. Then we'll examine ways to include emotion in decision making and thinking.

Disengagement from Emotion

Sometimes, emotions are too strong and too painful to bear. In such cases, we have many options and we can have a great deal of control over how we experience emotion. However, certain strategies have a cognitive cost associated with them. For example, we lose details and data if we continually try to suppress the emotional experience.

Disengaging ourselves from emotion means that we are aware of and process only the nonemotional data. We deal directly, and only, with concrete data and information.

Avoidance of Emotions

We can simply turn away from the event, remove ourselves from the event, or not get involved in the first place. An example of this emotional avoidance strategy is when one avoids going to an emotionally powerful movie if the costs would appear to outweigh the benefits. Knowing that you experience very strong feelings when you watch certain movies, you can view only those powerful movies with a message that you want to, and are ready to, hear. As a matter of course, you shouldn't go to horror movies or movies with gratuitous violence.

Emotional avoidance, like any emotional strategy, has its uses and its misuses. If we avoided all emotional situations, life would be fairly empty, and we would miss out on opportunities to learn, grow, and develop personally.

Denial of Emotions

If you can't *avoid* a strong emotional situation, then you can engage in another emotion-limiting strategy: emotional denial. This strategy can be employed after you are exposed to a powerful emotional event in order to minimize its impact on you.

Many of us learn emotional denial strategies early in our lives. Some little boys are exhorted to "be a man" and are told that "big boys don't cry." Both boys and girls are sometimes taught to turn away from powerful emotional events and scenes.

As an adult, have you attended a presentation when a member of the audience said something indirectly insulting to the presenter? On many occasions, the presenter just smiles a forced smile, shakes his head, and proceeds. It is likely that the speaker is actively trying to deny and block out the surprise and the anger. Whether this denial strategy will be effective depends on many factors, the most important being that the underlying emotion behind the verbal assault be determined and the information communicated correctly analyzed. Was the audience member angry for some other reason? Is he frustrated about some aspect of the plan or trying to sabotage the presentation because his voice has not been heard?

We often selectively suppress our reaction to an emotional event. Perhaps you feel that it isn't appropriate to show your feelings in front of people. You simply "bite your lip" or smile, even though you are very angry or very sad. You choose not to act, that is, you use your brain to control the impulse to show your emotions. But remember the cognitive costs of suppressing your emotions: you lose data and information. There must be a better strategy.

Engagement of Emotion

We can actively engage with emotion at various levels. Let's examine different strategies for emotional engagement.

Emotional Reappraisal

Another way to lessen the power of a subjective emotional experience is to change the way we view it. If you are going to have a painful medical test conducted, you might see the procedure as a way to get or stay healthy and focus on the positives of the experience rather than on the negative aspects of the procedure. The process of prescribing emotions is similar. When we prescribe emotions, we recast the emotional experience in a way that is more acceptable to our workplace environment.[11]

Emotional Acknowledgment

This is the Scarlett O'Hara strategy, named for a character in *Gone With the Wind*. One of her most famous lines is, "I'll think about it tomorrow," which Scarlett utters toward the end of the book (and movie), when she must confront death, devastation, and destruction, literally at her doorstep. The Scarlett strategy applied to emotion management is one in which you acknowledge the emotion but do not attempt to solve the problem. In this strategy, you recognize the emotion but then move on. This is the strategy to use when you want to seem like you're in touch with the issue but cannot deal with it at that time. You indicate that you are in touch with the emotional component of a situation and then you quickly move on, out of that uncomfortable territory. (Of course, you may very well argue that Scarlett is an emotional avoider, but we like the term and we'll use it to describe emotional acknowledgment, even though it may make you, and us, somewhat uncomfortable.)

For example, let's say that your boss praises you for a top-notch job on a presentation to the team. She says in front of the entire group, "Joe did a superb job today. It looks like this team is meeting, or perhaps exceeding, all of its objectives." Your reaction? Pay lip service and move on, perhaps saying something along these lines: "Thanks, Jill, that was nice of you." At least you recognized the situation; you didn't blow it off. Perhaps praise makes you feel uncomfortable. Perhaps you don't want to get into this any deeper because you feel ill at ease.

Emotional Integration

If we are generally aware of emotion in ourselves and others, we can integrate emotion and thought, but our emotional strategy will be fairly basic. If we feel sad but wish to feel happy, we can manage our own mood or that of others. But we may not clearly understand and differentiate our feelings and may miss certain key bits of information.

We can also be aware of, and directly address, a specific emotion. Strategies that derive from this approach will be direct but also fairly basic. They may resolve the underlying problem, if the problem itself is a simple one.

The most comprehensive strategy of emotional intelligence coping must involve a good deal of processing of emotion at a deep and meaningful level. Emotional intelligence at its best will likely include the four steps of our Emotional Blueprint:

1. *Identify Emotions*
   Are you aware of your mood?
   How clear is it to you?
   Is this a typical mood for you?
   Is it okay to feel this way?
   How powerful is the feeling?
2. *Use Emotions*
   What is the meaning of the mood or emotion?
   What caused you to feel this way?
3. *Understand Emotions*
   What is the cause and the real issue or problem?
   What are some emotional "What next" questions?
4. *Manage Emotions*
   What is the desired outcome?
   What are possible actions to take?
   Ask emotional what-if questions to determine the efficacy of
      alternatives.

Advanced Course: Managing Anger at Work

The case of anger deserves a special place in *The Emotionally Intelligent Manager*. So in this section, we focus particularly on the management of angry feelings.

Aggression and Anger

When people are in a confrontational situation with another person that results in angry feelings, many feel like becoming verbally aggressive. Many people want to be physically aggressive. In fact, a full 82 percent feel like being verbally aggressive, and 40 percent feel like punching the other person.[12]

However, some people seem to just think about being aggressive. The actual behaviors they engage in look quite different, as shown in Exhibit 11.4.

Exhibit 11.4. What We Do When We Feel Angry.

Strategy	% Who Use Strategy
Calm themselves down	60%
Talk about it without anger	59%
Get verbally aggressive	49%
Talk to the person	39%
Be extra nice	19%
Get physically aggressive	10%

In the next section, we'll help you manage intelligently *with* anger. This means that your feeling of anger is a signal that an injustice has been committed, that a wrong needs to be addressed.[13]

Constructive Use of Anger

Feeling angry and *acting* out of anger are different. Anger can be a powerful and *constructive* emotion or a powerful and *destructive* emotion. We'll first deal with the destructive, emotionally unintelligent side of anger.[14]

We start at the beginning, which, in our emotional intelligence model means we start with accurately identifying feelings. If anger doesn't work, then it is likely there was some problem with identifying the feeling. You need to identify carefully what event or action made you feel angry to begin with. This is when your mood and emotion filters are most clear and can be examined. If you have a tendency to be easily irritated or frustrated, you must come up with alternative explanations as to *why* the person who made you angry did what he or she did. Ask yourself whether it is reasonable to be angry. Consider how another person would view the situation. Next, question your own perceptions of the situation, for instance, ask yourself whether your boss is really out to get you.

You might find that you have incorrectly attributed the cause of your feeling of anger to the acts of another person when, in reality, you were just in a bad mood. You might discover that the smirk you saw on your colleague's face was not a smirk at all, but a look of thoughtfulness. Anger is always destructive and always leads to a negative outcome when we act on a feeling of anger that has no basis in the external world.

If you incorrectly identify the cause of your angry feelings, and you don't stop to question your perceptions, then it is likely you are already hurtling down a destructive path. Your focus narrows; you perceive the other person as a threat. You begin a chain of reasoning that finds other examples of anger-producing actions. Then you either act on the anger in a direct way, or you keep it inside, hiding it from view. Or so you think. Remember our discussion of the difficulties of hiding one's feelings? And how we use vital thinking power when we actively try to suppress our experience of emotion? We might think we're hiding, but a perceptive colleague will know better. And we might believe we are still paying attention to what is going on during the rest of the meeting, but in reality, we are missing critical information as we seethe inside.

How to Disengage from Anger

Here is an example of how an emotionally intelligent manager disengaged from anger by following the four steps of our model. First, here's a description of the situation:

> You are making a presentation to the team. One of the team members asks a question that challenges some of your basic points. You answer the question and move to the next slide in your presentation. The same person interrupts and again asks a question that directly challenges your basic assumptions. The questions he is asking are repetitive and do not seem relevant to your discussion. You are feeling quite irritated.

And here's how the manager followed the four steps:

> *Identify emotion:* It's clear that you're getting frustrated. It also seems from the nature of the questions and the way the questions are being asked that the person does not have a hostile intent. This is the key: *a threat does not exist.* However, a problem does exist, and it's a problem that you must solve efficiently and quickly.
>
> *Use emotion:* Taking his perspective for a moment, you try to see his point of view (use your emotion to help you think). The questions concern the remote possibility of failing to gain timely regulatory approvals.

The approval process is straightforward, and ample time has been allotted to this phase of the product launch plan. But he is still concerned about this issue, and for him, your entire product presentation is about the approvals process.

Understand emotion: At this point, you understand that your answers have only made his worries intensify. If you do not address his underlying concerns right now, he will become anxious and fearful. Then things will really start to unravel on you. It's not just that this one person will have an emotional meltdown. You realize that negative emotional contagion can infect the entire team unless you take action.

Manage emotion: Because his questions are generated by his anxious mood rather than an accurate gut feel for a problem, you are safe to ignore this team member's emotional signals but you do address his unstated question.

What can you do? It depends in large part on your personal style. Here is one way an emotionally intelligent manager might handle the situation.

You stop your presentation and walk closer to the questioner. You pause and then look at him. In a quiet, calm, and reassuring tone, you tell him, "I hear your concern about the regulatory approvals. We already have preliminary approvals in place, but of course that is no guarantee. It would be a shame if we were delayed by an approvals issue, and so I agree with you that we must deal with that possibility. I'd like to hear more about your concerns and ask you to help us find a way to avoid those problems. I would like to share the rest of the plan with the group right now so that you have the complete picture. That should help you develop a more effective approvals strategy. Will that work for you?"

He may back down and calm down. But he may not. If this approach does not work, then it is time to take more direct emotion management action. He'll need to be emotionally isolated so he does not infect the rest of the group. You might, depending on your leadership style, indicate that the issue has been addressed in the full plan and that you need to move on.

Our four-step approach does not dictate either how to feel or how to act. How you disengage from these feelings of frustration and annoyance will be up to you, but we believe that you'll find the model a helpful tool.

When to Get Angry

There are lots of self-help books, workshops, and seminars on anger management, and many of these books and programs are helpful. There are thousands of managers who certainly need these services; many ruin their careers and the lives of their employees because of their uncontrolled anger.

We're going to talk about a different side of anger management—teaching people *how to get angry*, not how to rid themselves of anger. We admit that it's a tricky subject, and we'll be careful to go easy on the recommendations. There will be no boxing lessons. But if you have ever experienced a situation in which someone's rights were trampled on, unfair advantage was taken of someone, or a corporate bully verbally beat up on a weaker foe, then you may see the need to get angry at times.

If you've felt anger and tried your best to ignore the feeling, you're not alone. Remember that 19 percent of people in an anger-causing situation act extra nice to the other person, and 60 percent try to calm down (our guess is they try to calm down and forget about the anger-causing incident and person).

Anger can be justified, and it can be intelligent. The way to determine whether it's smart to be angry is to use our emotionally intelligent approach. Here is how we suggest you manage *with* anger.

How to Manage with Anger

Constructively managing with anger is an extremely difficult task. It requires highly developed emotional skills and is based on a complete and accurate emotional identification. We'll use the complete, four-step model of emotional intelligence again.

> *Identify emotion:* You have used your mood and emotion filter analyses and discovered that these are not giving rise to your growing frustration. Now you can ask whether there exists an injustice, an issue of integrity, or honesty. Is this a case of bias, bigotry, or prejudice?
>
> Even though you can get easily frustrated at times, you are very clear about how you feel, and you are clear about how typical this feeling is. You determine that other people in the same situation would also perceive it as anger-provoking.
>
> *Use emotion:* This ability will help to make sure that acting with anger is a constructive, not a destructive, process. If you feel what the

other person feels, it will not be possible to act in a way that is unduly harsh. Feeling from the other person's perspective also gives you a deeper level of insight into her world, allowing you to devise a plan of effective action that will make a difference to her.

You should also ask, "Am I too focused on looking for problems, injustice, feelings of being wronged or hurt? If I expand my view, what else might I discover about the person and the situation?"

Understand emotion: You'll next want to pinpoint the underlying cause for the feeling of anger. "When did it start, and how did I feel just a short time ago? Will the feelings intensify or gradually pass and subside?"

It is important to use your what-if analyses to evaluate alternative courses of action. And you'll certainly want to ask what the outcome will be if you take no action.

Manage emotion: If my feeling of anger is justified, that is, there has indeed been an act of injustice, then what do I do with this feeling? It will all depend on your desired outcome. What do you want to happen? What is the desired feeling-based outcome? Do you want the other person to recognize his mistake? Do you want him to change his behavior or to simply stop what he is doing?

For each of the possible strategies you come up with, you'll evaluate them by using your emotional what-if planning skill to try to predict the possible result. Feeling empowered by your anger, you may now be ready to act out of anger but not act angrily. You can't fall asleep at the wheel. You must continually monitor the environment, both how you feel and how the other person feels. Your focus of attention has to constantly shift, and you need to switch perspectives to truly understand the situation. As the situation changes, so must your actions.

❖   ❖   ❖

Learning to manage your feelings and the feelings of others first requires some insight about the characteristic ways in which you experience your emotions. Once you master this step, you are ready to learn and use emotion management strategies. We hope that the discussion and exercises in this chapter will help you begin the process of being more open to feelings, getting to know them even better, and learning ways to effectively and intelligently manage with emotions.

The next part of the book helps you apply the skills you have acquired through case studies and the Emotional Blueprint.

PART 4

Apply Your Emotional Skills

We've outlined some ways to enhance your emotional skills. The next step is to help you to implement these skills in an organized and efficient manner. In the next two chapters, we present cases that suggest ways of applying our model of emotional intelligence to yourself and others. The objective is to provide concrete applications of the four-skill model. From these, you can generalize and apply your understanding of emotional intelligence to your own work-life.

CHAPTER 12

Managing You
Applying Your Emotional Intelligence Skills

We start by reviewing the four emotional intelligence skills incorporated in the Emotional Blueprint described earlier in this book. Each skill is associated with an objective, as shown in Exhibit 12.1, along with a general idea of how to achieve that objective.

Exhibit 12.1. Emotional Blueprint.

Step	Objective	What to Do
Identify Emotions	Stay open to your emotions and those of others around you.	Observe, listen, ask questions, confirm understanding.
Use Emotions	Reflect on these emotions and consider their influence on thinking.	Determine how these feelings influence thinking. Change the tone if necessary.
Understand Emotions	Examine the causes of feelings and what may happen next.	Consider reasons for the feelings and how they will likely change if various events occur.
Manage Emotions	Don't minimize the feelings, and don't blow the feelings out of proportion.	Include rational, logical information with emotional data for an optimal decision.

Successful emotional intelligence requires that you approach any situation with the right questions in mind. Each emotional intelligence step (identify, use, understand, manage) has a series of questions that you can ask to help you obtain good information and to make optimal decisions:

1. How do you feel? How strongly do you feel it?
   Label your feelings and their intensity.
2. What are you thinking about?
   How are these feelings influencing your thoughts?
3. Why do you feel this way?
   What was the cause? How have these feelings progressed? How will they change further?
4. What can you do with the emotions? Do they need to be modified?
   How can you manage these feelings so they are used adaptively in decision making and in motivating behavior?

We recommend analyzing emotionally charged situations in more detail using the full Emotional Blueprint. In Appendix 2, we've provided guidelines for using the blueprint, along with many more questions to consider.

It is easy to discover one of the most important, yet most neglected, customers of every manager and every leader. All you need to do is to look in the mirror. Managing the ups and downs of corporate politics and governance requires tremendous internal resources. However, many managers we work with forget about managing this difficult customer within. That's why we focus on *internal* emotion management in this chapter and show you how the Emotional Blueprint can be applied to your life as a manager.

Knowing Who You Are: Living with Complexity

The Story: Not Your Typical Industrialist

Many executives do not engage in perspective taking; their role is to hew to the company line carefully in order to keep their stock price flying high. Some industries require greater focus on the company line and avoidance of thinking uncomfortable thoughts than others. Tobacco companies are one example, and the auto industry is another. Auto executives live in an insular world and are quick and eager to denounce environmental and safety regulations as unnecessary and unproductive. Their companies build machines that kill tens of thousands of people annually and that pollute the air and water; their employees toil in behemoth factories like Ford's Rouge River plant. To this mix, we add economic and competitive uncertainties and, in the case of Ford, a company bleeding cash.

Enter William Clay (Bill) Ford III, the great-grandson of the company's founder. Ford was not your typical big, bad industrialist. Known for his pro-environmental stance, Ford rocked the industry when he admitted that gas-guzzling SUVs are not earth-friendly. He has talked at great length about his concern for Ford employees as well, and he has demonstrated this concern over the years.

When he was made CEO and chairman of Ford Motor Company, he literally and figuratively inherited a host of seemingly insurmountable problems. He then backtracked on some of his environmental proclamations and, in the eyes of some, turned out to be all talk and no action around earth-friendly issues, among others. According to this view, Ford sold his soul to the corporation.

The Emotionally Intelligent Manager Analysis

Or did he? Ford demonstrates many of the skills of an emotionally intelligent manager. He is able to identify how others feel and to feel what others do. Ford has emotional empathy, and he connects and establishes rapport with a wide range of individuals. One of his early talks to auto workers was described as a "chills-down-your-spine speech."[1] Ford also demonstrated his compassion when he raced to the scene of an explosion at the mammoth Rouge River plant that killed several employees.

He understands the complex "people" issues of the company and has accurately diagnosed the problems previous managers created that alienated suppliers, customers, and dealers. "We need to rebuild relationships," Ford said. "I'll be spending a lot of time with Wall Street, dealers, employees, suppliers. A lot of those relationships are broken or not healthy."[2]

As an avid environmentalist running one of the world's largest industrial companies, Ford stays open to, and integrates, conflicting and complex emotions. The uncomfortable feeling that we all get when one of our ideas is knocked can lead us to close down and reject the criticism as inherently faulty. But it has been said that Ford is a great listener and is open to feedback and input, especially feedback that is not supportive of his position.

Emotions can fuel perspective taking, as well as the generation of a vision for an organization or for an individual. Ford has described his vision for his company in terms that are quite unexpected and unusual for a chief executive: "I don't know if a company can have a soul, but I like to think it can," he says. "And if it can, then I'd like our soul to be an old soul—and everything that implies. I like to talk about things like values and soul. These things aren't transient. These are things you build forever."[3]

The ability to deal with complexity, to understand that the world is not so simple that it can be partitioned into black or white, is an ability that may be based on one's level of emotional intelligence. Perspective taking assumes that you can see the world through the eyes of another, and it can lead to some pretty interesting, yet uncomfortable, realizations.

A Plan for the Emotionally Intelligent Manager

Perspective taking can be viewed as consisting of emotional awareness (identifying emotions) and emotional empathy (using emotions) and can be richly described with emotional language (understanding emotions). But what about the fourth emotionally intelligent ability—managing emotions? Ford's effectiveness as chief executive, and perhaps his feelings of satisfaction and commitment, might be based on this ability of emotion management. Certainly, we are not implying that the success or failure of Ford Motor Company is tied to the four abilities we've described, but our model can help Ford—indeed every manager—better define his role and succeed in it.

Ford will need to identify the problems, screening out the background noise of daily problems from long-term and serious issues requiring his time and attention. He can leverage his emotional empathy—his ability to use emotions—to take on the perspective of key stakeholders and to create and communicate a vision for Ford Motor. By running emotional what-if analyses, Ford will be better equipped to plan and strategize for key meetings and decisions. Last, he must be able to stay open to increasingly tough news, to stay open to positions in direct conflict with some of his personal values. Ford has to be able to take action based on doing the right thing, whether analysts, family members, or the Sierra Club agree or disagree with him. He has to make decisions that address and resolve the real problems of the organization so it can be a growing and healthy company.

The Outcome and Lessons Learned

Ford has an unenviable job—a job he is making more complex when he declares, "I believe that business goals can best be achieved by also addressing social and environmental needs."[4] An emotionally intelligent manager might be better equipped to handle such strife and conflict.

Bill Ford's story and that of Ford Motor Company is being written, and will continue to be written, for decades to come. His performance to date can teach us a number of things about the role and qualities that many leaders need in order to manage effectively. Let's look at another case.

Smiling Your Way Through: Making a Tough Decision

The Story: Yuki

After the organization she worked for decided to leave New York City, Yuki quickly concluded that she would stay in New York anyway. Yuki had been an anomaly in Japan—a successful businesswoman working in finance. In New York, she sought to begin a small venture fund, and she was successful in raising an initial sum of capital from a wealthy Japanese investor.

Yuki was introduced to an American company based in Seattle that was seeking funding. A meeting had been set up; Yuki was to fly to Seattle, but the intermediaries were not able to arrange the details in time for her to make the trip. Disappointed, she called the CEO of the Seattle firm and was told that he would be coming to New York the following week. A date for a meeting was set up.

Yuki was a very positive person. She struggled with negative emotion and avoided negative feelings. She noted that her reaction to bad news was to immediately attempt to calm herself. Her emotional coping skills were well developed, but she applied them the moment a negative feeling came over her. And that sometimes led to problems. We also know that Yuki scored in the below-average range on the Using Emotions part of the MSCEIT: the ability to use emotions to facilitate thinking.

The Emotionally Intelligent Manager Analysis

Being optimistic is one thing, but not allowing yourself to experience negative emotions is another. Yuki was slated to make her first major investment. If the CEO of the Seattle company was persuasive enough, Yuki was ready to hand over a substantial portion of her total investment fund to support his ideas.

We know that people in a positive mood tend to focus on possibilities and see the big picture. They are not as tuned in to details, nor do they process information by looking for problems. Knowing that Yuki warded off negativity and encouraged positive feelings, there was a real danger that she would not cast a critical enough eye over the CEO's presentation.

Yuki clearly understood what was at stake. She knew that she focused on positive emotions, and she was open to the idea that this was not always the optimal mood to be in. In fact, she came up with several previous situations in which that positive mood had gotten her into trouble. She was aware of the issues but wasn't at all clear what to do about them—or even whether anything could be done.

It was therefore critical that Yuki be able to approach this situation in a manner that got her the information she needed to make a great investment decision. Because Yuki had already bought into the utility of the company's product line and vision, she needed to evaluate the risks the company faced. She practiced some of the emotional intelligence mood induction techniques she had learned, attempting to create a negative mood in herself to counterbalance her typical need to stay positive.

A Plan for the the Emotionally Intelligent Manager

During the CEO's presentation, Yuki reported that she felt herself getting caught up in his excitement. But as she did so, she was able to trigger a thought: Is this how I want to feel right now? Yuki began to calm herself but with a different goal in mind: to bring her mood down from an upbeat and optimistic one to a more neutral, even a slightly negative one.

She was more focused on the marketing plan and the intended roll-out into other geographic markets. Yuki was able to access her critical thinking skills and apply them to these aspects of the plan, with the result that she discovered a number of flaws in their reasoning. They were serious flaws but, in her estimation, correctable. With this information, she engaged the CEO in a constructive discussion and indicated what assurances she required before she was willing to make the investment.

Yuki said that the CEO appeared to be surprised by her insight and comments and perhaps a bit embarrassed that his team had not anticipated the problems.

The Outcome and Lessons Learned

Yuki was able to follow the four-step Emotional Blueprint. First, she identified her own feelings and those of the others in the meeting. She was able to generate the mood that helped her attend to and focus on details. Next, Yuki attempted to understand the underlying issues, how people felt, and why they felt that way. Last, by staying open to uncomfortable feelings, Yuki could process the information that was contained in the emotions and arrive at a satisfactory conclusion. How did she accomplish all of this? Yuki had the Emotional Blueprint process literally in front of her. She had the model in her head, and she used it to help her plan her approach. She practiced alternative scenarios, both in her imagination and in real life with colleagues and friends with whom she felt comfortable.

Getting in the Mood: Generating New Ways of Thinking

And now, here's another story that exemplifies putting emotional intelligence into practice by learning to experience new moods and use them to facilitate certain cognitive tasks.

The Story: Russell

Russell was never known as an upbeat kind of guy. He wasn't sad, but he was somber and reserved. For most of his career, Russell's performance was good-to-excellent, and most of the people he worked for felt that he handled things well.

Russell was in the compliance business. His job was to make sure that the deals the traders and bankers put together were legal. He had to understand fully the intricacies of the securities and banking laws and regulations, explain them to his clients, and then approve the deal. He had a knack for spotting inconsistencies and errors. Russell could wade through pages and pages of figures, tables, and hype, and find the places where the smartest MBA in the company had messed up.

He was doing such a good job that he was given a major promotion. In his new role, Russell was being asked to make recommendations to the investment banking community on how to better approach regulatory issues. The role was an exciting one on paper, as it provided for a friendly interchange between the folks in compliance and the investment banking sides of the house.

But Russell floundered in his new role. He couldn't seem to switch gears and wrap his mind around the job. Russell continued to focus on what was wrong with the system and how the bankers failed to understand compliance. Russell had neither a plan nor a vision for the future.

The Emotionally Intelligent Manager Analysis

Russell scored above average on the identifying emotions component of the MSCEIT, and he was able to identify accurately how people felt. He also had insight into others and was skilled at figuring out why people felt the way they did—understanding emotions. Russell's challenges and issues seemed to be due to his lower levels of skill in using emotions to facilitate thought and in managing emotions.

Russell dealt with negative and neutral emotions well. A low-key guy, his typical mood was also low-key (neutral), and he could easily get into a slightly negative mood. He did this without thinking about it. For him, it became part of his work routine. In his new role, focusing on what was wrong and on details didn't cut it anymore. The negative mood, which was adaptive in his previous job, was proving to be maladaptive now.

A Plan for the Emotionally Intelligent Manager

The plan for developing Russell's emotional intelligence was quite easy: what he needed to do was to recognize the emotion-thinking link and match his mood to the task at hand. Learning that there's a connection between thinking and feeling was not easy for Russell. As an extremely analytical person who valued rational thinking and judgment, Russell rejected any notion of emotions as having a place at work, especially in *his* work. Yet this very obstacle—his analytical ability—would soon come to his assistance.

Russell wanted data. He wanted numbers. He wanted to be convinced that emotional intelligence was real and that it amounted to something more than being a "nice guy." He readily took to the notion that emotional intelligence was a set of skills, though, and he enjoyed learning about emotions' role in thought. He was hooked. Now came the harder part—teaching Russell how to generate emotions and reason with them.

He monitored his daily moods, noting how they would change and how they would change his outlook. Russell created an emotion diary in which he attempted to link events and thoughts to a change in mood. This provided the critical information.

With these data, Russell was well armed with information on how to construct personal mood generation strategies. For example, Russell was an avid fly fisherman, and thoughts of boyhood trips with his dad to lakes up in Northern Ontario elevated his mood. In short, he became mildly happy and content, as well as much less negative and critical. He was able to generate several other scenarios that induced different positive moods, and he learned to access these memories at appropriate times.

The Outcome and Lessons Learned

After months of hard work, Russell became fairly adept at mood generation. A few more months after that, Russell appeared to be able to think more creatively and to feel what others felt; his client relations improved overall.

By then, Russell, who had been a low-key guy with a low-key typical mood, was still a low-key guy with a low-key mood. This was the mood state he preferred and with which he was most comfortable. He had not changed his personality, and his disposition was what it always had been. But Russell had added an important new skill to his tool kit.

Doing the Right Thing: Managing Ethical Conflict

The Story: Marcy

Flexibility and perspective may be two of the core traits of the emotionally intelligent manager. Take the example of the nurse-turned-CPA, Marcy. We like this case a lot because it illustrates all four of the skill sets in our model of emotional intelligence.

Marcy was a nurse for many years, working mainly in neurosurgery. She was good at what she did, and she loved her work, but after a motorcycle accident she found herself almost unable to walk. After extensive rehabilitation, she was able to walk again but was forced to consider a new career—one that did not require her to be on her feet for hours at a time.

Marcy reinvented herself by going back to school, graduating with honors, and becoming a CPA. She gravitated toward internal audit, which she found to be similar to the crisis management environment of the operating room. Marcy used her diagnostic skills to put the case together and then handed the case off to someone else, just as she had in the operating theater.

Hired into the financial unit of a large manufacturing firm, Marcy was conducting a routine internal audit when she discovered a $12.5 million mistake in how a division was booking future revenue, and claiming it as current revenue. Marcy's interpretation was that it was just that—a mistake. She assumed that the company would do the right thing, which meant admit the mistake, restate its earnings, and aggressively act to correct the root cause of the problem. That is not what Marcy's boss, the Chief Financial Officer (CFO), wanted to hear, and he asked Marcy to "get one of her people on the situation and make it go away."

That was advice with which Marcy did not agree, and she refused to let one of her subordinates cook the books. But the CFO got his way. A month after Marcy was asked to cover up the error, she received a surprise visit from her HR representative, Brad. It took him quite a while, but when he finally got around to it, Brad told Marcy that the company no longer required her services. Of course, there was no connection, he said, between her being fired and standing up to the CFO.

The Emotionally Intelligent Manager Analysis

Marcy's emotional intelligence skills (shown in Figure 12.1) are part of her strength, and our analysis leads us to conclude that these skills probably were, in part, to blame for her employment being terminated! Our analysis starts with identifying emotions.

Marcy knew that something was up when she had a meeting with Brad, her HR representative. Brad "always taps his fingers" when nervous, and "he looks away" from you when he talks. Well, Brad was tapping away and hardly looked at her during this meeting. She started to pay closer attention.

Figure 12.1. Marcy's MSCEIT Results.

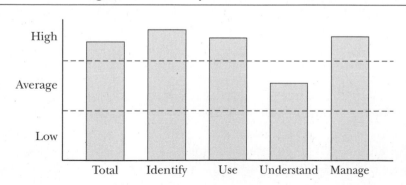

When Brad finally came to the point, Marcy was fully prepared. She was told that her position was being eliminated and that her services were no longer required. Marcy was not happy about the decision, and she was upset that the company had failed to do the right thing in this case. Yet, as she noted, "If I was angry, I would focus for the wrong reason." Marcy needed to hear Brad's message, to see the world through the eyes of the company, both Brad's eyes and those of the CFO. Marcy's ability to generate an emotion and reason with it—to use emotions—allowed her to get this part just right.

Marcy understood the dynamics of the situation. She recognized Brad's discomfort; she saw and understood the CFO's predicament. She knew how they felt and why they felt this way, showing some understanding of emotions. Later on, she was asked whether this was fair. "It depends on your perspective," she noted. "They saw me as a loose cannon. I can understand that."

Marcy pushed the company as hard as she could to recognize the accounting error and confront their problems head-on. Attempting to ignore the issue would not make it go away, no matter how much everyone wanted that. Uncomfortable feelings are just that—uncomfortable—and we often try to push them away. Marcy demonstrated her ability to manage emotions, as she was able to stay open to the feeling and use this feeling to motivate her to act in the best interests of the company. Her actions were not successful, but she made a glorious and passionate attempt to do the right thing.

A Plan for the Emotionally Intelligent Manager

Whether on the operating room floor or handling a tough audit situation, Marcy tried to bring the human side to everything. Marcy is not a strong leader, as she readily admits. She prefers to be in a number-two position. This allows her to leverage her insight, understanding, and big-picture perspective.

But it wasn't enough in this situation. In spite of her skills, Marcy failed to achieve her objective, and this story doesn't have a happy ending. When asked about this, Marcy admitted that she wished things had ended differently. She also noted that she could have handled things differently and that perhaps someone else would have been more successful. But she was adamant that she would not have made a decision that compromised her values and ethics. She was willing and able to take a stand in the face of some very stiff resistance.

We wonder whether Marcy could have achieved a different result if she had used an Emotional Blueprint for this situation. Perhaps. If the desired goal is to have the CFO accept Marcy's recommendations, then we need to better understand how the CFO is feeling and how these feelings are directing his thinking. Our what-if analysis needs to consider how the CFO will react to various suggestions and how the news is delivered. Managing the CFO's feelings in order to allow him to stay open to his discomfort and fear may provide him with the insight, desire, and ability to do the right thing.

The Outcome and Lessons Learned

The outcome was that Marcy did not have a job, and her ex-boss did. Although it didn't take her long to find a new position, it still does not seem fair or just that Marcy's honesty and integrity went unrewarded. And it is not fair. We don't know if this outcome could have been altered, but we do know what the lesson is: that leveraging the power and data in feelings is the right thing to do, even when the world around us does not always reward emotionally intelligent behavior.

The "Good" Manager

Is the emotionally intelligent manager necessarily a "good" person? From the start, we have recognized that these emotional skills can be used for many purposes. It's similar to the dilemma of charisma. Charismatic leaders can use their power for the good of the group or for their own glory.[5] A manager who is expert in managing emotions can use this ability to manipulate employees. Yet, if managers are truly emotionally intelligent, they also have a good deal of emotional empathy, that is, they feel what their employees feel. The emotionally intelligent manager's moral perspective is, we hope, well developed.[6] It is hard to imagine that this manager will intentionally or unnecessarily inflict pain on others. It is our hope that the emotionally intelligent manager will not just do things right but will "do the right thing."[7]

We've never come right out and said it, so let's say it now: *the skills of emotional intelligence do not guarantee health, wealth, or happiness.* In fact, the emotionally intelligent manager may often feel sad and anxious. Like Marcy, we also believe that the rewards awaiting the emotionally intelligent manager may not be measurable in money, power, or prestige but in the desire and the ability to do well for oneself and for others.

◆　◆　◆

"Managing you" is a difficult and often overlooked task. We hope that these applications of the Emotional Blueprint inspire you to think about ways of applying the skills of emotional intelligence to your own work life. Managing others, that is, leading effective teams and organizations, requires that you successfully leverage the wisdom of your feelings. In the next chapter, we will discuss the application of emotional intelligence skills to managing others.

CHAPTER 13

Managing Others
Applying Emotional Intelligence Skills with Others

The emotionally intelligent manager must manage him- or herself and interact with many other people as well. Once you're comfortable with the Emotional Blueprint approach, you can enhance your management capabilities by adding an additional element to the blueprint: the emotions of other people.

You can expand the Emotional Blueprint by again considering the set of emotional intelligence questions, only this time your view expands to include the emotions of a group of people. Ask yourself these questions:

1. How do the people in this situation feel?
2. How are their feelings influencing their thoughts?
3. Why do these people feel this way? How will their feelings change as various events unfold?
4. What can you do with their emotions? How can you pay attention and include their emotions in your thinking and decisions? How can you help them stay open to the data in their feelings and integrate the feelings into their thinking and behavior?

Notice how these questions are focused not just on you but on others. In this chapter, we provide some case examples that illustrate how this version of the Emotional Blueprint can help you to better manage the complex and critical interpersonal interactions faced by every manager and leader. We again begin with a case of an executive you may be familiar with. However, our analysis may surprise you.

Managing Change: Getting the Soft Stuff Right Is Hard Work

It's no longer considered a very profound insight to note that managing people, teams, or a company means navigating your way through a sea of change. The emotionally intelligent manager does not just steer a course through the sea. Such a manager sets the course.

Managers are better able to see where they need to go and get their ships to that distant land by creating change. How do they do this? One method of creating change is to leverage the four emotional abilities and follow a general approach, or Emotional Blueprint, to management.

The Story: Jack Welch

Mr. Tough-Guy himself, Jack Welch, the former CEO of General Electric, might be considered an emotionally *un*intelligent leader. He was known for his rude and blunt style, as well as his impulsive and, at times, nasty behavior.

For instance, Welch relates a speech he gave to the Elfun Society, an elite social organization whose ranks were drawn from GE's management. Invited as the guest of honor to a large Elfun Society meeting, Welch bluntly told the assembled group that they were an anachronism and of little value. Not surprisingly, his speech was not received with a great deal of warmth. In fact, as he writes, "There was stunned silence when I ended the speech. I tried to soften the blow by milling around the bar for an hour. However, no one was in the mood for cheering up."[1]

The Emotionally Intelligent Manager Analysis

Certainly, any leader with half an ounce of emotional intelligence would not have been surprised at the feelings generated by such a speech in this self-congratulatory environment. This was Welch at his worst—blunt, aggressive, and angry. Or was it? His words were not encouraging and did not support the group's current efforts. Not only did he surprise the hundred or so participants but he likely alienated and angered them. We suppose that if Welch really understood emotions, he should not have been surprised by how his speech was received. But we wonder whether Welch, on some level, knew exactly what he was doing and could have predicted, with some accuracy, how people would feel when he was done with his message.

This message delivered a strong dose of medicine that was needed because the patient—the Society—was sick. Welch administered the cure, and it hurt. The Elfun Society re-engineered itself sometime after Welch's attack—an attack we might now view as a wake-up call and a challenge. The Society's members heard the call and rose to the challenge, becoming a community-service-driven group that made itself both relevant and important again to GE, as well as to its members.

There may have been softer ways of generating change but perhaps not many more effective means of generating such change in this entrenched organization. Sometimes, the emotionally intelligent leader must confront others and generate conflict as well as negative feelings in order to be effective. The key is to know when and how to do it, just as Welch did during that dinner speech.

A Plan for the Emotionally Intelligent Manager

Did Welch use the Emotional Blueprint in these situations or during his long tenure at the helm of GE? We don't know the answer to this question, but we can apply the blueprint for him and, by doing so, perhaps help you see how it can help you become an emotionally intelligent manager. Here's our emotional intelligence analysis concerning how Welch handled this situation.

Identifying Emotions: the group's mood is complacent, content, and happy.

Using Emotions: the group is narrowly focused, and their focus is internal, on themselves. They don't see or feel the bigger picture.

Understanding Emotions: A wake-up call would shock them out of their complacency. They would be surprised, then angry.

Managing Emotions: Once they were awakened, their complacent worldview could be challenged, and this emotional discord could motivate them to grow and develop.

Welch's ability to communicate a vision and passion also appears to reflect keen emotional ability. One of our hypotheses regarding the ability to use emotions is that it is the underlying engine that drives charismatic leaders and the ability to create and communicate a vision. Mind you, we do not yet have solid data to back this claim. It is, essentially, our own gut feeling.

The Outcome and Lessons Learned

Is Welch an emotionally intelligent individual or manager? There are a number of examples of emotionally unintelligent behavior on Welch's part outside the workplace, and his workplace demeanor was not always pleasant or supportive. Yet we cannot help but be impressed by the many examples of Welch's actions and decisions that seem to us to reflect at least certain of the four emotional intelligence abilities.

Managing through tough times requires making tough decisions. If you cannot make these tough decisions, if you are too nice and are unable to handle negative emotion and conflict, you might be an effective manager when times are good but flail around helplessly in times of trouble. We do not advocate toughness, meanness, or outbursts as a management tool. But we do advocate for the identification, use, understanding, and management of the entire spectrum of our emotions.

Supervising People: I Can't Believe You Did That!

The failure to manage emotions appropriately is the downfall of many a manager. Such a failure can make life tough, but when these problems are played out in supervisory relationships, they are greatly magnified and become nearly impossible to ignore. We would like to share the case of Henry, an attorney—a case about the failure of emotion management in the context of a supervisory relationship.

The Story: Henry

Attorneys tend to be smart. At least they usually have a great deal of analytical intelligence. Henry was no exception. His educational pedigree and his occupational choice indicated a high level of cognitive ability. He spoke with erudition, was extremely well read, and had a good deal of knowledge about many subjects.

Apparently, he had befriended Cheryl, his administrative assistant, some months back. They occasionally had lunch together and often shared anecdotes about their respective weekends, their favorite sports teams, and other innocuous topics. For someone else, this may not have been dangerous ground to tread. But it was for Henry. Displaying incredibly poor judgment, Henry started to hang out with his assistant. He claimed that they were buddies and that there were no sexual overtones. Although Henry was not romantically involved with anyone at the time, Cheryl had a steady, live-in boyfriend who also happened to be an attorney.

His desire for companionship, coupled with his comfort in routine, meant that Henry preferred Cheryl's company to going out socially. A creature of habit, he wanted to meet his social needs in an easy way that didn't force him into new situations. The trouble began when Henry didn't control his needs for socializing and instead let his impulsive nature get the best of him. He made a series of really bad decisions. Treating Cheryl like an old college drinking buddy, he began to behave in ways not considered appropriate to a manager-employee relationship. In addition to hanging out with Cheryl on some weekends, he started to act even more inappropriately, sending her sexually explicit e-mail messages. Lack of judgment? Absolutely! Could it get worse? It did. One weekend, Henry not only e-mailed pornographic material to Cheryl but he used his corporate e-mail account to send the messages to Cheryl's corporate e-mail account. Monday morning came; Cheryl chatted with colleagues around her desk as she fired up her computer. She opened a few e-mail messages from her boss and was greeted by gasps and screams from her colleagues as they watched pictures of men, women, and animals in various compromising positions appear on her computer screen.

The Emotionally Intelligent Manager Analysis

Henry seemed to have a lot going for him, but somewhere along the line, he made a series of very bad decisions. Henry was mildly anxious and a bit depressed but well able to handle stress. He was very open to emotions and ideas but somewhat set in his ways. Henry was outgoing and pleasant, but not overbearing. He enjoyed a number of activities and seemed well suited to the practice of law in general.

Henry was remarkably good at identifying emotions in others. He was terrific at generating emotions on demand and using his emotions to help his thinking. He had a rich emotional vocabulary and a good emotional understanding of people. But these high scores on the first three abilities of emotional intelligence were not reflected in his score on the fourth ability: managing emotions.

Henry seemed to have no clue as to how to manage his own and others' emotions. He made dumb mistakes and bad decisions that resulted in outcomes that he neither expected nor wanted.

A Plan for the Emotionally Intelligent Manager

We met Henry some years ago, and yet each time we tell his story, we cannot help shaking our heads in disbelief and saying to ourselves, "I can't believe he did that!" At the same time, as a very smart guy there was hope for Henry. He could learn the process of the Emotional Blueprint and enhance his emotion management ability to avoid the traps he routinely set for himself.

Henry had the data available to him. It was only a matter of helping him recognize the validity of these emotional and seemingly nonrational bits of data to turn him around. By learning to leverage his emotional what-if skills, Henry could run emotional simulations to see what the likely outcome of various behaviors might be.

By role playing and practicing likely scenarios, we could provide Henry with an emotional inoculation against such problems. Henry might never become a master of emotion management, but he could certainly end up engaging in emotionally smarter behavior.

The Outcome and Lessons Learned

Alas, we never got the chance to help Henry develop and implement such a plan. The fact is, Henry was an outplacement client—he had been fired from his job.

Henry claimed that he was set up, but Cheryl's complaint against him, bolstered by copies of e-mails and the observations of many people in the office, eventually led to Henry's dismissal. Talking about the events that led to his being fired, Henry still wasn't sure what happened or why he got caught. He expressed naïve astonishment and said that he wished that he could have made smarter decisions.

Henry's lack of emotional decision-making ability led to his downfall. If he could have put two and two together, stayed open to the data of emotions, and incorporated the data into his decisions and actions, the outcome may have been quite different.

Managing Client Relationships: When Smoke Gets in Your Eyes

Here's a story that reveals a relatively complex emotional situation, in part because it involves ethical compromises.

The Story: Helen and Dan

Helen and Dan were excited about the client—a major ad agency—they were calling on that morning. It was the first time they had been asked to submit a proposal of this type to the agency. After a conference call the previous week with the vice president in charge of the project from the agency, there was an air of mystery surrounding it. The VP and his staff asked several questions about different projects that Helen and Dan's firm had conducted, asked about their expertise and background, and gave a few hints as to what the new project might entail. But they indicated that they did not want to reveal either the name of their client or the nature of the project—a bit mysterious and quite intriguing.

After a few introductions and the typical pleasantries were exchanged, the meeting began. However, the VP's assistant, Ed, left the room and returned in a few minutes with a handful of forms. "Our non-disclosure agreement," he indicated on his return. "We just need you to sign this. We do it all the time." The VP noticed Helen and Dan's surprise and added, "Read it first, of course. We just want to make sure that you keep the information we're disclosing confidential. That wouldn't be a problem, would it?"

It was Helen's client, and Dan was assisting her in the project. Looking up at her, he saw her smile, nod her head, and ask for a pen. Dan followed suit, although he had some misgivings. But, he reasoned, "I don't want to screw this up for Helen. She'd be mad if I said something."

"Great!" Ed said as he took the signed confidentiality agreements from Dan and Helen. "Now, let me tell you about the client and the project. The client is a cigarette company, and we're looking for a creative way to market one of their brands." Ed paused, looked at Helen and Dan, and continued. "That's not a problem, is it?" he inquired. With a laugh, he added, "Some people have a problem with that," and he looked over at Helen for a reaction. Dan did so as well.

Again, Helen smiled, and said, "Oh, no, that's okay with me. But how about you, Dan? Is that okay with you?" Dan felt trapped—what else could he do except to say, "Sure. No problem."

But it was a problem. Dan's father had died two years earlier from heart disease. A heavy smoker, his dad quit five years earlier when he had his first heart attack. Dan was not a fan of cigarettes, and he felt sick to his stomach when he heard what the project would entail. The meeting continued for another hour. Helen looked to Dan's expertise, and Dan became animated about what the firm could do for the client. He had a few creative ideas that he shared at the meeting. At the end of the meeting, he said that he'd need to think this through before coming up with a proposal. As Helen and Dan left the building, she looked at him and said, "I was surprised that you were so positive about this. I really hate the whole idea!" Dan was dumbfounded. He was only playing along with what Helen wanted, and he turned to her to say, "I can't believe that! Smoking killed my father, and I hate the smell of cigarettes. The whole idea stinks! Why did you lead me on that way?"

What happened to Dan and Helen? And what will they do about it?

The Emotionally Intelligent Manager Analysis

The essential problem in this story is that Dan was aware of his own emotions but misperceived Helen's. He could have picked up on how she shifted in her seat, indicating discomfort, or that she often looked down, indicating some degree of uncertainty, or pressed her lips in a sign of displeasure and disagreement. The cues were there, but Dan failed to see them or, perhaps, to accurately identify them. Then Dan proceeded to ignore his own discomfort with the whole idea. Dan felt guilty and a little angry with himself and with Helen. Helen felt annoyed that she was trapped into offering a proposal to her client—a proposal that she really did not want to make. The ad agency people were happy and content, as they believed that Dan would come up with an exciting and innovative solution to their problem.

However, not recognizing Helen's reaction to the client during the meeting, Dan dutifully forged ahead in his support of Helen's client and the new business opportunity. As Dan went ahead to try to develop a proposal, he created additional problems. He was later taken aback when Helen revealed her feelings about the client.

A Plan for the Emotionally Intelligent Manager

The challenge was for Dan and Helen to find a way to get out of the project without damaging their relationship with the agency.

Let's use the emotional intelligence model to help Dan and Helen figure out what to do. Here are the steps:

1. *Identify Emotions:* How does the client feel?
   They were feeling happy and content.
2. *Use Emotions:* What are they thinking about?
   They may be brainstorming about new ideas and how to move the project forward.
3. *Understand Emotions:* Can Dan and Helen make emotional predictions? What would happen if Dan called to say that he can't work with a tobacco company? Being happy and content and expecting a positive outcome, if the actual outcome is negative, the client may become frustrated, irritated, and angry.
4. *Manage Emotions:* What should Dan do?

The goal is to get out of the project. Ideally, Dan and Helen would also maintain a positive relationship with the client and, perhaps of greater importance, with each other. This last point is one that many people fail to consider.

What happened next? Dan apologized to Helen, indicating that he was trying to be supportive but that he misread the situation entirely. He offered to try to think of a way to rescue the client relationship.

Dan called the client and said that, on discussing the plan with Helen and reviewing possible options, he needed to bow out of the project. "I wanted to be as helpful as possible to you, and my enthusiasm got the better of me. Back here, I've been trying to come up with a way that I can help you meet your goals, but I can't do it. I came back to the office and started to do some research on the concept I proposed. I found out that it can't be done. I can suggest a few alternatives to you, and I'll write them up and e-mail them to you by tomorrow afternoon. I'm really sorry that I can't help. Helen has spoken about you many times, and I also feel that I let her down, as well as you."

Dan did generate some ideas for the clients to consider and, after e-mailing them, followed up with a phone call to see whether they understood the concepts and wanted to proceed with any of his suggestions. He repeated his apologies, making clear that it was his problem, not Helen's.

The Outcome and Lessons Learned

After Dan apologized, he provided information to Helen on the ethical considerations surrounding the project. With Dan's okay, she contacted the client, apologized for the confusion they had created, and underscored Dan's concerns about the ethical issues. She wanted to give them a "heads up" and suggested that they rethink the strategy and, certainly, involve their legal department in future planning.

The relationship between Dan and Helen was strained by this conflict, but it weathered the storm and recovered. They remained an effective team and worked together on many other projects. Dan learned a few lessons from this experience. One thing he has tried to do is to be much clearer—with himself—about the information contained in his emotions.

A year later, the client had not sent any business Helen's way. However, her relationship with her contact at the agency was, and is, solid.

Managing Politics: Trust, But Verify

Sometimes an individual's failure to understand emotions leads them to misperceive the motives of other people. This story illustrates what happens in such a circumstance.

The Story: Charles and Erik

After the firm closed down the mutual fund that Charles was to manage, he decided to pursue a start-up fund on his own. The guy who had hired him and later fired him, Erik, was running his own independent fund, which was fully financed. Charles decided to go ahead with his new venture fund, and his "pal" Erik indicated that he would assist Charles in his efforts. In fact, Charles reported, Erik was willing to travel with him to Tokyo to help with the negotiations with a Japanese investment firm to obtain seed financing for Charles's fund.

When asked about the agenda for the trip, Charles indicated that Erik would also be discussing his own fund—one that had been started months earlier and had $200 million raised already. The Tokyo bank was supposed to be a major backer of Erik's fund.

The Emotionally Intelligent Manager Analysis

Erik is very happy with the situation and does not feel that anything is amiss. It's Charles who is the client and the focus of the emotional intelligence plan.

Charles needed to begin at the beginning. He first had to identify how Erik was feeling (see Exhibit 13.1).

Charles gleaned critical information about the situation by attending to Erik's emotions. Next, Charles needed to determine what these feelings meant for Erik and how they affected him (see Exhibit 13.2).

Exhibit 13.1. Identify Emotions.

Question	Answer
How does Erik feel?	Happy and a bit guilty
Is he aware of his feelings?	Probably not of guilt
Is Erik expressing his feelings?	He shows his happiness, but he seems to be masking and hiding his negative or guilty feelings.

Exhibit 13.2. Use Emotions.

Question	Answer
Where is Erik's attention directed?	To his new venture
Is the mood helpful?	Not for Charles's needs
Does Erik have empathy for Charles?	Probably not

Charles is in a tough place. Erik is focusing on his own needs and goals, and he may view Charles as a distraction. Charles is in a very uncertain and tenuous position, whereas Erik is happily moving forward. Attempting to understand emotions, Charles reflects on the questions in Exhibit 13.3.

Exhibit 13.3. Understand Emotions.

Question	Answer
Why does Erik feel this way?	He's happy that his venture is going quite well but feels guilty that things may not work out for Charles.
How will feelings change?	Erik might focus on happiness.

If happiness is Erik's key feeling, and if it indeed will continue or intensify, Charles needs to plan around that fact. Including the data from emotions, even though it makes him feel uncomfortable, is what Charles must now do, leveraging his ability to manage emotions (see Exhibit 13.4).

A Plan for the Emotionally Intelligent Manager

Charles was a "nice guy." Such a description is usually a positive thing to say about a person. In this case, however, being nice meant that Charles was a bit naive and too trusting of people.

As a nice guy, Charles found it very difficult to see the bad in people. He knew there were bad people out there, and he was well aware that people can lie, cheat, and steal. But he took people at

Exhibit 13.4. Manage Emotions.

Question	Answer
How does Erik handle uncomfortable feelings?	He ignores them and focuses on the positive.
Is the feeling exaggerated?	He may minimize the negative feelings.
Is Erik aware of the emotion and its influence?	He is aware that the positive feelings enhance his venture and that feeling "bad" right now would not be helpful.

their word and at face value. If Erik said he was anxious and eager to help Charles, then Charles believed that Erik truly meant it.

Charles can try to feel and understand Erik's point of view. Charles realizes that he and Erik are on a different page, in terms of their business plan but emotionally speaking as well.

Charles informed Erik that he was going to attend the first meeting in Tokyo and that he wanted to schedule a final session with the Japanese investors, without Erik. Charles also decided to pursue his own fund, independent of Erik, since he felt that Erik was focused on his own interests and would really not have the time or energy to expend on helping Charles.

The Outcome and Lessons Learned

Charles and Erik visited Tokyo together, and Erik attended the first, and last, meeting with Charles, despite Charles's efforts. However, aware that Erik may have a different agenda, Charles stayed on his toes, observed Erik more closely, and represented his own fund with the investors. He didn't allow Erik to be his spokesperson.

Erik was somewhat annoyed with Charles, but he did not interfere with Charles's new agenda. The investors provided Charles with the requested start-up funds. Erik seemed a bit less comfortable with Charles afterwards. Charles felt bad about this later but came to see the change in Erik being due to Erik's heightened respect for Charles based on Charles' understanding of and leveraging the data in feelings.

Meeting Business Objectives: Happy Days Are Here

Negative outcomes, just like negative emotions stories, can teach us important lessons. In our next story, we describe the unfortunate outcome when a project manager ignored his feelings about a decision and went along with his team, despite his initial reluctance.

The Story: Jeff

Jeff was smiling. His teammates thought that was as it should be. After all, the board had just appropriated $6 million for his new product development team's efforts. Some of his fellow team members were openly shocked, believing that the project never had a chance. It would be the company's largest expenditure of this sort—ever. In addition, the project development schedule was aggressive, and the market for the product was quite different from the company's traditional core market.

Actually, Jeff was both thrilled and shocked. His smile was fixed on his face. His goal was to get the plan as far as the board, and if they approved the plan, he had expected that they would have provided only a small amount of funding. Now Jeff had to deliver, and he was worried.

Jeff was worried for an extremely good reason. The development team needed to find an original equipment manufacturer for the main component of the new product. After months of searching for a product to meet the market requirements, engineering and purchasing had presented the options to the team. "It does it all. In fact, it's also twice as fast as what you were looking for," purchasing claimed. Jeff looked at his product specification document and asked questions about other features. Engineering said there was no way to meet all of the requirements. Jeff was very uncomfortable about the decision, as one key feature appeared not to meet his product specification, and this specification was part of the proposal to the board. But everyone else on the team thought it was great and, ultimately, product manager Jeff got caught up in the excitement. After all, it was just one feature out of many, and the team had significantly upgraded the spec in other areas. And time was running out. He agreed to support the team, and negotiations with the vendor began.

The next few months were anxious ones, as the team raced to meet the aggressive deadline for the product launch There was a strong sense of excitement, and the team met the deadline. It was the fastest development project in the history of the company.

The team forgot Jeff's concerns regarding the missing product feature, although Jeff had lingering doubts. He did not allow these doubts to surface, however, and never discussed them. After all, he was one of the guys and part of the team. Everyone seemed so happy with the product that he thought it would be okay. He ignored his emotions and got caught up in the excitement of others.

But the product did not sell. At first, the team blamed sales. Sales blamed service. Service blamed the product.

The Emotionally Intelligent Manager Analysis

What happened? Our emotionally intelligent analysis lets us get at the root cause of the problem.

The development team was in love with the product. Most wanted it more than anything in the world. Such optimism and passion were what fueled their drive and motivation. They logged hundreds of hours on the project. It was these feelings that motivated their plan and was the source of the enthusiasm that helped to sell the board. These emotions also motivated them to roll the product out in record time. In fact, the team was honored by the division president for their work.

But Jeff also had negative feelings about the product plan. His emotions should have been a signal to him that something was amiss, but he ignored the signal. It was his undoing. Had he attended to his feeling more closely, Jeff would have realized that the missing feature was much too important to disregard. He would have not participated in the irrational exuberance of the group, and he would have become more neutral or negative and focused on the details, when such a focus was necessary.

Jeff's failure as a product manager in this instance appears to be due to his neglecting to manage his emotions and minimizing his negative feelings.

A Plan for the Emotionally Intelligent Manager

Many organizations have an unstated policy that they will "shoot the messenger" or the bearer of bad news, and Jeff's company was probably no exception. The news was not good, but by using the Emotional Blueprint, Jeff had a chance to make a bad situation a little better.

Identifying the source of his discomfort could have allowed Jeff to focus his attention on the core of the issue: the fact that the product would not meet customer needs. Rather than panic, Jeff could have attempted to generate a sense of concern among his engineering team to get them to focus on the problem. He could have enlisted them to sign up to try to save their new baby and done the same with the sales managers. He could have generated emotional scenarios to tell him that, as the situation unraveled relationships would deteriorate, along with any sense of team.

Perhaps the team feeling could have been maintained and strengthened by having the group recognize that they faced a common enemy and concern. Perhaps a team spirit would have gotten the group to accept their problems but stay committed to the concept and to each other.

Guiding the group through the uncomfortable realization would not have been enjoyable and might have engendered some bad feelings. No matter what happened, there would have been conflict and negativity. But Jeff could have chosen between the experience of negative conflict leading to disaster and the experience of negative conflict leading to a partial success. Unfortunately, Jeff chose the first route.

The Outcome and Lessons Learned

The initial product plan called for 20,000 units to be sold over the first phase of the product life cycle. This phase was estimated to be about three years. But the product was pulled from the market twenty-two months after its much-celebrated launch. The company had sold just over 1,200 units.

There was a reorganization of Jeff's division soon after the demise of the "revolutionary" new product. It was at this time that Jeff found himself without a position in the company, after having served faithfully and quite rationally for almost nine years.

Every situation is complex, and the abilities of emotional intelligence can explain part of the complexity. But perhaps no case from our vast casebook illustrates the disastrous consequences that can result when the wisdom of our feelings is ignored, as this case does.

Taking on Reasonable Risk: The Case of Being Too Rational

Dealing with risk is a situation that is fraught with emotion. Depending on one's style, confronting risk can produce feelings of fear or of eager anticipation. Or both.

The Story: Rick

The firm is consistently ranked as number 1, 2, or 3 in almost all of the businesses in which it participates. Yet Rick's area ranked number 12, and that was in a good year. This deal would move them ahead by several steps and take them closer to the top tier. After months of hard work, Rick's team was ready to present the deal to management. It was a fairly complex arrangement, but Rick felt confident that he knew what risks they would face. He had suitable contingency plans and believed that the worst-case scenario would be to break even. The upside potential was enormous in terms of revenue but was more important in terms of the markets the deal would open up for the firm.

The final presentation before sign-off went extremely well. The questions were probing and serious, but Rick and his team handled all of them. They listened to the questions, understood the concerns and politics behind them, and addressed the underlying issues.

At the end of the team's presentation, the chief operating officer (COO) of the unit, stood up, shook his head, and said, "This was a great effort, folks. But it's not in the firm's interests to proceed in this direction. I'm not faulting your work, mind you, but I can't allow us to take on this type of risk. It's not a fit with where we want to take the business."

There may have been more, but Rick wasn't listening; nor was anyone else on the team. They were blown away, not only by the decision itself but by the quickness of it. "How the hell could he have thought about it?" one team member wondered later. "There's no way he was ever going to do this. We were set up, big time!"

The Emotionally Intelligent Manager Analysis

"It's not a fit. . . . " How many business decisions have been made with those words as a justification? In this case, that justification was based on fear, perhaps exaggerated fear about risk.

Upper management had a zero tolerance policy for failure in this business; someone was fired when any deal, no matter what the reason, did not pan out as expected. And this is in a business in which reasonable risks must be taken in order to remain a player. In other lines of business the firm participated in, losing money was accepted as part of the cost of growing the firm and achieving market share.

Why was Rick's management so fiercely opposed to taking on risk? The story of this emotion begins in the late 1980s, when (or so the story goes) a rogue trader lost $300 million for the firm. Ever since that incident, management has been wary of getting into this particular business in a major way. The painful memory of the loss lingers on, many years after the fact, and it paralyzes the group. Rick believed that it was an unreasonable fear. He believed that the nature of his deals were different from the area of the business victimized by those big losses of decades ago.

A Plan for the Emotionally Intelligent Manager

Rick identified the fear of the top management team, and he knew what he was up against. Exhibit 13.5 illustrates what happens when the COO is afraid. The fear must be addressed, but it might also be in Rick's interest if the emotions delineated in Exhibit 13.6 were created in the COO and team, with the described impact on their thinking and decision making.

Creating these feelings and progressing from one to the next could happen in several ways. One way to achieve Rick's goals is illustrated in Exhibit 13.7.

Exhibit 13.5. Feeling and Behavior.

Management feels:	Motivates this behavior:
Fear	Act now to avoid negative consequences.

Exhibit 13.6. Feeling and Behavior, Part Two.

Management should feel:	To motivate this behavior:
Surprise	Pay attention.
Interest	Let's look into that.
Acceptance	I like it.

Exhibit 13.7. Emotional Results.

Emotion:	Generated by:
Surprise	Agree with the senior managers' point of view. Don't argue with them or try to convince them that they are wrong.
Interest	Share ideas and reasoning as to why they are right and the team is wrong.
Acceptance	Stay open to their criticism, don't fight them, and praise their decision-making process.

Once the COO and his team are in an accepting state, they will likely be more open to other ideas. They are feeling less threatened and defensive and don't perceive Rick and his plans as threats.

With the openness that comes from a feeling of acceptance, Rick can begin over a period of time to raise issues and ideas and plans for general discussion. Although this can be done in a highly manipulative fashion, if Rick is really good at generating these feelings, he will also establish a good deal of emotional empathy for senior management, to feel what they feel and then to share, or at least understand, their perspective.

Ideally, Rick's perspective will change as well, as he will come to incorporate some of management's views and feelings. His team will generate deals and present them in such a way that they are more in line with the needs of the firm, as opposed to just being great deals from their own perspective.

If all goes well, we might expect that senior management's feelings and Rick's team's feelings will be similar and that the emotional intelligence work will result in the feeling of happiness—perhaps even joy. Joy, in turn, says to everyone: "That was great, let's do it again!"

The Outcome and Lessons Learned

After several more meetings in which Rick highlighted the relative safety of the deal, the COO tentatively approved a scaled-back version in which the firm would play a minor role. Rick seized the opportunity, despite his disappointment, figuring that being a minor player was better than not playing at all.

A few months later, though, when firmwide revenue did not meet analysts' expectations, Rick was told to cut his staff back by 20 percent. That was easy, since several people on his team had already read the writing on the wall and were actively engaged in a job search. Five staff people agreed to leave the firm, with a decent severance package. At the same time, the deal flow survived, as did the group as a whole, benefiting the individuals, the team, the clients, and the firm.

The fearful mood of the leadership team was not based on current events; it was a left-over mood from a financial disaster in the firm's ancestral past. Fear-motivated decision making, as rational-seeming as it appeared, was neither rational nor emotionally intelligent. When Rick identified this mood and its cause, he could address the root cause of the decision-making impasse. He didn't ignore the data of these feelings but incorporated the data into his proposal and discussion.

◆ ◆ ◆

It's important to recognize that you simply don't have a choice when it comes to dealing with feelings. Emotions are woven into our everyday lives as managers, employees, customers, and leaders. This emotional world can be a difficult environment in which to manage, but its very complexity makes it an exciting and rewarding challenge to face.

The Emotional Blueprint doesn't provide you with handy answers to life's complex questions. Don't look for it to give you quick recipes for emotional situations. Instead, leverage this analytical tool to help you view your role differently and to give you the insight you need to do the right thing.

CHAPTER 14

Building the Emotionally Intelligent Manager

As you've probably discerned, becoming an emotionally intelligent manager is not an easy task. The skills needed and the path to acquiring them that we've described for you are not suitable for everyone. Nor can the skills of emotional intelligence replace technical expertise, general analytical intelligence, specific competencies, or experience. Sometimes, just plain luck will be the critical factor in achieving success. However, be assured that the emotional skills we outline *do* provide you with a valuable set of tools that can help you in your everyday work life, whether as a team member, project manager, or CEO. Any role you might be called upon to play in life can be enhanced when you apply emotional intelligence.

How to Build an Emotionally Intelligent Manager

There is no single, best way to build an emotionally intelligent manager. You might already have a warm, people-oriented managerial style or a more instrumental, direct managerial style. Both styles can be effective, in different ways. Perhaps when you began this book, you possessed the kind of excellent management and leadership skills depicted in Quadrant B of Figure 14.1. If so, working on another set of skills—emotional skills—may help you become a more effective manager, moving you to Quadrant A. For emotionally intelligent readers who may have been hesitant about leveraging their skills (Quadrant D), perhaps the examples we've

Figure 14.1. Building an Emotionally Intelligent Leader.

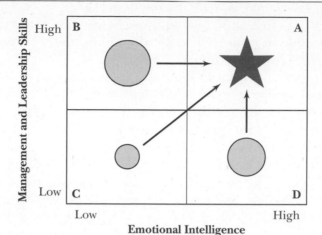

offered in this book will motivate you to step up to a new role. If you are new to a management role and lack emotional skills (Quadrant C), we've got you covered for part of the development you'll need.

Just reading this book means that you are interested in learning more about making a positive difference in your life and in the lives of others. We hope you have acquired just one or two things to help you make such a difference, and now's the time to think about the possibilities—think about what can you do to move forward.

The Emotionally Intelligent Manager as Leader

Throughout this book, we have emphasized the interaction between emotion and cognition, feeling and thinking, passion and reason. We hope we have convinced you that rational thinking involves the emotions and that the two cannot easily be separated. So let's say you're convinced. Where does the idea get you? We say it can get you a long way toward becoming a leader rather than simply a manager.

We don't want to overpromise what emotional intelligence can do for you. You probably shouldn't expect to acquire some emotional intelligence and suddenly become a "master of the universe" type of leader.[1] But we think if you learn and apply it, you'll have a chance to become something even better: a leader of teams and organizations that show lasting, positive qualities that can give them an edge in terms of loyalty and commitment, as well as in striving to do the right thing.

If you examine current theories of leadership or descriptions of trusted leaders, it is clear that emotional competencies—and "doing the right thing"—may play at least as important a role as technical competencies and industry knowledge, perhaps even more so.[2] Leadership gurus James Kouzes and Barry Posner argue that there are five keys to success as a leader: (1) *modeling how you want others to act* on your values, (2) *inspiring a shared vision,* (3) *challenging the usual processes* for getting things done by searching for opportunities to innovate, (4) *enabling others to act* by fostering collaboration and sharing power, and (5) *encouraging the heart,* by which they mean recognizing the contributions of others and creating a spirit of community.[3] It is difficult to imagine accomplishing these goals without emotional intelligence.

With your enhanced understanding and feel for emotional intelligence, you are probably making your own connections between what you do as a manager and the skills we've discussed in this book. Now let's take a look at how emotional intelligence can help you with six core challenges of management and leadership that we talked about in the Introduction to this book:

1. Building Effective Teams
2. Planning and Deciding Effectively
3. Motivating People
4. Communicating a Vision
5. Promoting Change
6. Creating Effective Interpersonal Relationships

Building Effective Teams

Teams are built, not born. As Steve Zaccaro notes, an effective team manager builds trust between individuals and then leverages and generates the bonds of trust across a group of people to build a cohesive team.[4] Before leaders can model desired actions, they must clarify their values and align their actions with these values. But how? One way is by listening to feelings. What ideas inspire pride? What values (even undesirable ones) inspire guilt or shame instead? In order to find your voice, as Kouzes and Posner encourage leaders to do, you must first clarify your feelings.

Early and frequent communications among team members are also critical in the development of a shared identity. A team's "ability to optimize the quality of team members' interactions through resolution of dissent, utilization of cooperative behaviors, or the use of motivational reinforcing statements" is the key to developing productive team member interactions.[5]

It is often the leader's role to make sure this happens. As Major General (retired) Lon Maggart notes, "Leadership is the essential ingredient in developing the trust necessary for building cohesion in an organization and the only source I know of for heart, grit, determination, endless hope and tenacity. The leader is the only one who can lead subordinates past mere understanding into the realm of doing."[6] Enabling others to act by fostering collaboration and sharing power again relies on the ability to empathize, to walk a mile in others' moccasins. Moreover, managers must have sufficient self-confidence to allow others to take credit for positive outcomes (while also not automatically blaming others for failure).

Creating an effective team—one that accomplishes tasks and does so as a cohesive unit—is perhaps one of the most important and difficult challenges faced by managers. Now, let's take a look at how one manager built an extremely effective team. This team example, however, is not drawn from the world of business but from the world of sports. Even if you're not a sports fan, read on. Our focus here is on a terrific example of emotionally intelligent team building, not on the sport itself. Therefore, consider the story of Grady Little, former manager of the Boston Red Sox baseball team.

The Situation: Grady Little

A single gut decision by baseball manager Grady Little was widely believed to have cost the Boston Red Sox the 2003 American League Championship, as well as a chance to play in the World Series. The Red Sox, whose unofficial slogan might be "wait until next year," were once again left at the altar, and the blame fell squarely on their manager (now their ex-manager). Grady Little was skewered by the press: "The Red Sox had a chance to win the American League pennant, dancing atop the mound at Yankee Stadium. They blew it, in large part because of a stunningly poor decision by the manager."[7]

After his ace pitcher, Pedro Martinez, showed signs of fatigue, Little walked to the pitcher's mound. The expectation was that Little would pull Pedro and put in a relief pitcher. A left-handed batter was due up next, and Little had a lefty relief pitcher warmed up and ready to go. However, Little stayed with Pedro. Pedro looked tired, but Little asked him if he could face another batter, and Pedro indicated that he could. This was a big game—*the* game—and Little had shown his ability to create a sense of team spirit and motivate players during the long season. Pedro said he could do it, and Little showed his confidence in his star pitcher, going with a gut decision. The rest, as they say, is history. Little, despite managing teams that won more than ninety games in two consecutive seasons, has been banned in Boston.

At the risk of our being banished forever from the hallowed ground of Fenway Park, the home of the Red Sox, we must beg to differ with popular opinion. First, let's examine the Red Sox 2003 season; then, we'll take a closer look at manager Grady Little. The Red Sox lost the final game of a seven-game series with the mighty New York Yankees after playing eleven innings of terrific ball (a game usually has nine innings, but when the score is a tie at the end of nine innings, teams continue to play until one takes the lead). The same team, under Little, pulled off a stunning upset against Oakland's Athletics for the chance to play in the championship series.

What Was Said About Little

The public wanted Little's head. But those who worked most closely with him were uniform in their praise of his managerial style and ability to build and to lead the team. Pedro Martinez stood up for his manager and the decision to leave him in the game. Pedro went so far as to shoulder the entire responsibility for the outcome of the decision, noting, "I am responsible for the pitches and decisions I make. Grady did a great job all season, and it's not fair to blame Grady for whatever decision was made out there."[8]

Even the guy who fired Little—general manager Theo Epstein— acknowledged Little's big accomplishments, noting how Little created a sense of team and a feeling of mutual support, and a team that enjoyed the fun of the sport. Said Epstein: "They set a really high standard, and that's what we're going to expect of every Red Sox team from now on in, in its own unique way."[9]

The praises kept coming. A player who is a "starter" is supposed to play almost every game, certainly every big game. But that was not the case in the play-offs for second baseman Todd Walker. Yet, even though Little benched Walker for a critical play-off game, Walker had only the most positive things to say about Grady Little: "He was honest, up front and very approachable as a manager."[10]

Perhaps it was first-baseman Kevin Millar who said it best: "There were times we could have collapsed, but he [Little] didn't let us. . . . We all love Grady Little."[11]

The Analysis

Whether or not Little made the right decision to leave Pedro Martinez in the game, the data support Little's ability to identify, use, understand, and manage emotions. It is this skill set, in our opinion, that enabled Little to take a group of prima donnas and develop a cohesive and high-functioning team.

Clearly, Little knew how Pedro felt. He sensed the fatigue. But he also sensed Pedro's motivation, purpose, and desire to win. As Little said later on, "I knew the condition and mind-set of every player before the game and during the game. Me and every player in that clubhouse and that dugout . . . that's who they wanted on the mound. There was no doubt in my mind."[12]

Of the loss, Little noted: "Yes, we came up short of our goal, and to the Red Sox Nation, I say I hurt with each of you. It was painful for all of us."[13] Little displayed a deep sense of emotional empathy.

Even Red Sox president, Larry Lucchino, had to admit that Little, with his "bountiful gifts," would be hard to replace.[14] Watching the Red Sox play and interact with each other, it seemed clear that this was a team sport and that the sense of team was created by Little. And unlike many super-star teams playing on their home field, Red Sox players often autographed baseballs, programs, and other items for their throngs of fans.

The Result

Little was a team builder in Boston, no doubt about it, and the public record is clear on this point. But we'd like to tell you a more private story about Little. Consider it an emotional intelligence exposé of sorts.

During one of the last games of the 2003 spring training season, we had the chance to watch the Red Sox, and Little, up-front and up-close in the intimate ballparks of Florida. During one such game, a young fellow of fourteen slipped a scrawled note to coach Mike Cubbage, asking Cubbage if he could give the paper to manager Grady Little. Little folded the note and put it in his back pocket. During a lull in the game, Little pulled the note out, read it, and put it back in his pocket. The note was brief. The young man related the story of his best friend, a die-hard Red Sox fan who had suffered a spinal stroke a few months earlier and was in a wheelchair. The note asked if it was possible for someone on the team to call his friend after the game to cheer him up.

At the game's end, as Little was walking toward the press for a post-game interview, the young man called out to him. Little waved and said, "I've got to talk to these guys now. We can't call your friend, but we'll do something for him." The young man was disappointed but not surprised at what he thought was a brush-off. At the very least, Little read the note, kept it, and actually responded to the young man's verbal inquiry. That's a lot more than most professionals would do. It indicates a person with some understanding of emotions and of people.

It was perhaps a week or two later when that same best friend called the young man to tell him that a large package, postmarked Boston, had arrived. In it were photos, autographs, and Red Sox souvenirs—and a note from manager Grady Little. Spring training had ended, the team had packed its bags for the journey north, and Grady Little must have hung on to that hand-written note.[15]

The Outcome and Lessons Learned

Will you win more ball games if you are emotionally intelligent? Perhaps, perhaps not. But emotionally intelligent managers do seem to have an edge over their rivals: they are able to see the big picture, consider multiple points of view, and do the right things. These are the actions of a leader who builds and maintains effective teams. Little, by doing the right thing, created a sense of trust and belonging, and we think these feelings, and the team he created, were effective.

Planning and Deciding Effectively

Of the six core managerial functions, planning is the most concrete and rational, and the least likely to require a high degree of emotional intelligence. Maybe. Planning is a logical activity, but effective planning requires you to stay open to many forms of information and data—data that are factual and that are sometimes emotional.

The manager who claims that "it doesn't matter how they feel about it, they just have to do it" can get away with this approach, but not too many times. Reasonable and realistic goals and schedules can only be created if you are open to, accurately perceive, and then integrate how your team will feel about the goals and schedules. The planning and decision-making process itself benefits from emotionality to help generate possible alternative scenarios and what-if analyses.

Using an Emotional Blueprint

We've leveraged the power of the Emotional Blueprint a number of times in this book because it provides us with a structured way to approach a myriad of situations faced by all managers and leaders. The various examples and cases provided should make you feel more comfortable using the blueprint on your own, but this time, let's create an informal blueprint for the core management function of planning. Consider a meeting where you need to make a decision about shedding a traditional line of business that your company has been involved in for decades. People are attached to the business, and it is part of your culture and identity. Although the business unit has not turned a profit in seven consecutive quarters, the losses are narrowing somewhat. This decision, like so many critical business decisions, is not being made in a data vacuum; you have tons of information about the business, the competition, and market trends. If you have all of the necessary data, just as many corporate managers do, then why are so many decisions bad decisions?

An Emotional Blueprint for effective decision making hinges on your ability to stay open to uncomfortable facts and to the data that are at your fingertips. Staying open to information that makes us feel uncomfortable starts with accurate awareness of the emotions we are experiencing at the moment. Emotionally intelligent decisions made in a meeting or team setting must also identify the feelings of the others who are involved in the planning meeting.

Staying Open to Emotion

Anne Mulcahy, CEO of Xerox, illustrates the ability to listen to critical information and criticism in general. She may not agree with it, but she does seem to have the openness to consider the criticism. Discussing how decisions need to be made, Mulcahy noted, "People around you want to please. That's where honest critics can play an important role. Encourage them to tell it like it is."[16] Not only do people have to feel empowered to provide their boss with honest feedback, but the boss, in this case the CEO, has to be able to *handle* the feedback—the core of managing emotions.

When experiencing the shock of unsettling news, many managers suppress or ignore the feeling. Not only does that mean they ignore the data of feelings but they must use cognitive resources to suppress feeling and therefore cannot pay as close attention to the problem as they need to. They are doubly handicapped.

You and your competitors are all smart, and you all have a lot of informative data. The key to effective decision making and planning is to use all the data you have available intelligently—the facts from competitive intelligence, the data of market plans, and the wisdom of feelings.

Motivating People

The most explicitly emotional aspect of leadership, according to Kouzes and Posner, is to encourage the heart by showing appreciation for others' accomplishments and celebrating community. Here managers need to be able to understand complex feelings. How can we make sure that celebrations of coworkers' successes produce a basking in reflected glory rather than mere envy? What kinds of ceremonies feel genuine? How do we reward accomplishment without undermining intrinsic motivation? These are all challenges for the emotionally intelligent manager.

Who Do We Serve?

Developing others forces leaders to ask, "Who does a leader serve?" Does the leader serve him- or herself first, or the needs of his or her team, shareholders, and customers? The concept of a servant leader has regained some interest recently.[17] A servant leader is motivated to serve the needs of people first and to acquire the interest in, and skills of, leadership later. In essence, the focus of the servant leader is on the needs of employees and their continued growth and development. Such a person may be great to work for, but we're not so sure that a servant leader will necessarily be effective in other domains.

But the concept of a servant leader reminds us that one of the goals of a good leader and, we believe, of an emotionally intelligent leader, is to do the right thing for people. A leader's resources *are* the people of the organization, the human capital. A good leader gets things done with and through the wise use of these resources, while at the same time replenishing these human resources. We have found that those higher in emotional intelligence tend to be more interested in developing and helping people.[18] The emotionally intelligent manager, then, should be able to focus on the development of these human resources.

Pretend for a moment that you are a product manager. In this matrix management environment, your development team does not report to you. You have just received a preliminary engineering analysis indicating that the costs and schedule for the product are way out of line. This will be a surprise to the team. You need them to get motivated and to find a way to make this development effort work, given these changed parameters. What do you do?

Emotionally Intelligent Management

There are a number of ways to approach this situation that seem quite reasonable but will not be very effective. For example, many

managers slap a smile on their face and try to motivate the team
through sheer happy will power. There are indeed times when we
need to grin and bear it, but the team will pick up on a phony
smile. When that happens, the falseness of your assurances becomes apparent, and any trust that had been developed previously
will be lost.

There is no single, best answer to the question faced by this
product manager. Stepping through a series of Emotional Blueprint questions, however, may begin to shed some light on possible solutions:

1. *Identify Emotions:* How are you feeling about this interaction?
   How might the team be feeling about this interaction? What
   about the engineers who did the analysis?
2. *Use Emotions:* How will these feelings influence your approach
   and thinking about this interaction? How will the team approach and think about this interaction?
3. *Understand Emotions:* How will the team react? What are they expecting from you? For example, how will they feel if you ask
   them to "work harder" on the problem?
4. *Manage Emotions:* How will you manage your feelings about this
   interaction? What will you do to manage the feelings of the team
   so that they recognize the seriousness of the problem and get
   to work on it right away?

You might discover that your initial panic led you to believe
that the project was hopeless and beyond being rescued. Now
you've come back more to an emotional center and see that the
news is bad but perhaps not as bad as you thought at first. You
sense the concern of your project team and leverage your somber
mood and theirs to stay focused on details and problem finding.
You prepare the team for the bad news—you don't sugarcoat it—
but you also don't claim it's the end of the world. You might indicate that you felt it was the end of the project when you first heard
the news but that additional analyses brought you toward a slightly
different conclusion.

You express empathy for the team; you understand their confusion, anger, surprise and fear. Because the news is bad but not
devastating, you realize and communicate that this particular show

must go on; the team is going to stay intact and find a way out of the mess. Now is the time for the motivational speech that is delivered with emotional directness and intellectual honesty. If you truly believe, as does the engineer, that you can salvage the product, then it is up to you to effectively communicate this message to your team, just as you have communicated it to yourself. Reflecting on your emotional transition can give you the map or blueprint you need to help direct the team toward the same goal.

The path to achieving such a goal, almost by its nature, will be a rocky one, and the team will experience a number of setbacks. Your job, as a manager, is not to anticipate every possible problem but to have an idea of how to manage yourself, and your team, when confronted with a setback. Benazir Bhutto, the first female government head of an Islamic nation, knows what it is to experience obstacles and setbacks. As Bhutto, former prime minister of Pakistan, concluded, "Leadership is very much predicated on the capacity to absorb defeat and overcome it."[19]

Communicating a Vision

As researcher Ed Salas notes, "communication acts as the glue which links together all other teamwork processes."[20] When the glue isn't strong enough, teams fall apart, leading Salas to conclude that communications-related problems of a team are one of the top reasons for project failures. Salas's work with airliner crews further suggests that such communications failures are also a leading cause of airline crashes.[21]

We're not proposing some new theory of communications. Yet effective communication must be based on delivering a message you want to deliver and delivering it in such a way that it is heard and understood by others. Message content and tone need to reflect how the recipient currently feels, and these feelings will be directing their attention toward, or away from, the message.

Inspiring a shared vision is part of the communication process of effective leaders. Without the ability to understand how others are feeling and to empathize, leaders will have difficulty encouraging others to buy into their views of the future. A starting point for articulating a shared vision is, of course, understanding others' current concerns and attitudes.

The Vision as a Guide

Creating a vision for an organization is relatively simple. The difficult part is communicating it so it does what it is intended to do: to motivate, direct, and energize an organization toward a meaningful objective. The vision has to make sense for the business, and its message has to be sent so that people understand it, feel it, and make it their own. This is where the abilities of the emotionally intelligent manager play a role.

Consider a product vision of the Sony Corporation, "digital dream kids." It's a cute phrase, but it communicates a meaning at several levels. This vision recognizes the changing nature of Sony's customers—the kids who are growing up in a digital world. The phrase is also delivered as a challenge to Sony employees to get them to think like kids in a digital age. The person credited with the vision, Nobuyuki Idei, chairman of Sony, exhorted his employees to "become *dream kids* to continue creating new products that will meet our future customers' expectations."[22]

The Use of Fear

There are, of course, many possible alternative vision statements for Sony and any organization. It is common to read about some CEO threatening the end of the world if his employees don't wake up and smell the coffee. This is a vision of fear, where the message is, "change, run faster, or die," or some similarly soothing and subtle proclamation. Fear is a terrific motivator, a lifesaver, literally, but fear doesn't work all that well in the long run. Fear just burns us out after a while. Fear is not forward-looking; it is a here-and-now emotion.

The emotionally intelligent manager must manage the fear of uncertainty that employees and customers experience. Fear will focus all parties on potential threats. But once you have everyone's attention, it's time to refocus their attention and direct their adrenaline toward an objective. This is where your vision comes in.

The vision has to feel right and make sense to people. If you understand your employees, customers, and stakeholders, you will be able to try out alternative vision statements using your emotional theater of the mind and emotional what-if analyses.

Promoting Change

Challenging processes by innovating, experimenting, and taking risks requires leaders to rely on emotion management skills. The highly anxious manager becomes risk averse, avoiding setbacks and losses at all costs. Conversely, the overly optimistic manager may take on too much risk and fail to consider the impact of various outcomes.

We are taught that we must embrace change, create change, and manage change, but the fact is, change is difficult for many people. Change is not only difficult, but it can face concerted and strong resistance in many corporate environments. Take the example of the Hewlett-Packard Company (HP) and their famed "HP Way." The HP Way—the corporate culture of ideas and entrepreneurial individualism fostered and nurtured by company founders David Packard and Bill Hewlett—was threatened by the then-new CEO, Carleton (Carly) Fiorina.

Fiorina took the culture of HP head-on. It wasn't that she devalued ideas, but she believed that the culture had become "a shield against change."[23] To her, the culture of HP was having the opposite effect from the one initially intended. Fiorina noted, "When culture turns into groupthink, when culture turns into closed minds, when culture turns into 'act the same, be the same, look the same,' that is when culture starts to kill a company."[24] She identified the need for change, and she identified one of the obstacles to change. The question is then, "Now what?"

Identify Emotions

It takes a great deal of courage and self-assuredness to promote change in any organization, but especially in a culture such as HP's. In order for a change-management effort to be successful, you have to start out with facts and data. This is where your ability to identify emotions comes in handy. As the change agent, you must ask yourself, "What do I think of the current process and methods? How do I feel about the current state of things?" If you sense a problem, you have to follow your lead and next try to ferret out the cause of the problem.

Gain Perspective

With your focus trained on the bigger picture of the area of change, which in the case of HP was the fundamental worldview of HP people, you can begin to see the situation from various perspectives. Now you are tapping into your ability to effectively use emotions.

Unraveling the history of the organization and the process that you've identified as needing some sort of change requires a deep understanding of cause and effect and of corporate and emotional history. The ability to understand emotions and generate and play out alternative what-if scenarios provides you with the data you need to solve the problem of change and figure out an action plan.

The best change efforts will fail unless the action plan not only addresses the surface needs for change but considers how those affected by change will react. Now you identify the feelings of the people involved in the change effort, and try to recognize those who will become angry, those who will become terrified by change, and the people who might not be happy but who will take a wait-and-see attitude. Managing change next asks you to consider the points of view of these people and to be able to generate a feeling in the organization that the direction of change will result in some pain but, ultimately, in a stronger organization.

For HP, this was not an easy task. As Fiorina noted, "The difficulty comes in communicating not just what a company is trying to do, but how it is trying to do it. Any corporation can sit down and write a high-minded statement of values. But we all know: it is in living those values that is the hard part."[25] Managing change, like managing emotions, requires that one must live the change and demonstrate the new rules in your every behavior and action.

Creating Effective Interpersonal Relationships

More than in any other area, emotionally intelligent managers show their stuff in daily interactions with their peers, employees, and customers. This is perhaps the most active research area in the nascent emotional intelligence field. In research conducted by psychologist Marc Brackett, emotionally *un*intelligent people reported having significantly more problems with their peers than do their more emotionally intelligent counterparts.[26] Lower EI (at least among men) was also related to getting into fights, using illegal drugs, and consuming excessive amounts of alcohol. Similar results for interpersonal relationships were obtained by researcher Paulo Lopes. Lopes found that those higher in EI got along better with people and reported fewer negative interactions with close friends. Work by Lopes also shows that supportive team interactions are related to emotional intelligence.[27]

Creating effective relationships requires a great deal of effort. It requires the ability and the willingness to support as well as to confront. It requires you to offer positive feedback for a job well done and sincere criticism to help the other person realize and recognize an error.

Emotionally Intelligent Development of a Helpful Interpersonal Relationship

Consider this supervisory scenario: It is a mid-year review for one of your direct reports. You believe that he feels positive about his performance. However, your analysis indicates that he is failing to meet two of his five critical objectives for the year. Many managers have a difficult time giving negative feedback, even though such feedback is critical to the success of the person receiving it. In our experience, it is all too common for an employee to be truly surprised by their performance evaluations, the meager size of their bonus check, or the promotion that was not realized. You can take the "nice" approach to management, and as a result, people reporting to you might really like you a lot. But this is not what we mean by effective relationships. In this case, you might be a nice guy, but if your niceness means that you fail to develop your employees, then you might not really be so nice after all.

One example of providing effective feedback to people is illustrated by Jack Welch. In an earlier chapter, we mentioned how Welch managed change. His approach to feedback also bears some exploration. (We're not nominating Welch for an emotionally intelligent manager-of-the-year award, it's just that there are so many detailed examples of his management style available.) Welch discussed how he approached performance issues with his managers, giving them advance warning that they were on a perilous path. His "in-your-face" style ensured that the manager was clear regarding what the problem was and what he needed to do to solve the problem. If the performance issue continued, that manager was dismissed. Welch's understanding of people, along with his toughness, gave his managers the information they needed to predict their own future—their career future and their *emotional* future. As Welch noted, "no one should ever be surprised when they are asked to leave (the company). By the time I met with managers I was about to replace, I would have had at least two or three conversations to express my disappointment and to give them a chance to turn things around. . . . That first talk is when the surprise and disappointment, if any, should occur—not when the person is asked to leave."[28] This what-if analysis is the core of understanding emotions.

Attending to core emotional data can assist you, but how you create and nurture effective relationships will reflect your own unique style and values. Ask yourself these questions:

1. *Identify Emotions:* How are you feeling about this interaction? How might the employee be feeling about this interaction?
2. *Use Emotions:* How will this feeling influence your approach and thinking about this interaction? If you are extremely anxious about the meeting, will you rush through it, will you fail to attend to your employee's reaction, or will you ignore some of the more difficult, negative feedback?
3. *Understand Emotions:* How will the employee approach and think about this interaction? How will the employee react? What is the person expecting?
4. *Manage Emotions:* How will you manage your feelings about this interaction? What will you do to manage the employee's feelings so he or she stays open and listens?

Remember that emotions contain data and that these data are primarily communicating information about people and relationships. Being accurately aware of emotions and their meaning provides the emotionally intelligent manager with a solid base of understanding of themselves and of others. This is the basis of effective interpersonal interactions.

A Conclusion About Emotional Intelligence in Managers

You need not wait to find an opportunity to develop and leverage your emotional intelligence skills. Each moment affords you many such rich opportunities. Your next phone call, greeting in the hallway, team meeting, or thought about what's coming next are all opportunities for growth. You will feel and think and decide in each of these situations, so why not try an emotionally intelligent approach to just one of them?

This is the time to ask yourself how you are feeling, how these feelings are guiding your thinking, why you are feeling this way, and how your feelings might change, and then harnessing the wisdom of these feelings as you think, decide, and act.

And what if the attempt is a failure? It is a failure not to make the attempt, which the emotionally intelligent manager recognizes. By stretching the boundaries of your understanding and actions, you are developing your emotional abilities. Building the emotionally intelligent manager happens piece-by-piece, situation-by-situation, and emotion-by-emotion. It happens by being smart about emotions and having emotions help you to be smarter.

The emotionally intelligent manager will also look for successes. With a myriad of opportunities to test out your newfound skills, you will also have successes, big or small. These must be recognized and celebrated, as the feelings of happiness, satisfaction, or joy will motivate you to continue when you experience obstacles and when successes do not come with ease.

This chapter underscores the most important message of this book: *emotions provide data that assist us in making rational decisions and behaving in adaptive ways.* To ignore this source of data is to neglect an important aspect of the information available to us. When engaging in the work of leaders and managers by building effective teams, planning and deciding effectively, motivating people, communicating a vision, promoting change, and creating effective interpersonal relations, we must rely on our emotions as a source of inspiration and feedback. The emotional system is an intelligent system; that's why it evolved in animals, including humans. Our emotions point us in the right direction and motivate us to do what needs to be done. In that spirit, we close with the words of one of our favorite emotions theorists, someone who recognized the intelligence of the emotions decades ago, Sylvan Tomkins: "Out of the marriage of reason with affect there issues clarity with passion. Reason without affect would be impotent, affect without reason would be blind."[29]

Appendix 1: Assessing Your Emotional Style

Questions to Help You Assess Your Emotional Style

Successfully using emotional intelligence depends in large part on our desire and ability to understand ourselves. Asking ourselves questions about our approach to situations, especially powerful and meaningful situations, can help us obtain insight into our emotional style.

This section provides a means to help you develop additional insight into these issues. These are not scientifically validated psychological tests. The questions in this section simply provide a structured way for you to consider your emotional skills.

The questions are designed to help you think about and sometimes actually feel the skills of emotional intelligence. Unlike our MSCEIT ability test of EI, there are *no* right or wrong answers here. Just reading the questions can help you become more aware of your own self-image with respect to these skills and behaviors.

Use, Don't Abuse, Your Results

The point of the quizzes and exercises in Appendix 1 is to get you to think about how you handle emotions. The questions don't diagnosis any condition, nor can they serve as a proxy for a true measure of your emotional skills.

Emotional Style Questions

We've put together four different sets of questions:

1. Emotional Intelligence Self-Study: Overview of the Four Skills of EI
2. Problem-Solving Style: Find Your General Approach to Problems
3. Emotional Processing Survey: Understand Your Handling of Specific Emotions
4. Mood Filters: Determine How You View Situations

Emotional Intelligence Self-Study: Overview of the Four Skills of EI

Objective

The four parts of this section can help you to become more aware of your confidence and understanding of your emotional intelligence skills.

Instructions

Simply read each question and select one response—a, b, or c—that you feel best describes yourself.

Part 1. Identifying Emotions: Assess your emotional awareness.

1. Awareness of emotions
a [ ] Almost always aware of how I feel.
b [ ] At times am aware of my feelings.
c [ ] Don't pay much attention to my feelings.

2. Expression of feelings
a [ ] Can show others how I feel through emotional expression.
b [ ] Can show some of my feelings.
c [ ] Not good at expressing my feelings.

3. Reading of other people's emotions
a [ ] Always know how someone else feels.
b [ ] Sometimes pick up on others' feelings.
c [ ] Misread people's feelings.

4. Ability to read subtle, nonverbal emotional cues
a [ ] Can read between the lines and pick up on how the person feels.
b [ ] At times, can read nonverbal cues such as body language.
c [ ] Don't pay much attention to these cues.

5. Awareness of false emotions
a [ ] Always pick up on lies.
b [ ] Usually am aware of when a person is lying.
c [ ] Can be fooled by people.

6. Perception of emotion in art
a [ ] Strong aesthetic sense.
b [ ] At times can feel it.
c [ ] Am uninterested in art or music.

7. Ability to monitor emotions
a [ ] Always aware of feelings.
b [ ] Usually aware.
c [ ] Rarely aware.

8. Awareness of manipulative emotions
a [ ] Always know when a person is trying to manipulate me.
b [ ] Usually know.
c [ ] Rarely know.

Part 2. Using Emotions to Facilitate Thought: Assess your ability to generate emotions and use them to think.

1. When people describe experiences to me,
a [ ] I can feel what they feel.
b [ ] I understand what they feel.
c [ ] I focus on facts and details.

2. I can generate an emotion on demand
a [ ] Easily, for all emotions.
b [ ] For most emotions.
c [ ] Rarely, or with great difficulty.

3. Before an important event,
a [ ] I can get into a positive, energetic mood.
b [ ] I may be able to psych myself up for it.
c [ ] I keep my mood just the same.

4. Is my thinking influenced by my feelings?
a [ ] Different moods affect thinking and decision making in different ways.
b [ ] It may be important to be in a certain mood at certain times.
c [ ] My thinking is not clouded by emotions.

5. What is the influence of strong feelings on my thinking?
a [ ] Feelings help me focus on what's important.
b [ ] Feelings have little impact on me.
c [ ] Feelings distract me.

6. My emotional imagination is
a [ ] Very strong.
b [ ] Mildly interesting.
c [ ] Adds little value.

7. I can change my mood
a [ ] Easily.
b [ ] Usually.
c [ ] Rarely.

8. When people describe powerful emotional events,
a [ ] I feel what they feel.
b [ ] My feelings change a bit.
c [ ] My feelings stay the same.

Part 3. Understanding Emotions: Assess your emotional knowledge.

1. My emotional vocabulary is
a [ ] Very detailed and rich.
b [ ] About average.
c [ ] Not very large.

2. My understanding of why people feel the way they do usually yields
a [ ] Excellent insights.
b [ ] Some insight.
c [ ] Some missing pieces.

3. My knowledge of how emotions change and develop is
a [ ] Sophisticated.
b [ ] Somewhat developed.
c [ ] Limited and of little interest to me.

4. Emotional what-if thinking yields
a [ ] Accurate prediction of outcome of various actions.
b [ ] At times, good prediction of feelings.
c [ ] Tend not to project how people will feel.

5. When I try to determine what causes emotions, I
a [ ] Always link the feeling to the event.
b [ ] Sometimes link a feeling to a cause.
c [ ] Believe that feelings don't always have a cause.

6. I believe that contradictory emotions
a [ ] Can be felt, such as love and hate at the same time.

b [ ] May be possible.
c [ ] Make little sense.

7. I think emotions
a [ ] Have certain patterns of change.
b [ ] Sometimes can follow other emotions.
c [ ] Usually occur in a random order.

8. My emotional reasoning could be described this way:
a [ ] I have a sophisticated emotional vocabulary.
b [ ] I can usually describe emotions.
c [ ] I struggle for words to describe feelings.

Part 4. Managing Emotions: Assess your emotional management.
1. I attend to feelings
a [ ] Usually.
b [ ] At times.
c [ ] Rarely.

2. I act on my feelings
a [ ] Immediately.
b [ ] At times.
c [ ] Hardly ever.

3. Strong emotions
a [ ] Motivate me and help me.
b [ ] At times take over.
c [ ] Should be controlled and forgotten.

4. I am clear about how I feel
a [ ] Usually.
b [ ] At times.
c [ ] Rarely.

5. The influence feelings have on me
a [ ] Is usually understood in terms of how feelings affect me.
b [ ] Is understood at times.
c [ ] Is rarely processed or felt.

6. I process strong emotions
a [ ] In order not to exaggerate or minimize them.
b [ ] At times.
c [ ] So as to either minimize or maximize.

7. I am able to change a bad mood

a [ ] Usually.

b [ ] At times.

c [ ] Rarely.

8. I can keep a good mood going

a [ ] Usually.

b [ ] At times.

c [ ] Rarely.

What Does It Mean?

A minute or so more of your time can help you better understand your relative emotional intelligence skills and confidence level.

Indicate how many times you selected a, b, or c responses for each of the four sets of questions. Then create a score for each of the four parts of the self-assessment survey by giving yourself 2 points for every "a" response, 1 point for a "b" response, and 0 points for a "c" response.

Area	a (2)	b (1)	c (0)	*Your Score*
Identifying Emotions	—	—	—	—
Using Emotions	—	—	—	—
Understanding Emotions	—	—	—	—
Managing Emotions	—	—	—	—

Let's say that a lower score is one that is around 8 or less, and a higher score one that is about 9 or above. This is meant only as a means to stimulate your thinking and feeling about these issues, not to measure your actual skills.

You can interpret these scores as follows:

Identifying Emotions: Your score indicates how you feel about identifying emotions accurately. Do you attend to this source of data, or do you ignore it? And if you do try to figure other people out, are your guesses accurate or not?

Using Emotions: Your score gives you an idea of whether you use your feelings to help you gain insight into others or to enhance the way you decide and think.

Understanding Emotions: Your score for this set of questions helps you better understand the depth of your emotional knowledge.

Managing Emotions: Your score on managing emotions indicates the extent to which you allow your feelings to positively affect your decision making.

Consider your highest area and ask yourself:

- What strengths do I have?
- How might I approach a situation?

Consider your lowest area and ask yourself:

- What obstacles do I face?
- What possible problems might I have in a given situation?

Problem-Solving Style: Find Your General Approach to Problems

Objective

What is your approach to various problems? How do you handle yourself? What input and information do you seek? Understanding your approach to problem solving can help you better understand your emotional style.

Instructions

Read about each situation and select the action with which you are most likely to agree or to use in the workplace.

1. A team member who is scheduled to present the new plan to the CEO found out that his dog had died unexpectedly. What would you do?
a [ ] Since he is prepared, I'd just have him do the presentation.
b [ ] Console him and see if he wishes to present the plan.
c [ ] Send him home.

2. You are trying to influence the team to decide on a certain course of action. It's an extremely emotional topic and everyone is passionate. How would you proceed?
a [ ] Stress the analysis of the problem.
b [ ] Say that the feelings people have about it are as important as the objective analysis.
c [ ] Intensify people's passions on the subject in order to gain their attention.

3. You've been asked to do a final review of the entire budget for the following year to look for discrepancies and errors before it gets submitted to Finance. You are feeling really upbeat and positive as you sit down at your desk to tackle the assignment.
a [ ] I would get right to work.
b [ ] I would calm down a bit and then focus on the budget.
c [ ] I would make sure that I stayed positive as I worked through the details.

4. You have been offered a new and important job and are very excited about it. Which strategy would you employ to make a decision about the job?

a [ ] Get as many facts about the position as possible.
b [ ] Consider what I would enjoy about the job and what I wouldn't enjoy.
c [ ] Because it seems to be an exciting opportunity, I would accept the offer.

5. *Your boss made a decision that you disagree with. How do you handle such a situation?*
a [ ] Give her all the facts regarding the decision.
b [ ] Give her the facts and how I feel about them.
c [ ] Tell her how I feel about the decision.

6. *Your boss is trying to decide whether to promote you or another person in your department. A colleague told you that your boss feels more comfortable with the other person. How would you handle a meeting with your boss to discuss your promotion?*
a [ ] Focus on my skills and accomplishments.
b [ ] Talk about what I have done for the group and how much I enjoy the work.
c [ ] Discuss why I feel that decisions like this should not be personal.

7. *You have an annual feedback and job review meeting scheduled with an employee. You are a bit tired and cranky, and it seems that the employee is as well.*
a [ ] Separate the facts and feelings and hold the meeting.
b [ ] Generate a more positive mood before the meeting.
c [ ] Reschedule it for a time when we are all feeling better.

8. *The job performance of a person who has worked for the company for several years has been poor. He has made many costly errors in the last several months. What would you do?*
a [ ] The only issue to consider is whether the employee is doing his job or not.
b [ ] We should balance the needs of the company with the employee's needs.
c [ ] The employee's emotional health and needs come first.

9. *You are working with another member of your team. He lacks experience, and his ideas are not well developed. What would you do?*
a [ ] Ask him to work harder and more carefully on the ideas.
b [ ] Make suggestions and ask questions.
c [ ] Encourage him and support him.

10. A colleague says that she is ready to quit her job because it just isn't working out the way that she planned. You feel that the job is a good fit for her and this is just a temporary reaction. What do you say to her?
a [ ] Tell her she must put her feelings aside.
b [ ] Ask her what it means that she feels that way.
c [ ] Encourage her to share her feelings.

11. In general, how would you characterize your decision-making style?
a [ ] My decisions focus on rational, objective thinking.
b [ ] My decisions combine my thinking with how I feel.
c [ ] My decisions are from the gut, based on how I feel.

What Does It Mean?

This simple survey examines possible approaches to workplace problems and behavior. Each of the problems had a choice of three responses. The first response (a) suggests that you prefer or value a rational and logical approach to solving workplace situations. The third response (c) indicates that you prefer an emotion-based approach, in which feelings and emotions are given the most important role. It is the second response (b) that indicates you integrate your thinking with your feelings. This is the Emotionally Intelligent style.

A. Overly Rational Style. We have heard people admonished for being overly emotional. Yet it is just as dangerous to decision making for us to be overly rational. An emphasis on logical thinking, to the exclusion of feeling, leads us down the garden path of sub-optimal decisions and limited understanding.

Many of us try to be as consistently logical and rational as possible while at work. After all, that's what we are being paid to do—to think and act in a thoughtful manner. Perhaps we should redefine what our role as a manager or leader is: to set and to accomplish critical goals with others. To do so effectively is not the job of pure rationality.

C. Overly Emotional Style. The criticism of being too emotional can often be a valid one. There will of course be times when we are motivated by a feeling of intense joy or sadness or fear. We are not being too emotional when we seek comfort and solace after we hear news of a major downsizing or when we high-five a fellow team member in joy when we hear the news that we won the big contract.

When we mistake the influence of a mood for the data of an emotion, we can be too emotional—or perhaps incorrectly emotional. When we check our reasoning at the door, we can become too emotional.

When emotion overwhelms and swamps us, and we unjustifiably lash out in anger at an imagined opponent, then we are being overly emotional. When we accept a bold new plan in a gush of enthusiasm, even though it will lead to devastating results, we are being overly emotional. If the emotion is true—if it is well founded—then perhaps we cannot be overly emotional.

B. *Emotionally Intelligent Style.* If there are two points that we want you to take away from this book, they are that (1) emotions contain valuable information and that (2) decision making must combine feeling and thinking to be effective. If we ignore our emotions and those of others, we do so at our own peril. We ignore warning signs and signal-flares of trouble ahead. We miss opportunities to learn, to develop, and to explore.

An emotionally intelligent style integrates the rational and logical elements of a situation with the underlying core emotion components.

Emotional Processing Survey: Understand Your Handling of Specific Emotions

Objective

We process different emotions in different ways. Let's take a look at how you see your style of processing different kinds of feelings.

Instructions

Simply read each of the questions and select one response—"Never" through "Always"—that you feel fits best.

Part 1. Awareness of feelings

How well do you understand your emotions? For each feeling listed in the table, rate how accurately you can "read" yourself as you experience that feeling.

	Never	Seldom	Sometimes	Usually	Always
Set A					
Afraid					
Angry					
Sad					
Disgusted					
Set B					
Interested					
Surprised					
Accepting					
Happy					

Analyze Your Results

Refer to the next chart to give yourself points for each of the feeling ratings. Indicate the number of times you used each rating, and then multiply the number of ratings by the points. Write this number in the Total column. Finally, add the points.

Rating	#	Points	Total
Never		0	
Seldom		1	
Sometimes		2	
Usually		3	
Always		4	
Total			

Now, add up your points for the first four feelings and, in a separate step, for the second set of four feelings:

Set	Points
Set A	
Set B	

What Does It Mean?

Interpret Your Results

The higher your total score, which can range from 0 to 32, the more likely you are to experience feelings and to be aware of them.

The *Set A* feeling words are negative emotions, and the *Set B* feeling words represent positive emotions. These scores can range from a low of 0 to a high of 16. Some people are more open to negative than they are positive emotions, whereas others are more open to positive emotions than they are negative ones. Similar scores for Sets 1 and 2 suggest that you process both types of emotions in a similar manner.

Use Your Results

If you have a high score, then you probably don't need to work on emotional awareness. Instead, take the next step in emotional intelligence and learn how to leverage this awareness and knowledge.

A lower score may lead you to more carefully consider your attitude and feelings toward—feelings. Focus your efforts on developing greater awareness.

Part 2. Expression of feelings

Now, think about *how* you typically express yourself when you are feeling a certain way. For each feeling listed here, rate how you *express* that feeling.

	Block It Out	Act It Out Impulsively	Express Indirectly in Tone	Express Directly in Words	Express in Words and Tone
Set A					
Afraid					
Angry					
Sad					
Disgusted					
Set B					
Interested					
Surprised					
Accepting					
Happy					

Analyze Your Results

Refer to the chart shown next to give yourself points for each of the expression ratings. Indicate the number of times you used each rating, and then multiply the number of ratings by the points. Write this number in the Total column. Finally, add the points.

Rating	#	Points	Total
Block		0	
Act Out		1	
Indirect		2	
Words		3	
Words/Tone		4	
Total			

Now, add up your points for the first four feelings, and separately for the second set of four feelings:

Set	Points
Set A	
Set B	

What Does It Mean?

Interpret Your Results

The higher your score, which can range from 0 to 32, the more likely you are to directly express your feelings.

Again, you can also look at whether you express negative and positive emotions differently (scores for Set A and B range from 0 to 16). Expression of negative (Set A) emotions may or may not be different than expression of positive (Set B) emotions for you.

Use Your Results

High-scoring people act on their emotions and inform others of their feelings by using emotion and feeling words. Very high scorers combine words and tones, as well as other nonverbal signals, to get a message across to people.

Those with very low scores may try to keep emotions at arm's length and defend against them. Perhaps emotions are neither important nor relevant to you.

Part 3. Experience of emotion

In this section, we take a closer look at how you handle and process specific emotions.

1. When I am feeling sad,
a [ ] I imagine something to improve the way I feel.
b [ ] I keep the feeling going.
c [ ] I just accept the feeling.

2. When I am feeling angry,
a [ ] I imagine something to improve the way I feel.
b [ ] I keep the feeling going.
c [ ] I just accept the feeling.

3. When I am feeling afraid,
a [ ] I imagine something to improve the way I feel.
b [ ] I keep the feeling going.
c [ ] I just accept the feeling.

4. When I am feeling disgusted,
a [ ] I imagine something to improve the way I feel.
b [ ] I keep the feeling going.
c [ ] I just accept the feeling.

Analyze Your Results
Enter the number of times you selected each of the responses—a, b, or c—in the table.

Rating	#
a	
b	
c	

What Does It Mean?

Interpret Your Results
There are three major ways to experience negative emotions:

1. Mood Repair: Try to make yourself feel better and experience a more positive mood. (Response "a")
2. Mood Maintenance: Actively maintain the feeling at the same level of intensity. (Response "b")
3. Mood Acceptance: Accept the feeling without trying to change it. (Response "c")

Use Your Results

How we process our emotions has important implications for emotional intelligence. Engaging in mood repair—that is, the use of the "a" strategies—can be productive and healthy. At the same time, it may distort our experience and our view of reality if we try to fix our moods all the time.

Keeping the emotion can be appropriate or not, depending on the situation. The key to mood maintenance is that the feeling continues, without being distorted in any way.

Acceptance of the feeling is a passive strategy. We stay open to the feeling and it takes its own course, without our help.

Part 4. Experience of emotion

Now consider your experience of a different set of emotions.

1. When I am feeling really happy,
a [ ] I imagine something to bring the feeling down.
b [ ] I keep the feeling going.
c [ ] I just feel the feeling.
d [ ] I try to make the feeling stronger.

2. When I am feeling loving,
a [ ] I imagine something to bring the feeling down.
b [ ] I keep the feeling going.
c [ ] I just feel the feeling.
d [ ] I try to make the feeling stronger.

3. When I am feeling very interested,
a [ ] I imagine something to bring the feeling down.
b [ ] I keep the feeling going.
c [ ] I just feel the feeling.
d [ ] I try to make the feeling stronger.

4. When I am feeling trusting,
a [ ] I imagine something to bring the feeling down.
b [ ] I keep the feeling going.
c [ ] I just feel the feeling.
d [ ] I try to make the feeling stronger.

Analyze Your Results
Enter the number of times you selected each of the responses—a, b, c, or d—in the table.

Rating	#
a	
b	
c	
d	

What Does It Mean?

Interpret Your Results
There are four major ways to experience positive emotions:

1. Mood Dampening: Dampen the mood by bringing your feelings down so that you feel more in control. (Response "a")
2. Mood Maintenance: Actively maintain the feeling at the same level of intensity. (Response "b")
3. Mood Acceptance: Accept the feeling without trying to change it. (Response "c")
4. Mood Enhancement: Enhance the mood to feel even better. (Response "d")

Use Your Results
Positive feelings can be overwhelming. That's why many people try to *dampen* positive emotions. They don't want to appear foolish or ridiculous. Dampening positive emotions is a very common strategy in the workplace.

Yet positive emotions can provide us with information and feedback on how we are performing. They can motivate us and broaden our perspective. Maintaining the feeling or accepting it may be the best strategy in certain situations. But feeling even more positive can allow us to take a feeling of happiness to the level of joy.

Part 5. Understanding emotion

Answer each of the following questions. Don't think too much about your responses, and try to answer based on what you typically or usually do.

1. When I am feeling happy,
a [ ] I understand the reasons for feeling this way.
b [ ] I am not sure of why I feel this way.
c [ ] I don't think about what may have caused me to feel this way.

2. When I am feeling afraid,
a [ ] I understand the reasons for feeling this way.
b [ ] I am not sure of why I feel this way.
c [ ] I don't think about what may have caused me to feel this way.

3. When I am feeling angry,
a [ ] I understand the reasons for feeling this way.
b [ ] I am not sure of why I feel this way.
c [ ] I don't think about what may have caused me to feel this way.

4. When I am feeling surprised,
a [ ] I understand the reasons for feeling this way.
b [ ] I am not sure of why I feel this way.
c [ ] I don't think about what may have caused me to feel this way.

5. When I am feeling sad,
a [ ] I understand the reasons for feeling this way.
b [ ] I am not sure of why I feel this way.
c [ ] I don't think about what may have caused me to feel this way.

6. When I am feeling interested,
a [ ] I understand the reasons for feeling this way.
b [ ] I am not sure of why I feel this way.
c [ ] I don't think about what may have caused me to feel this way.

7. When I am feeling disgusted,
a [ ] I understand the reasons for feeling this way.
b [ ] I am not sure of why I feel this way.
c [ ] I don't think about what may have caused me to feel this way.

8. When I am feeling accepting,
a [ ] I understand the reasons for feeling this way.
b [ ] I am not sure of why I feel this way.
c [ ] I don't think about what may have caused me to feel this way.

Analyze Your Results
Enter the number of times you selected each of the responses—a, b, or c—in the table.

Rating	#
a	
b	
c	

What Does It Mean?

Interpret Your Results
How do you approach your reasoning about feelings? Do you

1. Reflect on the mood, and successfully understand it? (Response "a")
2. Reflect on the mood but fail to determine its cause? (Response "b")
3. Have no interest in emotional reasoning? (Response "c")

Use Your Results
If you are not interested in reasoning about emotions, you may be missing out on an important data source. There are laws of emotional cause and effect and change, just as there are laws of gravity. Perhaps the emotion laws are not as well defined at this point in our history, but emotions arise and develop according to certain principles.

Being willing to think about this is part of understanding emotions. One must also understand the emotion laws and accurately apply the right rule to the right situation.

Part 6. Integration of emotion

Answer these questions fairly quickly so that you provide responses based on how you usually act or feel.

1. When I am feeling happy,
a [ ] My feeling has little impact on my decisions or thoughts.
b [ ] My feeling influences my decisions or thoughts for the better.
c [ ] My feeling influences my decisions or thoughts for the worse.

2. When I am feeling afraid,
a [ ] My feeling has little impact on my decisions or thoughts.
b [ ] My feeling influences my decisions or thoughts for the better.
c [ ] My feeling influences my decisions or thoughts for the worse.

3. When I am feeling surprised,
a [ ] My feeling has little impact on my decisions or thoughts.
b [ ] My feeling influences my decisions or thoughts for the better.
c [ ] My feeling influences my decisions or thoughts for the worse.

4. When I am feeling angry,
a [ ] My feeling has little impact on my decisions or thoughts.
b [ ] My feeling influences my decisions or thoughts for the better.
c [ ] My feeling influences my decisions or thoughts for the worse.

5. When I am feeling interested,
a [ ] My feeling has little impact on my decisions or thoughts.
b [ ] My feeling influences my decisions or thoughts for the better.
c [ ] My feeling influences my decisions or thoughts for the worse.

6. When I am feeling sad,
a [ ] My feeling has little impact on my decisions or thoughts.
b [ ] My feeling influences my decisions or thoughts for the better.
c [ ] My feeling influences my decisions or thoughts for the worse.

7. When I am feeling accepting,
a [ ] My feeling has little impact on my decisions or thoughts.
b [ ] My feeling influences my decisions or thoughts for the better.
c [ ] My feeling influences my decisions or thoughts for the worse.

8. When I am feeling disgusted,
a [ ] My feeling has little impact on my decisions or thoughts.
b [ ] My feeling influences my decisions or thoughts for the better.
c [ ] My feeling influences my decisions or thoughts for the worse.

Analyze Your Results
Enter the number of times you selected each of the responses—a, b, or c—in the table.

Rating	#
a	
b	
c	

What Does It Mean?

Interpret Your Results
What effect do your moods and feelings have on your thinking?

1. Moods do not influence you.
2. Moods help you think.
3. Moods negatively influence your thinking.

Use Your Results
1. Moods influence our thinking, whether you believe it or not. If you consistently selected rating "a," you should seriously reconsider the fundamental premise of emotional intelligence: moods influence thought, whether we are aware of their impact or not.
2. The ideal situation is one in which you experience the feeling to the fullest, without minimizing or exaggerating it. The emotion—and the data it contains—can then be a powerful, productive, and effective influence. (Response "b")
3. Perhaps moods do influence you, but you exaggerate them and their influence and are ruled by them. They swamp your thinking and lead to false conclusions and ineffective strategies. (Response "c")

Mood Filters: Determine How You View Situations

Objective

Do you have a predisposition to filter in or to filter out certain feelings? One way to begin to think about this issue is to answer the questions that follow. They are designed to get you to reflect on your propensity, if any, to focus on certain types of feelings.

Instructions

For each question in each set, simply answer Yes or No.

Set 1
> I often have a lot on my mind.
> I tend to be tense or anxious.
> Mostly, I feel calm and at ease.
> I worry about many things.
> I often feel nervous.
> I don't worry about things.

Set 2
> Sometimes, I feel sad or depressed.
> I am often discouraged.
> It's rare for me to feel down or depressed.
> There are times when I feel very down.
> I am somewhat moody.
> I am usually in a positive, happy mood.

Set 3
> Certain people really annoy me.
> I am impatient.
> I get easily frustrated.
> I am very accepting of people.
> I often feel angry or frustrated.
> It takes a lot to make me angry.

Set 4
> I am easy to get along with.
> I get along with people.
> I am very competitive.
> I am not a team player.

I'm not a pushy person.
I often share the credit with others.

Set 5

I believe I will be successful.
I usually look at things in a positive way.
My expectations for myself are low.
Things usually work out for the better.
Life has too many obstacles to overcome.
I look on the bright side.

Set 6

I generally trust people.
I give people the benefit of the doubt.
People are basically trustworthy.
It's not a good idea to trust people.
Most people are basically honest.
People will take advantage of you if you're not careful.

Set 7

I cope well with stress.
I feel like I'm falling apart when under a lot of stress.
Life overwhelms me at times.
There are times when I feel overburdened.
I handle stress very well.
At times I feel totally overwhelmed.

Scoring: You will get either a 0 or a 1 for each question. To determine your score, refer to the key that follows. For example, if you answered Yes to a question with a key of N, your score for that question would be a 0. Once you compute your score for each item, add up the numbers for each set to get a total Set Score.

Your Response	Key	Your Score
Yes	Y	1
Yes	N	0
No	N	0
No	Y	1

Key

Set 1

   Y   I often have a lot on my mind.

   Y   I tend to be tense or anxious.

   N   Mostly, I feel calm and at ease.

   Y   I worry about many things.

   Y   I often feel nervous.

   N   I don't worry about things.

Set 1 Score:

Set 2

   Y   Sometimes, I feel sad or depressed.

   Y   I am often discouraged.

   N   It's rare for me to feel down or depressed.

   Y   There are times when I feel very down.

   Y   I am somewhat moody.

   N   I am usually in a positive, happy mood.

Set 2 Score:

Set 3

   Y   Certain people really annoy me.

   Y   I am impatient.

   Y   I get easily frustrated.

   N   I am very accepting of people.

   Y   I often feel angry or frustrated.

   N   It takes a lot to make me angry.

Set 3 Score:

Set 4

   Y   I am easy to get along with.

   Y   I get along with people.

   N   I am very competitive.

   N   I am not a team player.

   Y   I'm not a pushy person.

   Y   I often share the credit with others.

Set 4 Score:

Set 5

   Y   I believe I will be successful.

   Y   I usually look at things in a positive way.

   N   My expectations for myself are low.

   Y   Things usually work out for the better.

   N   Life has too many obstacles to overcome.

   Y   I look on the bright side.

Set 5 Score:

Set 6

   Y   I generally trust people.

   Y   I give people the benefit of the doubt.

   Y   People are basically trustworthy.

   N   It's not a good idea to trust people.

   Y   Most people are basically honest.

   N   People will take advantage of you if you're not careful.

Set 6 Score:

Set 7

   N   I cope well with stress.

   Y   I feel like I'm falling apart when under a lot of stress.

   Y   Life overwhelms me at times.

   Y   There are times when I feel overburdened.

   N   I handle stress very well.

   Y   At times I feel totally overwhelmed.

Set 7 Score:

Set	Your Score
1	
2	
3	
4	
5	
6	
7	

What Does It Mean?

Each set of questions looks at a specific dispositional trait. Traits are personal characteristics we all have. They provide us with a baseline understanding of how we experience and view our lives.

Take a look at each of your Trait scores. As with any quiz of this sort, the questions make you think in a structured way about a certain issue. The table of results offers you hypotheses about your experience of the world, not objective truths.

Trait	What to think about with a score that is lower (0–4)	What to think about with a score that is higher (5–6)
1. Anxiety	May block out worries and threats.	Hypervigilant; focuses on threats.
2. Depression	Rarely experiences sadness.	Focuses on sadness. Mood may fluctuate independently.
3. Anger	Accepting of others; avoids seeing unfairness.	Propensity to see injustices and wrongs.
4. Pleasantness	Competitive; open to fault-finding.	Avoids conflict with others.
5. Optimism	Open to negative emotions.	Focuses on positive emotions.
6. Trust	Will be able to consider other people's faults, negative emotions.	Sees people as good and less capable of negative emotion.
7. Stress	Open to stressful situations.	Blocks out emotional situations.

Anxiety

Worry and anxiety are often viewed negatively. However, anxiety can play a positive role in our lives. Anxiety means that we are scanning our environment, fearful that something is going to happen. It forces us to consider our options and plans.

What, then, is the problem with anxiety? The problem is that at some point, too much worry can paralyze you. You can worry about all sorts of possibilities and not have the mental, or even physical, energy to deal with your life. If you are always vigilant, there is a cost—you might feel tired and drained. Or others might see you as nervous, fidgety, or edgy. Too little anxiety may mean that you block out feelings of worry, anticipation, or fear. You may not be vigilant enough and may not adequately guard against danger signals.

Anger

When you are insulted, ignored, or hurt by another person, you may become angry. You might say to yourself, "It's not right" or "It's not fair." Indeed, you may be correct. But perhaps an angry reaction is due as much to the actions of others as it is to your interpretation of the events. A high score may cause you to filter events in a way that you personalize the situation and feel a sense of injustice and anger.

A person with a low score may defend against anger and similar feelings. You may turn away from such experiences and actively try to filter them out.

Depression

Loss often results in sadness. When we lose something that we hold dear or is important to us, we may feel sad or depressed. If you have experienced the death of a loved one, chances are you know what deep sadness is. Job loss can also result in feelings of sadness.

However, depression is the feeling of loss without the actual loss. You may feel that things are just not worth the effort. You may, at times, feel dejected and hopeless. Many depressed people are not always sad. Some days, they are up and positive and on other days, down and depressed. When depression is serious and lasts a while, it can cause us to give up hope. It's very important to recognize signs of depression and to take action if you are depressed. This means that you should consult a mental health professional.

A low score on this trait may mean that you block out or filter signs of loss and sadness.

Stress Resistance

We don't measure how much stress you are currently experiencing. It may be a great deal or nothing much at all. Stress resistance is a measure of your coping skills. Consider two people, one low and one high on Stress Resistance. Then pretend that we have just invented a stress you can measure and put in a box. Take this standard unit of stress—let's say it's a flat tire—and apply it to the vulnerable person. This person won't cope well with the flat tire. He will get upset and feel overwhelmed. A high score may mean that you get easily overwhelmed and may also exaggerate negative emotions.

In contrast, the person who is not vulnerable to stress will take it all in stride. If your score is in the low range, it means you are tough and hardy, and can absorb a good deal of stress. A very low score may lead to the minimization of negative emotions.

Optimism

Is that *another* mountain up ahead? Are we there yet? Our lives will have a number of obstacles. If we view these obstacles as insurmountable, then we'll turn around and go home. It is an optimistic outlook that keeps us going in the face of failure or when confronting the inevitable obstacles on a difficult, but worthwhile, journey. A low score on Optimism can be reason to investigate whether you filter events through a negative lens.

Optimism is not the same thing as positive thinking. Optimism is a belief that you will—you must—succeed, whereas positive thinking is often a technique to block out negative thoughts, even if these thoughts are realistic and reality-based. Optimism, by the way, is thought to be the single most important predictor of success in sales-based careers, and it is also a key component of charismatic leadership. However, wishful thinking may lead you to ignore emotional danger or warning signs.

Pleasantness

What is the opposite of being pleasant? Consider the man who told a story of how he was playing a game of chess with his son. His wife was upset that he was playing his best game rather than letting their son gain an advantage. The man said he felt that the best way for his son to really learn chess is to be challenged, which many people would endorse. This same individual scored very low on Pleasantness, which suggests that he is very competitive and aggressive and has a strong desire to win (at all costs). You should know that his son was turning five years old in a few weeks and was a beginning-level player. That's competitiveness—the opposite of Pleasantness.

Agreeable, pleasant people tend to be team players. They forgive and forget, and although they enjoy winning, they like to win as part of a team effort. They share the glory and the credit with others.

A high score here can lead people to see things in a nonconflictual way. That is, they may avoid disagreements or refuse to believe that a person can do something bad.

Trust

Trust means believing in people. It means that you give others the benefit of the doubt and that you have faith in human nature. This faith is often unshaken, even when others let you down. You keep on believing. If you are too trusting, you may be perceived as being naive and gullible. You could get taken advantage of as well. But trust is important in personal relationships and in many business settings.

Although learning to trust is a key developmental stage according to some psychological theories, not all of us resolve this core issue. Some people are very skeptical, and they rarely trust other people, especially at first. Their trust must be earned over a long period of time. A lack of trust makes you cynical and may make it difficult for you to form close, intimate relationships. At the same time, it's likely that you won't get fooled or tricked by unscrupulous people.

A trusting person may not want to believe the worst and will actively search for alternatives. Instead, they accept a person's statements at face value. The person sees a friend who is teary-eyed but claims, "No, I'm fine" and accepts that all is well.

Summary

Use your Trait Score analysis to determine whether you have difficulty with certain moods. Do you block certain feelings, filter emotions, or exaggerate emotions? Most of us do, so it's helpful to determine this for yourself.

Appendix 2:
The Emotional Blueprint

What follows is a useful tool to help you analyze an emotionally laden situation intelligently. There are no right and wrong answers in this set of exercises, and there's nothing to score. Rather, these questions are to help you become more skillful in organizing your thoughts and feelings about difficult situations.

We suggest that you begin developing an Emotional Blueprint for an event that has already occurred. Once you get the hang of it, you'll be ready to develop a blueprint for any critical situation that you will face.

Blueprint Primer

Analyze the Situation

1. What is the situation?
2. Who is involved?

Identify Emotions

How do the people in the situation feel? (Rate each feeling listed for each person.)

1 = Definitely do *not* feel this way.
2 = Somewhat do *not* feel this way.
3 = Neither feel nor don't feel this way.
4 = Somewhat do feel this way.
5 = Definitely do feel this way.

Feeling	You	Person 1	Person 2
Angry			
Happy			
Fearful			
Sad			
Love			
Jealous			
Ashamed			
Surprised			

Use Emotions

How do feelings affect these people's thinking? Put a check mark in each box that describes the thinking process of these people.

Thinking	You	Person 1	Person 2
Focused			
Attentive			
Distracted			
Detail-Oriented			
Full of Ideas			
High-Energy			
Calm			

Understand Emotions

What happened to make you feel this way? And the others?

	Cause of Feeling		
Feeling	You	Person 1	Person 2

Manage Emotions

What was your reaction? What did you do? And the others? What is your ideal outcome? What steps can you take to achieve this outcome?

Blueprint Advanced Steps

Each of the steps of the blueprint depends on asking the right questions. The next sections can help you do so. These questions can be applied to you as well as other people in a given emotional situation.

1. Questions to Help You Identify Emotions

How aware am I of my emotions?
Was I aware of how I felt during this situation?
How do I feel right now?
How did I feel during this interaction?
How emotional was I?
Did I express my feelings to others? Appropriately so?
Was I expressing my true feelings or trying to cover them up?
Was I focused only on my feelings, or was I aware of the other person's feelings?

2. Questions to Help You Use Emotions

Did it help you to feel this way?
Did your mood focus you on the issue or away from it?
Did you find yourself feeling negative or positive about things?
Did your mood help you see the other person's point of view?
Were you able to feel what the other person was feeling?
How much did you pay attention to the problem?
Did you try to feel the emotions or block them out?

3. Questions to Help You Understand Emotions

Why did you feel this way?
What caused you to feel the way you feel?
Describe the intensity of your feelings.
How will you feel next?

4. Questions to Help You Manage Emotions

What did you want to happen?
What did happen?
What did you do?
How did it work out?
Was there a better way to have handled it?
Why didn't you handle it better?
How satisfied were you with the outcome?
How satisfied do you think the other person was with the outcome?
What could you have done differently?
What did you learn from this situation?

Building the Emotionally Intelligent Manager with the Emotional Blueprint

We don't want to create managers who woodenly follow a four-step model of emotions for every challenging situation they face. The Emotional Blueprint is just a sketch and a suggestion to guide you. But you will know best what is going on and what to do. Keep in mind that rigidly adhering to any sort of emotional rules probably won't work.

Now consider a situation you are facing, and use the steps for developing an Emotional Blueprint to help you manage successfully.

Analyze the Situation

1. What is the situation?
2. Who will be involved?

Identify Emotions

If you have some experience with the main players, consider their baseline moods and how likely it is for them to feel a certain way. Is one person generally happy and upbeat? Is another a bit up and down? Knowing this, or having some emotional hypotheses going into the situation, can be very helpful.

When you are with these people, you'll need to actively identify emotions. You won't be rating their emotions, of course, but it will help if you have some sort of structured approach, or blueprint, in mind.

How do the people in the situation feel? (Rate each feeling listed next for each person.)

1 = Definitely do *not* feel this way.
2 = Somewhat do *not* feel this way.
3 = Neither feel nor don't feel this way.
4 = Somewhat do feel this way.
5 = Definitely do feel this way.

Feeling	You	Person 1	Person 2
Angry			
Happy			
Fearful			
Sad			
Love			
Jealous			
Ashamed			
Surprised			

Use Emotions

Next, you'll want to consider how the emotions of the various players will guide and affect their thinking. Will each person be open or closed to discussion? Will they be in a search for errors or seeking the big picture?

Thinking	You	Person 1	Person 2
Focused			
Attentive			
Distracted			
Detail-Oriented			
Full of Ideas			
High-Energy			
Calm			

Understand Emotions

Your emotional what-if skills will be severely tested. You can't predict the future, of course, but the intelligent use of the Emotional Blueprint will allow you to reduce uncertainty by some small, and hopefully meaningful, amount.

Consider various events that might occur during the interaction. What will the likely emotional result be on each person for each major event? Don't go overboard with this analysis. Perhaps you'll find it more efficient to analyze just those actions you are considering engaging in.

Manage Emotions

You'll need to plan and practice staying open to emotions that you might find uncomfortable. The minute you begin to close yourself off to the wisdom of your emotions, you'll be losing an important source of data and situational feedback.

Consider the real issues involved and how you can address them constructively. You can't always please everyone all of the time, nor should this be your goal. The idea is to manage the situation with enough emotional savvy to achieve a desirable outcome. After all, this is what *The Emotionally Intelligent Manager* is all about.

Appendix 3: Further Reading and Updates

Here we list books, journal articles, and chapters that we have written, based on the four-skill model of emotional intelligence. Other writers have conceptualized emotional intelligence in other ways, and the number of books and articles in this field grows every day. We have confined the list here to our work, but we're sure you would find the work of others interesting and relevant as well.

Books

Ciarrochi, J., Forgas, J., and Mayer, J. D. (eds.). *Emotional Intelligence in Everyday Life: A Scientific Inquiry.* Philadelphia: Psychology Press, 2001.

Feldman-Barrett, L., and Salovey, P. (eds.). *The Wisdom in Feeling: Psychological Processes in Emotional Intelligence.* New York: Guilford Press, 2002.

Mayer, J. D., Salovey, P., and Caruso, D. R. *Mayer-Salovey-Caruso Emotional Intelligence Test (MSCEIT): User's Manual.* Toronto, Ontario: Multi-Health Systems, 2002.

Salovey, P., Brackett, M.A., and Mayer, J.D. (eds.). *Emotional Intelligence: Key Readings About the Mayer & Salovey Model.* Port Chester, NY: Dude Press, 2004.

Salovey, P., and Sluyter, D. (eds.). *Emotional Development and Emotional Intelligence: Educational Implications.* New York: Basic Books, 1997.

Selected Articles

Brackett, M. A., Lopes, P., Ivcevic, Z., Mayer, J. D., and Salovey, P. "Integrating Emotion and Cognition: The Role of Emotional Intelligence." In D. Dai and R. Sternberg (eds.), *Motivation, Emotion, and Cognition: Integrating Perspectives on Intellectual Functioning.* Hillsdale, N.J.: Erlbaum, 2004.

Caruso, D. R., and Wolfe, C. J. "Emotional Intelligence and Leadership Development." In D. Day, S. Zaccaro, and S. Halpin (eds.), *Leadership Development for Transforming Organizations*. Hillsdale, N.J.: Erlbaum, forthcoming.

Caruso, D. R., Mayer, J. D., and Salovey, P. "Emotional Intelligence and Emotional Leadership." In R. E. Riggio, S. E. Murphy, and F. J. Pirozzolo (eds.), *Multiple Intelligences and Leadership*. Hillsdale, N.J.: Erlbaum, 2002.

Caruso, D. R., Mayer, J. D., and Salovey, P. "Relation of an Ability Measure of Emotional Intelligence to Personality." *Journal of Personality Assessment*, 2002, *79*, 306–320.

Lopes, P., and Salovey, P. "Toward a Broader Education: Social, Emotional, and Practical Skills." In J. E. Zins, R. P. Weissberg, M. C. Wang, and H. J. Walberg (eds.), *Building School Success on Social and Emotional Learning*. New York: Teachers College Press, 2004.

Lopes, P. N., Salovey, P., and Straus, R. "Emotional Intelligence, Personality, and the Perceived Quality of Social Relationships." *Personality and Individual Differences*, 2003, *35*, 641–658.

Mayer, J. D., and Salovey, P. "The Intelligence of Emotional Intelligence." *Intelligence*, 1993, *17*, 433–442.

Mayer, J. D., and Salovey, P. "Emotional Intelligence and the Construction and Regulation of Feelings." *Applied and Preventive Psychology*, 1995, *4*, 197–208.

Mayer, J. D., and Salovey, P. "What Is Emotional Intelligence?" In P. Salovey and D. Sluyter (eds.), *Emotional Development and Emotional Intelligence: Educational Implications*. New York: Basic Books, 1997.

Mayer, J. D., and Salovey, P. "Personal Intelligence, Social Intelligence, Emotional Intelligence: Measures of "Hot" Intelligence." In C. Peterson and M.E.P. Seligman (eds.), *The Classification of Strengths and Virtues: Values in Action Manual*. Philadelphia: Mayerson Foundation, forthcoming.

Mayer, J. D., Caruso, D., and Salovey, P. "Selecting a Measure of Emotional Intelligence: The Case for Ability Scales." In R. Bar-On and J.D.A. Parker (eds.), *The Handbook of Emotional Intelligence*. San Francisco: Jossey-Bass, 2000.

Mayer, J. D., DiPaolo, M., and Salovey, P. "Perceiving the Affective Content in Ambiguous Visual Stimuli: A Component of Emotional Intelligence." *Journal of Personality Assessment*, 1990, *54*, 772–781.

Mayer, J. D., Salovey, P., and Caruso, D. "Emotional Intelligence as Zeitgeist, as Personality, and as a Mental Ability." In R. Bar-On and J.D.A. Parker (eds.), *The Handbook of Emotional Intelligence*. San Francisco: Jossey-Bass, 2000.

Mayer, J. D., Salovey, P., and Caruso, D. "Models of Emotional Intelligence." In R. J. Sternberg (ed.), *The Handbook of Intelligence*. New York: Cambridge University Press, 2000.

Mayer, J. D., Perkins, D. M., Caruso, D. R., and Salovey, P. "Emotional Intelligence and Giftedness." *Roeper Review*, 2001, *23*, 131–137.

Mayer, J. D., Salovey, P., Caruso, D. R., and Sitarenios, G. "Emotional Intelligence as a Standard Intelligence." *Emotion*, 2001, *1*, 232–242.

Mayer, J. D., Salovey, P., Caruso, D. R., and Sitarenios, G. "Measuring Emotional Intelligence with the MSCEIT V2.0." *Emotion*, 2003, *3*, 97–105.

Pizarro, D. A., and Salovey, P. "Being and Becoming a Good Person: The Role of Emotional Intelligence in Moral Development and Behavior." In J. Aronson and D. Cordova (eds.), *Improving Academic Achievement: Impact of Psychological Factors on Education*. San Diego: Academic Press, 2002.

Salovey, P., and Mayer, J. D. "Emotional Intelligence." *Imagination, Cognition, and Personality*, 1990, *9*, 185–211.

Salovey, P., and Mayer, J. D. "Some Final Thoughts About Personality and Intelligence." In R. J. Sternberg and P. Ruzgis (eds.), *Personality and Intelligence*. Cambridge, England: Cambridge University Press, 1994.

Salovey, P., and Pizarro, D. A. "The Value of Emotional Intelligence." In R. J. Sternberg, J. Lautrey, and T. I. Lubart (eds.), *Models of Intelligence: International Perspectives*. Washington, D.C.: American Psychological Association, 2003.

Salovey, P., Mayer, J. D., and Caruso, D. "The Positive Psychology of Emotional Intelligence." In C. R. Snyder and S. J. Lopez (eds.), *The Handbook of Positive Psychology*. New York: Oxford University Press, 2002.

Salovey, P., Woolery, A., and Mayer, J. D. "Emotional Intelligence: Conceptualization and Measurement." In G.J.O. Fletcher and M. S. Clark (eds.), *Blackwell Handbook of Social Psychology: Interpersonal Processes*. Malden, MA: Blackwell Publishers, 2001.

Salovey, P., Bedell, B. T., Detweiler, J. B., and Mayer, J. D. "Current Directions in Emotional Intelligence Research." In M. Lewis and J. M. Haviland-Jones (eds.), *Handbook of Emotions*. (2nd ed.) New York: Guilford Press, 2000.

Salovey, P., Mayer, J. D., Caruso, D., and Lopes, P. N. "Measuring Emotional Intelligence as a Set of Abilities with the Mayer-Salovey-Caruso Emotional Intelligence Test." In S. J. Lopez and C. R. Snyder (eds.), *Positive Psychological Assessment: A Handbook of Models and Measures*. Washington, D.C.: American Psychological Association, 2003.

Salovey, P., Mayer, J. D., Goldman, S., Turvey, C., and Palfai, T. "Emotional Attention, Clarity, and Repair: Exploring Emotional Intelligence Using the Trait Meta-Mood Scale." In J. Pennebaker (ed.), *Emotion,*

Disclosure, and Health. Washington, D.C.: American Psychological Association, 1995.

Salovey, P., Kokkonen, M., Lopes, P., and Mayer, J. D. "Emotional Intelligence: What Do We Know?" In A.S.R. Manstead, N. H. Frijda, and A. H. Fischer (eds.), *Feelings and Emotions: The Amsterdam Symposium.* New York: Cambridge University Press, 2004.

Woolery, A., and Salovey, P. "Emotional Intelligence and Physical Health." In I. Nyklicek, L. R. Temoshok, and A. Vingerhoets (eds.), *Emotional Expression and Health: Biobehavioral Perspectives on Health and Disease Prevention* (vol. 6). New York: Harwood Academic Publishers, 2004.

Update and Contact Information

This is a fast-moving field, and we have set up a Web site to help you keep in touch with the latest developments in emotional intelligence.

We also want to hear how you have used the Emotional Blueprint in your work. Join us at EImanager.com!

Notes

Introduction

1. Kramer, M. W., and Hess, J. A. "Communication Rules for the Display of Emotions in Organizational Settings." *Management Communication Quarterly*, 2002, *16*, 66–80.

2. Darwin, C. *The Expression of the Emotions in Man and Animals.* (Definitive edition with introduction, afterword, and commentaries by Paul Ekman). New York: Oxford University, 1998. (Originally published 1872.)

3. Damasio, A. R. *Descartes' Error: Emotion, Reason, and the Human Brain.* New York: Avon, 1994.

4. Salovey, P., and Mayer, J. D. "Emotional Intelligence." *Imagination, Cognition, and Personality*, 1990, *9*, 185–211; Mayer, J. D., and Salovey, P. "What Is Emotional Intelligence?" In P. Salovey and D. Sluyter (eds.), *Emotional Development and Emotional Intelligence: Educational Implications.* New York: Basic Books, 1997.

5. There are many superb texts on management and leadership, including Bass, B. M. *Stogdill's Handbook of Leadership* (2nd ed.), New York: Free Press, 1981; Bass, B. M. *Leadership and Performance Beyond Expectations.* New York: Free Press, 1985; Bass, B. M. "Does the Transactional-Transformational Leadership Paradigm Transcend Organizational and National Boundaries?" *American Psychologist*, 1997, *52*, 130–139; Bennis, W. G. *On Becoming a Leader.* Reading, Mass.: Addison-Wesley, 1988; Brief, A. P. *Attitudes in and Around Organizations.* Thousand Oaks, Calif.: Sage, 1998; Fiedler, F. E. *A Theory of Leadership Effectiveness.* New York: McGraw-Hill, 1967; Hersey, P., and Blanchard, K. H. *Management of Organizational Behavior.* Englewood Cliffs, N.J.: Prentice Hall, 1988; Hogan, R., Curphy, G. J., and Hogan, J. "What We Know About Leadership." *American Psychologist*, 1994, *49*, 493–504; Kotter, J. P. *A Force for Change: How Leadership Differs from Management.* New York: Free Press, 1990; Kouzes, J. M., and Posner, B. Z. *The Leadership Challenge.* (3rd ed.) San Francisco: Jossey-Bass, 2002; Maccoby, M. *The Leader: A New Face for American Management.* New York: Ballantine, 1983.

6. *Benchmarks Facilitator's Manual.* Greensboro, N.C.: Center for Creative Leadership, 2000.

7. Kouzes, J. M., and Posner, B. Z. *The Leadership Challenge.* (3rd ed.) San Francisco: Jossey-Bass, 2002.

8. See, for example, Boyatzis, R. *The Competent Manager: A Model for Effective Performance.* New York: Wiley, 1982.

9. Cherniss, C., and Adler, M. *Promoting Emotional Intelligence in Organizations: Guidelines for Practitioners.* Alexandria, Va.: American Society for Training and Development, 2000; Cherniss, C., and Goleman, D. (eds.) *The Emotionally Intelligent Workplace: How to Select For, Measure, and Improve Emotional Intelligence in Individuals, Groups, and Organizations.* San Francisco: Jossey-Bass, 2001; Goleman, D., Boyatzis, R. E., and McKee, A. *Primal Leadership: Realizing the Power of Emotional Intelligence.* Boston: Harvard Business School Press, 2002.

10. Goleman, D. *Emotional Intelligence.* New York: Bantam, 1995.

Chapter One

1. For information on Althea Gibson, see Thomas, R. M., Jr. "Althea Gibson, the First Black Player to Win Wimbledon and U.S. Titles, Dies at 76." *New York Times,* Sept. 29, 2003, p. B8, and also Hasday, J. L. *Extraordinary Women Athletes.* New York: Children's Press, 2000.

2. Brown, C. "Case of the Caddie Who Couldn't Count." *New York Times,* July 23, 2001 (late ed., East Coast), p. D.4.

3. Roberts, S. "Agassi Lets His Emotions, and Rafter, Get the Best of Him." *New York Times,* July 7, 2001 (late ed., East Coast), p. D.1.

4. Staw, B. M., and Barsade S. G. "Affect and Managerial Performance: A Test of the Sadder-But-Wiser Vs. Happier-And-Smarter Hypotheses." *Administrative Science Quarterly,* 1993, *38,* 304–328. Also see Staw, B. M., Sutton, R. I., and Pelled, L. H. "Employee Positive Emotion and Favorable Outcomes at the Workplace." *Organizational Science,* 1994, *5,* 51–71.

5. Barsade, S. G., Ward, A. J., Turner, J.D.F., and Sonnenfeld, J. A. "To Your Heart's Content: The Influence of Affective Diversity in Top Management Teams." *Administrative Science Quarterly,* 2000, *45,* 802–836.

6. Jordan, P. J., Ashkanasy, N. M., Härtel, C.E.J., and Hooper, G. S. "Workgroup Emotional Intelligence: Scale Development and Relationship to Team Process Effectiveness and Goal Focus." *Human Resource Management Review,* 2002, *12,* 195–214.

7. Totterdell, P. "Catching Moods and Hitting Runs: Mood Linkage and Subjective Performance in Professional Sports Teams." *Journal of Applied Psychology,* 2000, *85,* 848–859; Totterdell, P., Kellet, S., Teuchmann, K., and Briner, R. B. "Evidence of Mood Linkage in

Work Groups." *Journal of Personality and Social Psychology,* 1998, *74,* 1504–1515.

8. Barsade, S. G. "The Ripple Effect: Emotional Contagion and Its Influence on Group Behavior." *Administrative Science Quarterly,* 2002, *47,* 644–675.

9. See, for example, Brief, A. P., and Weiss, H. M. "Organizational Behavior: Affect in the Workplace." *Annual Review of Psychology,* 2002, *53,* 270–307; Weiss, H. M., and Cropanzano, R. "Affective Events Theory: A Theoretical Discussion of the Structure, Causes and Consequences of Affective Experiences at Work." In B. M. Staw and L. L. Cummings (eds.), *Research in Organizational Behavior.* Greenwich, CT: JAI Press, 1996; Ashforth, B. E., and Humphrey, R. H. "Emotion in the Workplace: A Reappraisal." *Human Relations,* 1995 *48,* 97–125; George, J. M. "Emotions and Leadership: The Role of Emotional Intelligence." *Human Relations,* 2000, *53,* 1027–1055; Fisher, C. D., and Ashkanasy, N. M. "The Emerging Role of Emotions in Working Life: An Introduction." *Journal of Organizational Behavior,* 2000, *21,* 123–129; Ashkanasy, N. M., and Daus, S. D. "Emotion in the Workplace: The New Challenge For Managers. *Academy of Management Executive,* 2002, *16,* 23–45.

10. See, for example, Clore, G. L., Wyer, R. S., Dienes, B., Gasper, K., Gohm, C., and Isbell, L. "Affective Feelings as Feedback: Some Cognitive Consequences." In L. L. Martin and G. L. Clore (eds.), *Theories of Mood and Cognition.* Hillsdale, N.J.: Erlbaum, 2001; Schwarz, N. "Feelings as Information: Informational and Motivational Functions of Affective States." In R. M. Sorrentino and E. T. Higgins (eds.), *Handbook of Motivation and Cognition: Foundations of Social Behavior,* New York: Guilford, 1990.

11. Ekman, P. "Facial Expression and Emotion." *American Psychologist,* 1993, *48,* 384–392.

12. Literature on stress and coping skills offers detailed analyses of this role of mood. See Lazarus, R. S. *Emotion and Adaptation.* New York: Oxford University Press, 1991; Lazarus, R. S. *Stress and Emotion: A New Synthesis.* New York: Springer, 1999; Lazarus, R. S., and Folkman, S. *Stress Appraisal and Coping.* New York: Springer, 1984; Lazarus, R. S., and Lazarus, B. N. *Passion and Reason: Making Sense of Our Emotions.* New York: Oxford University Press, 1994.

13. Frijda, N. H. *The Emotions.* New York: Cambridge University Press, 1986; Plutchik, R. *Emotion: A Psychoevolutionary Synthesis.* New York: Harper & Row, 1980.

14. Alpert, R., and Haber, R. N. "Anxiety in Academic Achievement Situations." *Journal of Abnormal and Social Psychology,* 1960, *61,* 207–215.

15. Estrada, C. A., Isen, A. M., and Young, M. J. "Positive Affect Facilitates Integration of Information and Decreases Anchoring in Reasoning Among Physicians." *Organizational Behavior and Human Decision Processes,* 1997, *72,* 117–135; Estrada, C. A., Isen, A. M., and Young, M. J. "Positive Affect Improves Creative Problem Solving and Influences Reported Source of Practice Satisfaction in Physicians." *Motivation and Emotion,* 1994, *18,* 285–299.

16. Baumeister, R. F., Muraven, M., and Tice, D. M. "Ego Depletion: A Resource Model of Volition, Self-Regulation, and Controlled Processing." *Social Cognition,* 2000, *18,* 130–150.

17. Hochschild, A. R. *The Managed Heart: Commercialization of Human Feeling.* Berkeley: University of California Press, 1983.

18. Ashforth, B. E., and Humphrey, R. H. "Emotional Labor in Service Roles: The Influence of Identity." *Academy of Management Review,* 1993, *18,* 88–115; Ashforth, B. E., and Tomiuk, M. A. "Emotional Labour and Authenticity: Views from Service Agents." In S. Fineman (ed.), *Emotion in Organization.* (2nd ed.) London: Sage, 2000.

19. Ashforth, B. E., and Humphrey, R. H. "Emotion in the Workplace: A Reappraisal." *Human Relations,* 1995 *48,* 97–125.

20. Gibson, D.E. "Emotional scripts and changes in organizations." In F. Massarik (ed.), *Advances in Organization Development,* vol. 3. Westport, CT: Ablex, 1995.

21. Ekman, P. *Telling Lies.* New York: Norton, 1985; Ekman, P. *Emotions Revealed.* New York: Times Books, 2003.

22. Damasio, A. R. *Descartes' Error: Emotion, Reason, and the Human Brain.* New York: Avon, 1994.

23. Gibbs, N. "What's Your EQ?" *Time,* Oct. 1995, pp. 60–68.

24. See, for example, Bower, G. H. "Mood and Memory." *American Psychologist,* 1981, *36,* 129–148; Isen, A. "Positive Affect, Cognitive Processes and Social Behavior." In L. Berkowitz (ed.), *Advances in Experimental Social Psychology.* New York: Academic Press, 1987.

25. Fredrickson, B. L. "The Role of Positive Emotions in Positive Psychology: The Broaden-And-Build Theory of Positive Emotions." *American Psychologist,* 2001, *56,* 218–226; Fredrickson, B. L. "The Value of Positive Emotions." *American Scientist,* 2003, *91,* 330–335.

26. Harker, L. A., and Keltner, D. "Expressions of Positive Emotion in Women's College Yearbook Pictures and Their Relationship to Personality and Life Outcomes Across Adulthood." *Journal of Personality and Social Psychology,* 2001, *80,* 112–124.

27. Forgas, J. P. "Affect and Information Processing Strategies: An Interactive Relationship." In J. P. Forgas (ed.), *Feeling and Thinking: The Role of Affect in Social Cognition.* Cambridge, England: Cambridge

University Press, 2000; Leeper, R. W. "A Motivational Theory of Emotion to Replace 'Emotions as Disorganized Response.'" *Psychological Bulletin*, 1948, *55*, 5–21; Schwarz, N., and Clore, G. L. "How Do I Feel About It? The Informative Function of Affective States." In K. Fiedler and J. P. Forgas (eds.), *Affect, Cognition, and Social Behavior.* Toronto: Hogrefe, 1988.

28.   Plutchik, R. *The Psychology and Biology of Emotion.* New York: Harper-Collins, 1994.

29.   Although there are strong cultural differences in acceptable social behavior, our focus is on the display of emotions.

30.   Mayer, J. D., Caruso, D. R., and Salovey, P. "Emotional Intelligence Meets Traditional Standards for an Intelligence." *Intelligence*, 1999, *27,* 267–298.

31.   Eagly, A. H., Makhijani, M. G., and Klonsky, B. G. "Gender and the Evaluation of Leaders: A Meta-Analysis." *Psychological Bulletin*, 1992, *111*, 3–22. See also Shields, S. A. *Speaking from the Heart: Gender and the Social Meaning of Emotion.* Cambridge, England: Cambridge University Press, 2002.

Chapter Two

1.   Mayer, J. D., DiPaolo, M., and Salovey, P. "Perceiving the Affective Content in Ambiguous Visual Stimuli: A Component of Emotional Intelligence." *Journal of Personality Assessment,* 1990, *54,* 772–781; Salovey, P., and Mayer, J. D. "Emotional Intelligence." *Imagination, Cognition, and Personality,* 1990, *9,* 185–211.

2.   Gardner, H. *Frames of Mind: The Theory of Multiple Intelligences.* (10th Anniversary Ed.) New York: Basic Books, 1993 (originally published 1983). See also Sternberg, R. J. *The Triarchic Mind: A New Theory of Human Intelligence.* New York: Penguin, 1985. Sternberg, R. J. *Successful Intelligence: How Practical and Creative Intelligence Determine Success in Life.* New York: Plume, 1996.

3.   For more thorough descriptions of the four-skill model, see Mayer, J. D., and Salovey, P. "What Is Emotional Intelligence?" In P. Salovey and D. Sluyter (eds.), *Emotional Development and Emotional Intelligence: Educational Implications.* New York: Basic Books, 1997; Mayer, J. D., Salovey, P., and Caruso, D. "Models of Emotional Intelligence." In R. J. Sternberg (ed.), *The Handbook of Intelligence.* New York: Cambridge University Press, 2000; Salovey, P., Bedell, B. T., Detweiler, J. B., and Mayer, J. D. "Current Directions in Emotional Intelligence Research." In M. Lewis and J. M. Haviland-Jones (eds.), *Handbook of Emotions.* (2nd ed.) New York: Guilford Press, 2000.

Chapter Three

1. Darwin, C. *The Expression of the Emotions in Man and Animals.* (Definitive edition with introduction, afterword, and commentaries by Paul Ekman). New York: Oxford University, 1998. (Originally published 1872.)
2. For a more thorough discussion of identifying emotions, see Ekman, P. *Emotions Revealed.* New York: Times Books, 2003.
3. See, for example, Nolen-Hoeksema, S. *Women Who Think Too Much.* New York: Henry Holt, 2003.
4. Rosenstein, D., and Oster, H. "Differential Facial Response to Four Basic Tastes in Newborns." *Child Development,* 1988, *59,* 1555–1568.
5. Ekman, P. *Emotions Revealed.* New York: Times Books, 2003.
6. See, for example, Gobe, M. *Emotional Branding.* Oxford, England: Windsor, 2001; Martins, J. S. *The Emotional Nature of a Brand.* Sao Paulo, Brazil: Marts Plan Imagen, 2000.
7. Ekman, P. *Telling Lies: Clues to Deceit in the Marketplace, Marriage, and Politics.* New York: Norton, 1985.
8. Wilson, M. *The Music Man.* Milwaukee, WI: Hal Leonard Corporation, 1957.
9. Henley, N. M. *Body Politics: Power, Sex, and Nonverbal Communication.* Englewood Cliffs, N.J.: Prentice Hall, 1977.
10. Elfenbein, H. A., Marsh, A. A., and Ambady, N. "Emotional Intelligence and the Recognition of Emotion from Facial Expression." In L. F. Barrett and P. Salovey (eds.), *The Wisdom in Feeling: Psychological Processes in Emotional Intelligence.* New York: Guilford Press, 2002.

Chapter Four

1. Young, P. T. *Motivation of Behavior.* New York: Wiley, 1936, pp. 457–458.
2. See, for example, Schwarz, N. "Situated Cognition and the Wisdom in Feelings: Cognitive Tuning." In L. F. Barrett and P. Salovey (eds.), *The Wisdom in Feeling: Psychological Processes in Emotional Intelligence.* New York: Guilford Press, 2002.
3. Palfai, T. P., and Salovey, P. "The Influence of Depressed and Elated Mood on Deductive and Inductive Reasoning." *Imagination, Cognition, and Personality,* 1993, *13,* 57–71.
4. Proust, M. *Remembrance of Things Past.* (C.K.S. Moncrieff, trans.) New York: Random House, 1932.
5. Mayer, J. D. "How Mood Influences Cognition." In N. E. Sharkey (ed.), *Advances in Cognitive Science,* Vol. 1. Chichester: Ellis Horwood, 1986. Jamison, K. R. *Touched with Fire: Manic Depressive Illness and the Artistic Temperament.* New York: Free Press, 1993.
6. Adams, J. L. *Conceptual Blockbusting.* (2nd ed.) New York: Norton, 1979.

7.   Barach, J. A., and Eckhardt, D. R. *Leadership and the Job of the Executive.* Westport, CT: Quorum Books, 1996, p. 4.

8.   Ashforth, B. E., and Humphreys, R. H. "Emotion in the Workplace: A Reappraisal." *Human Relations,* 1995, *48,* 97–125. (Quote is from p. 111.)

9.   The speech is available online. See http://www.canadahistory. com/sections/documents/1940churchillfightspeech.htm.

10. Damasio, A. R. *Descartes' Error: Emotion, Reason, and the Human Brain.* New York: Avon Books, 1994. See also, Damasio's other work: Damasio, A. R. "Fundamental Feelings." *Nature,* 2001, *413,* 781; Damasio, A. R. *The Feeling of What Happens: Body and Emotion in the Making of Consciousness.* New York: Harcourt Brace, 1999.

11. Estrada, C. A., Isen, A. M., and Young, M. J. "Positive Affect Facilitates Integration of Information and Decreases Anchoring in Reasoning Among Physicians." *Organizational Behavior and Human Decision Processes,* 1997, *72,* 117–135; Estrada, C. A., Isen, A. M., and Young, M. J. "Positive Affect Improves Creative Problem Solving and Influences Reported Source of Practice Satisfaction in Physicians." *Motivation and Emotion,* 1994, *18,* 285–299.

12. Summarized in Gohm, C. L., and Clore, G. L. "Affect as Information: An Individual-Differences Approach." In L. F. Barrett and P. Salovey (eds.), *The Wisdom in Feeling: Psychological Processes in Emotional Intelligence.* New York: Guilford Press, 2002.

13. Summarized in Schwarz, N., and Clore, G. L. "How Do I Feel About It? The Informative Function of Affective States." In K. Fieldler and J. Forgas (eds.), *Affect, Cognition, and Social Behavior.* Toronto: C. J. Hogrefe, 1988.

14. Summarized in Mayer, J. D., and Salovey, P. "Personality Moderates the Interaction of Mood and Cognition." In K. Fieldler and J. Forgas (eds.), *Affect, Cognition, and Social Behavior.* Toronto: C. J. Hogrefe, 1988. Also see Mayer, J. D. "Emotion, Intelligence, and Emotional Intelligence." In J. P. Forgas (ed.), *Handbook of Affect and Social Cognition.* Mahwah, N.J.: Erlbaum, 2001.

Chapter Five

1.   See, for example, Ekman, P., and Davidson, R. J. *The Nature of Emotions: Fundamental Questions.* New York: Oxford University Press, 1994 (especially the first chapter). But for an opposing point of view, see Ortony, A., and Turner, T. J. "What's Basic About Basic Emotions?" *Psychological Review,* 1990, *97,* 315–331.

2.   Some years ago, Ekman modified his views regarding basic emotions, but he continues to argue that certain emotions appear to be experienced universally.

3. Plutchik, R. *The Psychology and Biology of Emotion.* New York: Harper-Collins, 1994.

4. See also, Izard, C. E. *The Psychology of Emotions.* New York: Plenum, 1991; Tomkins, S. S. *Affect, Imagery, and Consciousness: The Positive Affects.* New York: Springer, 1962; Tomkins, S. S. *Affect, Imagery, and Consciousness: The Negative Affects.* New York: Springer, 1963.

5. For detailed discussions of this idea, see the contributions to Scherer, K. S., Schorr, A., and Johnstone, T. (eds.), *Appraisal Processes in Emotion: Theory, Methods, and Research.* New York: Oxford University Press, 2001.

6. Lisa Feldman Barrett calls this *emotional granularity.* See, for example, Barrett, L. F., and Fossum, T. "Mental Representations of Affect Knowledge." *Cognition and Emotion,* 2001, *15,* 333–363.

7. A good introduction to emotion vocabulary can be found in Ortony, A., Clore, G. L., and Collins, A. *The Cognitive Structure of Emotions.* Cambridge, England: Cambridge University Press, 1988.

Chapter Six

1. Richards, J. M., and Gross, J. J. "Emotion Regulation and Memory: The Cognitive Costs of Keeping One's Cool." *Journal of Personality and Social Psychology,* 2000, *79,* 410–424.

2. For more information, see Gross, J. J., and John, O. P. "Wise Emotion Regulation." In L. F. Barrett and P. Salovey (eds.), *The Wisdom in Feeling: Psychological Processes in Emotional Intelligence.* New York: Guilford Press, 2002.

3. Schoeck, H. *Envy: A Theory of Social Behavior.* New York: Harcourt Brace, 1966.

4. Kelly, J. R., and Barsade, S. G. "Mood and Emotions in Small Groups and Work Teams." *Organizational Behavior and Human Decision Processes,* 2001, *86,* 99–130.

5. Bushman, B. J. "Does Venting Anger Feed or Extinguish the Flame? Catharsis, Rumination, Distraction, Anger and Aggressive Responding." *Personality and Social Psychology Bulletin,* 2002, *28,* 724–731.

6. Frijda, N. H. *The Emotions.* Cambridge, England: Cambridge University Press, 1986; see also, Frijda, N. H., Kuipers, P., and ter Schure, E. "Relations Among Emotion, Appraisal, and Emotional Action Readiness." *Journal of Personality and Social Psychology,* 1989, *57,* 212–228.

7. Aristotle. *The Poetics.* G. F. Else (trans.) Ann Arbor, MI: The University of Michigan Press, 1970. (Aristotle, circa 355 B.C.)

8. For a relevant discussion, see de Sousa, R. *The Rationality of Emotion.* Cambridge: MIT Press, 1987.

9. Damasio, A. R. *Descartes' Error: Emotion, Reason, and the Human Brain.* New York: Putnam, 1994.

10. Mischel, W., and Ebbesen, E. B. "Attention in Delay of Gratification." *Journal of Personality and Social Psychology,* 1970, *16,* 329–337; Mischel, W., Ebbesen, E. B., and Zeiss, A. R. "Cognitive and Attentional Mechanisms in Delay of Gratification." *Journal of Personality and Social Psychology,* 1972, *21,* 204–218.

11. Baumeister, R. F. "Ego Depletion, the Executive Function, and Self-Control: An Energy Model of the Self in Personality." In B. W. Roberts and R. Hogan (eds.), *Personality Psychology in the Workplace. Decade Of Behavior.* Washington, D.C.: American Psychological Association, 2001; Tice, D. M., Bratslavsky, E., and Baumeister, R. F. "Emotional Distress Regulation Takes Precedence Over Impulse Control: If You Feel Bad, Do It!" *Journal of Personality and Social Psychology,* 2001, *80,* 53–67.

12. Reviewed in Tangney, J. P., and Salovey, P. "Problematic Social Emotions: Shame, Guilt, Jealousy, and Envy." In R. M. Kowalski and M. R. Leary (eds.), *The Social Psychology of Emotional and Behavioral Problems: Interfaces of Social and Clinical Psychology.* Washington, D.C.: American Psychological Association, 1999; Tangney, J. P., and Dearing, R. L. *Shame and Guilt.* New York: Guilford Press, 2002; for earlier work, see Lewis, H. B. *Shame and Guilt in Neurosis.* New York: International Universities Press, 1971; for a charming book on embarrassment, see Miller, R. E. *Embarrassment: Poise and Peril in Everyday Life.* New York: Guilford Press, 1996.

13. Tice, D. M., and Bratslavsky, E. "Giving in to Feel Good: The Place of Emotion Regulation in the Context of General Self-Control." *Psychological Inquiry,* 2000, *11,* 149–159.

Chapter Seven

1. Paulus, D. L., Lysy, D. C., and Yik, M.S.M. "Self-Report Measures of Intelligence: Are They Useful as a Proxy IQ Test?" *Journal of Personality,* 1998, *66,* 525–554.

2. Borkenau, P., and Liebler, A. "Convergence of Stranger Ratings of Personality and Intelligence with Self-Ratings, Partner Ratings, and Measured Intelligence." *Journal of Personality and Social Psychology,* 1993, *65,* 546–553; Sharpley, C. F., and Edgar, E. "Teachers' Ratings vs. Standardized Tests: An Empirical Investigation of Agreement Between Two Indices of Achievement." *Psychology in the Schools,* 1986, *23,* 106–111.

3. Mayer, J. D., Salovey, P., and Caruso, D. R. *Mayer-Salovey-Caruso Emotional Intelligence Test (MSCEIT): User's Manual.* Toronto, Ontario: Multi-Health Systems, Inc., 2002; Mayer, J. D., Salovey, P., Caruso, D. R., and Sitarenios, G. "Measuring Emotional Intelligence with

the MSCEIT V2.0." *Emotion*, 2003, *3*, 97–105; Salovey, P., Mayer, J. D., Caruso, D., and Lopes, P. N. "Measuring Emotional Intelligence as a Set Of Abilities with the Mayer-Salovey-Caruso Emotional Intelligence Test." In S. J. Lopez and C. R. Snyder (eds.), *Positive Psychological Assessment: A Handbook of Models and Measures*. Washington, D.C.: American Psychological Association, 2003.

4. For a detailed description of how to identify smiles as real or posed, see Ekman, P. *Emotions Revealed*. New York: Times Books, 2003.

5. Wegner, D. *White Bears and Other Unwanted Thoughts: Suppression, Obsession, and the Psychology of Mental Control*. New York: Viking, 1989.

Chapter Eight

1. For more information, see Watson, D. *Mood and Temperament*. New York: Guilford Press, 2000.

2. A nice discussion of these issues can be found in Thayer, R. E. *The Biopsychology of Mood and Arousal*. New York: Oxford University Press, 1989; Thayer, R. E. *The Origin of Everyday Moods: Managing Energy, Tension, and Stress*. New York: Oxford University Press, 1996.

3. See Thayer, R. E. *Calm Energy: How People Regulate Mood with Food and Exercise*. New York: Oxford University Press, 2001.

4. Scherer, K. R. "Vocal Affect Expression: A Review and Model for Future Research." *Psychological Bulletin*, 1986, *99*, 143–165; Scherer, K. R., Banse, R., and Wallbott, H. G. "Emotion Inferences from Vocal Expression Correlate Across Languages and Cultures. *Journal of Cross-Cultural Psychology*, 2001, *32*, 76–92; also see Bachorowski, J. A., and Owren, M. J. "Vocal Acoustics in Emotional Intelligence." In L. F. Barrett and P. Salovey (eds.), *The Wisdom in Feeling: Psychological Processes in Emotional Intelligence*. New York: Guilford Press, 2002.

5. Ekman, P. *Emotions Revealed*. New York: Times Books, 2003.

6. Ekman, P. *Telling Lies: Clues to Deceit in the Marketplace, Marriage, and Politics*. New York: Norton, 1985.

7. Ekman, P. *Telling Lies*.

Chapter Nine

1. Fredrickson, B. L. "The Role of Positive Emotions in Positive Psychology: The Broaden-and-Build Theory of Positive Emotions." *American Psychologist*, 2001, *56*, 218–226.

2. Isen, A. M., Daubman, Kimberly A., and Nowicki, Gary P. "Positive Affect Facilitates Creative Problem Solving." *Journal of Personality and Social Psychology*, 1987, *52*, 1122–1131.

3. Bless, H. "Mood and the Use of General Knowledge Structures." In L. L. Martin and G. L. Clore (eds.), *Theories of Mood and Cognition: A User's Guidebook*. Hillsdale, N.J.: Erlbaum, 2001.

4. Lyubomirsky, S., and Tucker, K. L. "Implications of Individual Differences in Subjective Happiness for Perceiving, Interpreting, and Thinking About Life Events." *Motivation and Emotion,* 1998, *22,* 155–186; Seidlitz, L., and Diener, E. "Memory for Positive Versus Negative Life Events: Theories for the Differences Between Happy and Unhappy Persons." *Journal of Personality and Social Psychology,* 1993, *64,* 654–663.

5. Isen, A. M., Daubman, K. A., and Nowicki, G. P. "Positive Affect Facilitates Creative Problem Solving." *Journal of Personality and Social Psychology,* 1987, *52,* 1122–1131.

6. Bless, H. "Mood and the Use of General Knowledge Structures." In L. L. Martin and G. L. Clore (eds.), *Theories of Mood and Cognition: A User's Guidebook.* Hillsdale, N.J.: Erlbaum, 2001.

7. Clore, G. L., Wyer, R. S., Jr., Dienes, B., Gasper, K., Gohm, C., and Isbell, L. "Affective Feelings as Feedback: Some Cognitive Consequences." In L. L. Martin and G. L. Clore (eds.), *Theories of Mood and Cognition: A User's Guidebook.* Hillsdale, N.J.: Erlbaum, 2001.

8. LeDoux, J. "Fear and the Brain: Where Have We Been, and Where Are We Going?" *Biological Psychiatry,* 1998, *44,* 1229–1238.

9. DeSteno, D., Petty, R. E., Wegener, D. T., and Rucker, D. D. "Beyond Valence in the Perception of Likelihood: The Role of Emotion Specificity." *Journal of Personality and Social Psychology,* 2000, *78,* 397–416.

10. Gillham, J. E., Shatte, A. J., Reivich, K. J., and Seligman, M.E.P. "Optimism, Pessimism, and Explanatory Style." In E. C. Chang (ed.), *Optimism and Pessimism: Implications for Theory, Research, and Practice.* Washington, D.C.: American Psychological Association, 2001.

11. Palfai, T. P., and Salovey, P. "The Influence of Depressed and Elated Mood on Deductive and Inductive Reasoning." *Imagination, Cognition, and Personality,* 1993, *13,* 57–71.

12. Van Honk, J., Tuiten, A., de Haan, E., van den Hout, M., and Stam, H. "Attentional Biases for Angry Faces: Relationships to Trait Anger and Anxiety." *Cognition and Emotion,* 2001, *15,* 279–297.

13. Darwin, C. *The Expression of the Emotions in Man and Animals.* (Definitive edition with introduction, afterword, and commentaries by Paul Ekman). New York: Oxford University, 1998. (Originally published 1872.)

14. Forgas, J. P. "Feeling and Doing: Affective Influences on Interpersonal Behavior." *Psychological Inquiry,* 2002, *13,* 1–28.

15. For an excellent overview of emotion's role in persuasion, see DeSteno, D., and Braverman, J. "Emotions and Persuasion: Thoughts on the Role of Emotional Intelligence." In L. F. Barrett and P. Salovey (eds.), *The Wisdom in Feeling: Psychological Processes in Emotional Intelligence.* New York: Guilford Press, 2002.

16. Mayer, J. D., Gaschke, Y. N., Braverman, D. L., and Evans, T. W. "Mood-Congruent Judgment Is a General Effect." *Journal of Personality and Social Psychology,* 1992, *63,* 119–132.

17. Stanislavsky, C. *An Actor Prepares.* (E. R. Hapgood, trans.) London: Routledge, 1989.

18. Gardner, H. *Leading Minds: An Anatomy of Leadership.* New York: Basic Books, 1996.

19. Based on Velten, E. "A Laboratory Task for Induction of Mood States." *Behaviour Research and Therapy,* 1968, *8,* 473–482.

20. We thank Charles (Chuck) Wolfe for suggesting this exercise.

Chapter Ten

1. Russell, J. A. "A Circumplex Model of Affect." *Journal of Personality and Social Psychology,* 1980, *39,* 1161–1178. An alternative circular model but with different labeled dimensions was proposed by Watson, D., and Tellegen, A. "Toward a Consensual Structure of Mood." *Psychological Bulletin,* 1985, *98,* 219–235.

2. Miller, T. Q., Smith, T. W., Turner, C. W., Guijarro, M. L., and Hallet, A. J. "Meta-Analytic Review of Research on Hostility and Physical Health." *Psychological Bulletin,* 1996, *119,* 322–348.

3. Tangney, J. P., and Dearing, R. L. *Shame and Guilt.* New York: Guilford Press, 2002. For earlier work, see Lewis, H. B. *Shame and Guilt in Neurosis.* New York: International Universities Press, 1971.

4. For a charming book on embarrassment, see Miller, R. E. *Embarrassment: Poise and Peril in Everyday Life.* New York: Guilford Press, 1996.

Chapter Eleven

1. Mood regulation strategies are studied by Ralph Erber and others. See, for instance, Erber, R. "The Self-Regulation of Moods." In L. L. Martin and A. Tesser (eds.), *Striving and Feeling: Interactions Among Goals, Affect, and Self-Regulation.* Hillsdale, N.J.: Erlbaum, 1996.

2. An accessible introduction to Pennebaker's research can be found in Pennebaker, J. W. *Opening Up: The Healing Power of Confiding in Others.* New York: William Morrow, 1990. A statistical meta-analysis of research findings in this area is Smyth, J. M. "Written Emotional Expression: Effect Sizes, Outcome Types, and Moderating Variables." *Journal of Consulting and Clinical Psychology,* 1998, *66,* 174–184. For more general issues, see Kennedy-Moore, E., and Watson, J. C. *Expressing Emotion: Myths, Realities, and Therapeutic Strategies.* New York: Guilford Press, 1999.

3. Thayer, R. E. *Calm Energy: How People Regulate Mood with Food and Exercise.* New York: Oxford University Press, 2001.

4. For more on this idea, see Salovey, P., Mayer, J. D., Goldman, S., Turvey, C., and Palfai, T. "Emotional Attention, Clarity, and Repair: Exploring Emotional Intelligence Using the Trait Meta-Mood Scale." In J. Pennebaker (ed.), *Emotion, Disclosure, and Health.* Washington, D.C.: American Psychological Association, 1995.

5. Tomkins, S. S., and McCarter, R. "What and Where Are the Primary Affects? Some Evidence for a Theory." *Perceptual and Motor Skills,* 1964, *18,* 119–158.

6. Wolpe, J. *Psychotherapy by Reciprocal Inhibition.* Stanford, CA: Stanford University Press, 1958.

7. Sometimes, it is good to feel bad. See Parrott, W. G. "Beyond Hedonism: Motives for Inhibiting Good Moods and Maintaining Bad Moods." In D. M. Wegner and J. W. Pennebaker (eds.), *Handbook of Mental Control.* Englewood Cliffs, N.J.: Prentice Hall, 1993.

8. For a somewhat different but related distinction, see Feldman Barrett, L. A. "Valence Focus and Arousal Focus: Individual Differences in the Structure of Affective Experience." *Journal of Personality and Social Psychology,* 1995, *69,* 153–166.

9. We borrow liberally from the literatures on cognitive-behavioral and rational-emotive therapy for this section. However, although we employ some of the same terms and techniques, the focus is quite different. Our emotionally intelligent approach emphasizes the functionality of emotions and the need for emotions rather than the regulation of emotions.

10. Ashforth, B. E., and Kreiner, G. E. "Normalizing Emotion in Organizations: Making the Extraordinary Seem Ordinary." *Human Resource Management Review,* 2002, *12,* 215–235.

11. Ashforth, B. E., and Humphrey, R. H. "Emotion in the Workplace: A Reappraisal." *Human Relations,* 1995, *48,* 97–125.

12. Averill, J. R. "Studies on Anger and Aggression: Implications for Theories of Emotion." *American Psychologist,* 1983, *38,* 1145–1160.

13. Also see Fitness, J. "Anger in the Workplace: An Emotion Script Approach to Anger Episodes Between Workers and Their Superiors, Co-Workers and Subordinates." *Journal of Organizational Behavior,* 2000, *21,* 147–162.

14. Tice, D. M., and Baumeister, R. F. "Controlling Anger: Self-Induced Emotion Change." In D. M. Wegner and J. W. Pennebaker (eds.), *Handbook of Mental Control.* Englewood Cliffs, N.J.: Prentice Hall, 1983.

Chapter Twelve

1. Morris, B. "Can Ford Save Ford?" *Fortune,* Nov. 3, 2002. (see http://www.fortune.com/fortune/ceo/articles/0,15114,390071,00.html)

2. Cox, J., and Kiley, D. "Ford Jr. Takes On Role He Was Born to Play." *USA Today,* Oct. 31, 2001.

3. Sherrill, M. "The Buddha of Detroit." *New York Times Magazine,* Nov. 26, 2000. (See http:// www.nytimes.com/library/magazine/home/ 20001126mag-ford.html)

4. http://www.ford.com/en/company/about/leadership/WilliamClayFord. htm

5. Bass and Avolio differentiate between two types of charismatic leaders: those who are idealized and those who are idolized. These types are thought to differ in their level of morality. See Bass, B. M., and Avolio, B. J. *Transformational Leadership: Improving Organizational Effectiveness.* Thousand Oaks, CA: Sage, 1994.

6. See, for instance, Kegan, R. *The Evolving Self: Problem and Process in Human Development.* Cambridge, MA: Harvard University Press, 1982.

7. Bennis, W., and Nanus, B. *Leaders: The Strategies for Taking Charge.* New York: Harper & Row, 1985.

Chapter Thirteen

1. Welch, J., and Byrne, J. A. *Jack: Straight from the Gut.* New York: Warner Books, 2001. The quotes are from pp. 44 and 98.

Chapter Fourteen

1. The term is from Tom Wolfe's *Bonfire of the Vanities.* New York: Farrar, Straus and Giroux, 1987.

2. Boyatzis, R. *The Competent Manager: A Model for Effective Performance.* New York: Wiley, 1982. Goleman, D., Boyatzis, R. E., and McKee, A. *Primal Leadership: Realizing the Power of Emotional Intelligence.* Boston: Harvard Business School Press, 2002.

3. Kouzes, J. M., and Posner, B. Z. *The Leadership Challenge.* (3rd ed.) San Francisco: Jossey-Bass, 2002.

4. Zaccaro, S. J., Blair, V., Peterson, C., and Zazanis, M. "Collective Efficacy." In J. Maddux (ed.), *Self-Efficacy, Adaptation, and Adjustment.* New York: Plenum, 1995; Zaccaro, S. J., Marks, M., O'Connor-Boes, J., and Costanza, D. *The Nature of Leader Mental Models.* Alexandria, Va.: U.S. Army Research Institute for the Behavioral and Social Sciences, 1995; Zaccaro, S. J., and McCoy, M. C. "The Effects of Task and Interpersonal Cohesiveness on Performance of a Disjunctive Group Task." *Journal of Applied Social Psychology,* 1988, *18,* 837–851; Zaccaro, S. J., and Ardison, S. D. "Leadership in Virtual Army Teams." In D. V. Day, S. Zaccaro, and S. Halpin (eds.), *Leadership Development for Transforming Organizations.* Hillsdale, N.J.: Erlbaum, 2004.

5. Cannon-Bowers, J. A., Tannenbaum, S. I., Salas, E., and Volpe, C. E. "Defining Team Competencies and Establishing Team Training Requirements." In R. Guzzo, E. Salas, and Associates (eds.), *Team Effectiveness and Decision Making in Organizations.* San Francisco: Jossey-Bass, 1995.

6. Maggart, L. E. "Leadership Challenges for the Future." In D. V. Day, S. Zaccaro, and S. Halpin (eds.), *Leadership Development for Transforming Organizations.* Hillsdale, N.J.: Erlbaum, forthcoming.

7. "Red Sox Report: Inside Pitch." Sports Xchange, October 27, 2003.

8. Street, J. "Sox Stick with Pedro in Key Eighth: Players Defend Little for Leaving Ace in the Game." MLB.com, October 17, 2003.

9. Browne, I. "2003 Red Sox built on 'character.'" MLB.com, October 20, 2003.

10. Browne, I. "Millar: 'This Is a Sad Day.'" MLB.com, October 27, 2003.

11. Browne, I. "Millar: 'This Is a Sad Day.'"

12. Cafardo, N. "Little Intrigued by Orioles." *Boston Globe,* November 1, 2003.

13. Hohler, B. "Point of No Return: As Expected, Little Is Given the Ax by the Red Sox Brass." *Boston Globe,* October 28, 2003.

14. Hohler, B. "Point of No Return."

15. We've paraphrased these quotes and incidents from memory.

16. Kharif, O. "Anne Mulcahy Has Xerox by the Horns." *Business Week,* May 29, 2003). Available online: http://www.businessweek.com:/print/technology/content/may2003/tc20030529_1642_tc111.htm/tc.

17. Greenleaf, R. K. *Servant Leadership (25th Anniversary Edition): A Journey into the Nature of Legitimate Power and Greatness.* Mahwah, N.J.: Paulist Press, 2001.

18. Caruso, D. R., Mayer, J. D., and Salovey, P. "Relation of an Ability Measure of Emotional Intelligence to Personality." *Journal of Personality Assessment, 2002, 79,* 306–320.

19. Available online: http://www.achievement.org/autodoc/page/bhu0int-1.

20. Salas, E., Burke, C. S., and Stagl, K. C. "Developing Teams and Team Leaders: Strategies and Principles." In D. V. Day, S. Zaccaro, and S. Halpin (eds.), *Leadership Development for Transforming Organizations.* Hillsdale, N.J.: Erlbaum , 2004.

21. Salas, E., and Cannon-Bowers, J. A. "The Anatomy of Team Training." In S. Tobias and J. D. Fletcher (eds.), *Training and Retraining: A Handbook for Business, Industry, Government, and the Military.* New York: Macmillan, 2000; Salas, E., Burke, C. S., and Stagl, K. C. "Developing Teams and Team Leaders: Strategies and Principles." In D. V. Day, S. Zaccaro, and S. Halpin (eds.), *Leadership Development for Transforming Organizations.* Hillsdale, N.J.: Erlbaum, 2004.

22. Sony History, Chapter 13. Available online: www.sony.net/Fun/SH/.

23. "Catching Up with Carly Fiorina." *San Jose Mercury News,* April 13, 2003. Available onlne: www.siliconvalley.com/mld/mercurynews/business/5624255.htm

24. "Catching up with Carly Fiorina."

25. Fiorina, C. "Good Corporate Governance." Speech delivered to Confederation of British Industries. Manchester, UK, November 26, 2002. Available online: http://www.hp.com/hpinfo/execteam/speeches/fiorina/cbi02.html.

26. Brackett, M. A., Mayer, J. D., and Warner, R. M. "Emotional Intelligence and Its Relation to Everyday Behaviour." *Personality and Individual Differences,* forthcoming; Lopes, P. N., Brackett, M. A., Nezlek, J. B., Schutz, A., Sellin, I., and Salovey, P. "Emotional Intelligence and Social Interaction," *Personality and Social Psychology Bulletin,* forthcoming; Brackett, M. A., Warner, R. M., and Bosco, J. *Emotional Intelligence and Its Relation to Relationship Satisfaction Among Dating Couples.* Manuscript submitted for publication.

27. Lopes, P. N., Cote, S., Salovey, P., and Beers, M. *Emotion Regulation Abilities and the Quality of Social Relationships.* Manuscript submitted for publication. Lopes, P. N., Salovey, P., and Straus, R. "Emotional Intelligence, Personality, and the Perceived Quality of Social Relationships." *Personality and Individual Differences,* 2003, *35,* 641–658.

28. Welch, J., and Byrne, J. A. *Jack: Straight from the Gut.* New York: Warner Books, 2001, pp. 44, 98.

29. Tomkins, S. S. (1962). *Affect, Imagery, and Consciousness* (Vol. 1: *The Positive Affects*). New York: Springer, p. 112.

Acknowledgments

We are grateful for the support and assistance of a number of people. We have collaborated with John D. (Jack) Mayer, our friend and colleague, on emotional intelligence and other topics for more than twenty years. Charles J. (Chuck) Wolfe helped to apply our ability model in organizational settings. We value the insights provided to us by our colleagues at EQ Japan in Tokyo, especially Tohru Watanabe, Noriko Goh, Masami Sato, and Nao Takayama. Sigal Barsade has contributed much to the emotions-in-the-workplace literature, and she has been a consistent supporter of the ability approach and of this writing effort. Steven Stein and the crew at Multi-Health Systems in Toronto, the publishers of the MSCEIT, have provided helpful advice, and we especially appreciate their support of researchers using the MSCEIT.

There would not have been a book without the active efforts of our literary agent Ed Knappman of New England Publishing Associates, as well as Kristine Schiavoni. Susan Williams of Jossey-Bass truly understood our approach to EI and believed in it. Mary Garrett and Mary O'Briant did a terrific job getting a manuscript turned into a book, and Rob Brandt and Carolyn Miller of Jossey-Bass helped to get this book onto the shelves and into your hands.

Our clients have taught us a great deal about emotional intelligence and leadership, and we gratefully acknowledge their input and feedback. However, all names of clients have been changed, details of the situations have been altered or deleted, and in many cases, composites of different clients have been utilized.

The hard work of a number of students and collaborators has helped us to refine our thinking in this area in many ways. Our thanks to Brian Bedell-Detweiler, Michael Beers, Eliot Brenner, Heather Chabot, Stephane Côté, David DeSteno, Jerusha Detweiler-Bedell, Elissa Epel, Tony Freitas, Glen Geher, Jack Glaser, Susan

Goldman, Rocio Guil Bozal, Juliana Granskaya, Donald Green, Daisy Grewal, Cory Head, Lim How, Christopher Hsee, Marja Kokkonen, Paulo Lopes, Holly Lynton, Chloé Martin, Jose Miguel Mestre Navas, Anne Moyer, Tibor Palfai, David Pizarro, Susan Rivers, Alexander Rothman, Magdalena Smieja, Wayne Steward, Rebecca Straus, Carolyn Turvey, Laura Stroud, Sarah Wert, and Allison Woolery.

Many colleagues have provided us with valuable feedback, criticism, and challenges. Of course, we accept full responsibility for the material in this book, and the listing of a colleague's name certainly does not imply his or her endorsement of our approach or ideas! Thank you to Neal Ashkanasy, Marc Brackett, Karen Bryson, Cary Cherniss, Joseph Ciarrochi, Catherine Daus, Lisa Feldman Barrett, Mitsuyo Hanada, Peter Legree, Amy Van Buren, Joan Vitello, and the talented research staff of the Health, Emotion, and Behavior (HEB) Laboratory at Yale University.

We must thank our families for their support and also for putting up with our emotionally intelligent, and many emotionally unintelligent, moments as we were working on this project. Thank you Marta, Nancie, Rachel, Jonathan, and Ethan.

DAVID CARUSO
PETER SALOVEY

About the Authors

David R. Caruso is a management consultant specializing in management and organization development. After receiving his B.A. in psychology in 1979, he was awarded a National Institute of Child Health and Human Development predoctoral fellowship to conduct research on intelligence and individual differences at Case Western Reserve University. David received his M.A. and Ph.D. in psychology in 1982 and 1983 from Case. Upon graduation, he was awarded a postdoctoral fellowship and spent two years at Yale University conducting research on competence and intelligence.

David's career path took a sharp turn, which brought him from academia into corporate life. He next worked for ten years in Fortune 500 organizations as a market researcher, strategic planner, and product line manager. He led numerous product development teams, conducted sales training seminars, and developed a number of marketing plans for business and consumer products. As a product manager with P&L responsibility, he was responsible for launching a line of software products with first-year revenue of $11 million.

After he was downsized from his product-manager job, David began his own consulting practice in 1993. His practice areas include executive coaching, leadership development, and career assessment. He also teaches emotional skills to individuals and groups; he designed and now offers highly acclaimed interactive workshops on emotional intelligence. His practical, hands-on experience is complemented by his continuing research and academic work as a research affiliate in the Department of Psychology at Yale University. He has published a number of papers and chapters in the areas of intelligence and emotional intelligence.

Peter Salovey is dean of the Graduate School of Arts and Sciences at Yale University. He is the Chris Argyris Professor of Psychology and served as chair of the Department of Psychology from 2000 to 2003. Peter is also professor of management and of epidemiology and public health. He directs the Health, Emotion and Behavior Laboratory and is deputy director of the Yale Center for Interdisciplinary Research on AIDS. He has affiliations with the Yale Cancer Center and the Institution for Social and Policy Studies.

Peter received an A.B. in psychology and a coterminal M.A. in sociology from Stanford University in 1980. He holds three Yale degrees in psychology: an M.S. (1983), M.Phil. (1984), and Ph.D. (1986). He joined the Yale faculty as an assistant professor in 1986 and has been a full professor since 1995.

Peter's research has focused on the psychological significance and function of human moods and emotions, as well as the application of social-psychological principles to motivate people to adopt behaviors that protect their health. His recent work concerns the ways in which emotions facilitate adaptive cognitive and behavioral functioning.

With John D. Mayer, he developed a broad framework, coined "emotional intelligence," to describe how people understand, manage, and use their emotions. Peter's research has been funded by a Presidential Young Investigator (PYI) Award from the National Science Foundation and grants from the National Cancer Institute, National Institute of Mental Health, National Institute of Drug Abuse, American Cancer Society, Andrew W. Mellon Foundation, and the Ethel F. Donaghue Women's Health Investigator Program.

Peter has published about two hundred articles and chapters and has authored, coauthored, or edited eleven books. He edits the Guilford Press series *Emotions and Social Behavior,* and he has served as editor or associate editor for three scientific journals. He is also an award-winning teacher, having been honored with the William Clyde DeVane Medal for Distinguished Scholarship and Teaching in Yale College in 2000 and the Lex Hixon Prize for Teaching in the Social Sciences at Yale in 2002.

In his leisure time, Peter plays stand-up bass with The Professors of Bluegrass.

The author team first met in 1983, when David was a postdoctoral fellow at Yale University and Peter was a graduate student. More than ten years passed until they began their collaborative efforts. Since that time, they have worked together on book chapters, research projects, consulting assignments, and speaking engagements; they have coauthored two ability tests of emotional intelligence, along with colleague John D. Mayer.

You can contact the authors at EImanager.com.

Index

Van Buren, A., 92
Venting, 68, 72
Venture capitalist case studies, 163–165, 182–185
Verbal aggression, 150, 151
Video watching exercise, 92–93
Videotaping exercise, 87, 88
Violence, 117, 150, 151, 209
Virtual vacation, 46
Vision generation and communication, 51; emotional intelligence and, 162, 176, 196, 205–206; fear and, 206; happiness and, 101; managerial competency of, 205–206, *xix, xx*
Visualization exercises, 108–109, 110–111, 138–139
Vocabulary, emotional, 55–57, 58, 115, *x;* for acceptance, 124; for anger, 125; for anticipation, 124–125; basic emotions in, 57, 116–117; building, 116–121, 123–126; for disgust, 125–126; for fear, 126; for happiness, 124; importance of, 127; intensity levels in, 127; primer of, 116–117; for sadness, 126; in sample test, 78, 79; shades of emotion in, 57; for surprise, 125
Voice, finding your, 197
Voice tones, 91, 98

W

Waiting, 68

Walker, T., 199
Walking, 137
Web site, emotional intelligence, 256
Welch, J., 174–176, 209–210
Wharton School, 7
What-if-analyses, emotional, 29, 121, *x;* in conflict management, 53–54, 163, 171; to improve emotional management, 178; in interpersonal relationships, 210; predicting the future with, 60–61, 127–134; for vision creation, 206
"What's Your EQ?," 17
Wishful thinking, 242
Women, emotional intelligence of, 23
Woosnam, I., 4, 5
Worldviews: of anger and hostility, 103, 142; of depression, 142; of optimism, 142; of pleasantness, 142–143. *See also* Dispositional traits
Worry, 44–45, 118–119, 240–241
Writing, 136–137. *See also* Diary; Journals

X

Xerox, 202

Y

"Yuki" case study, 163–165

Z

Zaccaro, S. J., 196